T0133661

Advances in Biometrics for Secure Human Authentication and Recognition

Advances in Biometrics for Secure Human Authentication and Recognition

Edited by

Dakshina Ranjan Kisku

Phalguni Gupta

Jamuna Kanta Sing

CRC Press
Taylor & Francis Group
Boca Raton London New York

CRC Press is an imprint of the
Taylor & Francis Group, an **informa** business

CRC Press
Taylor & Francis Group
6000 Broken Sound Parkway NW, Suite 300
Boca Raton, FL 33487-2742

Printed on acid-free paper
Version Date: 20131023

International Standard Book Number-13: 978-1-4665-8242-2 (Hardback)

We dedicate this book to our parents.

Contents

List of Figures

List of Tables

Preface

The uniqueness of the physiological and behavioral characteristics of human beings is used to facilitate the identification or verification process, and it always results in correct classification. However, the distinctive evidence obtained from an individual does not guarantee a 100% matching be performed to the biometric characteristics corresponding another subject, even after considering all aspects of accurate recognition process. Tampered sensors, distorted evidence, recognition at a distance, and sometimes, motion of the target subject cause the identification process to be a weak one. Moreover, picking up the right algorithms for image enhancement, feature extraction, matching, classification, and decision in a biometric system are critical. Most of the commercial, off-the-shelf biometrics systems together cannot deal with all the intrinsic perspectives that could easily make the system unstable. Therefore, to cope with this problem, we should consider standard biometrics properties and algorithmic paradigms for the identification or verification of human beings. Hence, experiments of biometric systems at large with various biometrics traits could be a good approach to identify the correct and secure human recognition system. This book is a collection of biometrics solutions, which include both unimodal and multimodal biometrics. Also, it includes up-to-date biometrics algorithms with novel feature extraction techniques, computer vision approaches, soft computing approaches, and machine learning techniques under a unified framework used in biometrics systems.

This book has attempted to showcase some of the latest technologies and algorithms for human authentication and recognition. Recent developments made in pattern classification and image processing techniques have motivated researchers and practitioners to design cutting-edge biometric technologies and gain competitive advantages over conventional security applications by applying innovative thoughts and algorithms for real-life authentication problems. The need for biometrics systems is increasing tremendously in day-to-day activities such as airport security, medical diagnostics, ATM security, border security control, electronic data security, E-commerce, online banking transactions, cellular phones, national ID cards, drivers' licenses, corpse identification, criminal investigation, etc. The novel methods of biometric systems are evolving rapidly and boosting research areas in new directions. The book provides up-to-date reviews of intelligence techniques and theories used in biometric technologies for human authentication and identification.

The primary audience for the book includes researchers, scholars, graduate students, engineers, practitioners, and developers who work in biometrics and its related fields. We hope our efforts are able to benefit our readers.

Dakshina Ranjan Kisku
Asansol Engineering College, India

Phalguni Gupta
Indian Institute of Technology Kanpur, India

Jamuna Kanta Sing
Jadavpur University, India

MATLAB® is a registered trademark of The MathWorks, Inc. For product information, please contact:

The MathWorks, Inc.
3 Apple Hill Drive
Natick, MA 01760-2098 USA
Tel: 508 647 7000
Fax: 508-647-7001
E-mail: info@mathworks.com
Web: www.mathworks.com

Contributors

Sambit Bakshi
NIT Rourkela
Odissa, India

Ahmed Bouridane
Northumbria University
Newcastle upon Tyne, United
 Kingdom

Sheli Sinha Chaudhuri
Jadavpur University
Kolkata, India

N. G. Chitaliya
Sardar Vallabhbhai Patel
 Institute of Technology
Gujarat, India

Salim Chitroub
University of Sciences and
 Technology HB
Algiers, Algeria

Achintya Das
Kalyani Government
 Engineering College
Kalyani, India

Poulami Das
JIS College of Engineering
Kalyani, India

Amin Dehghani
Department of Electrical
 Engineering
K. N. Toosi University of
 Technology
Tehran, Iran

Maryam Dehghani
Department of Mathematics
University of Beheshti
Tehran, Iran

Nilanjan Dey
JIS College of Engineering
Kalyani, India

Hadi Farzin
Research Institute for ICT
Tehran, Iran

Manoj Singh Gaur
Malaviya National Institute
of Technology
Jaipur, India

Vijay John
University of Amsterdam
Amsterdam, Netherlands

Vijay Laxmi
Malaviya National Institute
of Technology
Jaipur, India

Banshidhar Majhi
NIT Rourkela
Odissa, India

Hans Varghese Mathews
Computer Society of India
Bangalore, India

Abdallah Meraoumia
Universite Kasdi Merbah
Ouargla
Ouargla, Algeria

Gayatri Mirajkar
Shivaji University
Kolhapur, India

Bijurika Nandi
CIEM Kolkata
Kolkata, India

Pouya Nazari
Department of Electrical
Engineering
Islamic Azad University
Najaf Abad, Iran

Elham Rajabian Noghondar
Gjøvik University College
Gjøvik, Norway

Pankaj Kumar Sa
NIT Rourkela
Odissa, India

Mohammad Hasan Saghafi
Amir Kabir University of
Technology
Tehran, Iran

Mohammed Saigaa
Universite Kasdi Merbah
Ouargla
Ouargla, Algeria

Preety Singh
LNM Institute of Information
Technology
Jaipur, India

A.I. Trivedi
Maharaja Sayajirao University
Gujarat, India

Hanif Vahedian
Department of Electrical
Engineering
K.N. Toosi University of
Technology
Tehran, Iran

PART I
GENERAL BIOMETRICS

1

SECURITY AND RELIABILITY ASSESSMENT FOR BIOMETRIC SYSTEMS

GAYATRI MIRAJKAR

Contents

Abstract

The problem of user authentication in identity management systems has a reliable solution provided by biometric recognition. Today, biometric systems have a widespread deployment in various applications—providing a powerful alternative to traditional authentication schemes. However, there are increasing concerns about the security and privacy of biometric technology. A biometric system is vulnerable to a variety of attacks aimed at undermining the integrity of the authentication process. These attacks are intended to either circumvent the security afforded by the system or to deter the normal functioning of the system. Vulnerability in a biometric system results in incorrect recognition or failure to correctly recognize individuals. Their existence in a biometric system is largely dependent on system design and structure, the type of biometrics used, and managerial policies. A high-level categorization of the different vulnerabilities of a biometric system is presented. Vulnerability analysis determines the imposter usage of the vulnerabilities with the aim of breaking the security policy. The chapter deals with vulnerability assessment and also presents a list of generalized vulnerabilities of a biometric system. Also, a framework for analyzing the vulnerabilities developed by the Biometrics Institute is presented. The proposed framework is capable of deriving useful metrics for the likelihood of a successful attack. As a solution for increasing the biometric system security, vitality detection and multimodal biometrics are also discussed. Given the right vulnerability analysis methodology and tools, it becomes easier for the system engineer to identify and analyze the potential points of attack and implement appropriate countermeasures for each.

1.1 Introduction

A reliable identity management system is the need of the day to combat the epidemic growth in identity theft and to meet the increased security requirements in a variety of applications ranging from international border crossings to securing information in databases [1]. Security is "freedom from risk of danger," whereas computer and data security is "the ability of a system to protect information and system resources with respect to confidentiality and integrity." Defining biometrics system security is difficult because of the ways biometric systems differ from traditional computer and cryptographic security. Biometric system security can be defined by its absence. Because biometrics is the "automated recognition of individuals based on their behavioral and biological characteristics," vulnerability in biometric security results in incorrect recognition or failure to correctly recognize individuals. This definition includes methods to falsely accept an individual (template regeneration), affect overall system performance (denial of service), or to attack another system through leaked data (identity theft). Vulnerabilities are measured against explicit or implicit design claims [2].

In their seminal work, Jain et al. [1,3,4] have emphasized the security and privacy concerns related to biometric systems and have also discussed in detail the vulnerabilities encountered in biometric systems. This chapter attempts to put forth these vulnerabilities under one roof. Because the adequate evaluation of the security of biometric technologies is currently an issue, vulnerability analysis—as discussed by Abdullayeva et al. [5]—is also presented here. The Biometric Institute's vulnerability assessment methodology [6] is considered next. The main aim of this assessment procedure is to provide a reliable level of assurance against a spoofing attack for a particular threat on a particular technology. The chapter concludes by presenting solutions for increased security, namely, vitality detection and multimodal biometrics [3].

1.2 Biometric System

Establishing the identity of a person is a critical task in any identity management system. Surrogate representations of identity such as passwords and ID cards are not sufficient for reliable identity determination because they can be easily misplaced, shared, or stolen. Commonly used biometric traits include fingerprint, face, iris, hand geometry, voice, palmprint, handwritten signatures, and gait (Figure 1.1) [1]. Biometric systems have a number of desirable properties over traditional authentication systems. They are inherently more reliable than password-based authentication because biometric traits

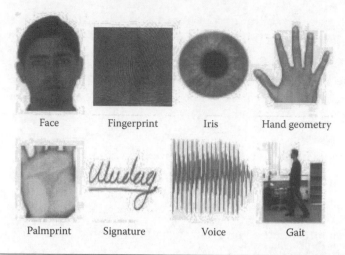

Face   Fingerprint   Iris   Hand geometry

Palmprint   Signature   Voice   Gait

Figure 1.1 Examples of body traits that can be used for biometric recognition. Anatomical traits include face, fingerprint, iris, palmprint, hand geometry, and ear shape; whereas gait, signature, and keystroke dynamics are some of the behavioral characteristics. Voice can be considered as an anatomical or behavioral characteristic. (From A.K. Jain et al., *Journal on Advances in Signal Processing* 2008, 17 pp., 2008.)

cannot be lost or forgotten (passwords can be lost or forgotten); biometric traits are difficult to copy, share, and distribute (passwords can be announced in hacker web sites); and they require the person being authenticated to be present at the time and point of authentication (conniving users can deny that they shared their password). It is difficult to forge biometrics (it requires more time, money, experience, and access privileges) and it is unlikely for the user to repudiate having accessed the digital content using biometrics. Thus, a biometrics-based authentication system is a powerful alternative to traditional authentication schemes. In some instances, biometrics can be used in conjunction with passwords (or tokens) to enhance the security offered by the authentication system [4]. All these characteristics have led to the widespread deployment of biometric authentication systems. However, there are still issues concerning the security of biometric recognition systems that need to be addressed to ensure the integrity and public acceptance of these systems.

There are five major components in a generic biometric authentication system, namely, sensor, feature extraction, template database, matcher, and decision modules (Figure 1.2). The sensor module is the

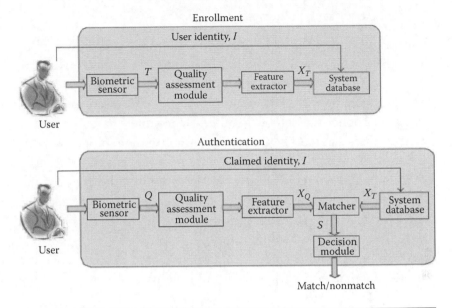

Figure 1.2 Enrollment and recognition stages in a biometric system. Here, *T* represents the biometric sample obtained during enrollment, *Q* is the query biometric sample obtained during recognition, X_T and X_Q are the template and query feature sets, respectively, and *S* represents the match score. (From A.K. Jain et al., *Journal on Advances in Signal Processing* 2008, 17 pp., 2008.)

interface between the user and the authentication system and its function is to scan the biometric trait(s) of the user. The feature extraction module processes the scanned biometric data to extract the salient information (feature set) that is useful in distinguishing between different areas. In some cases, the feature extractor is preceded by a quality assessment module that determines whether the scanned biometric trait is of sufficient quality for further processing. During enrollment, the extracted feature set is stored in a database as a template (X_T) indexed by the user's identity information. Because the template database could be geographically distributed and contain millions of records (e.g., in a national identification system), maintaining its security is not a trivial task. The matcher module is usually an executable problem that accepts two biometric feature sets X_T and X_Q (from template and query, respectively) as inputs, and outputs a match score (*S*) indicating the similarity between the two sets. Finally, the decision module makes the identity decision and initiates a response to the query [1].

1.3 Biometric System Vulnerability

Averting any potential security crisis requires the proper identification of biometric system vulnerabilities and their systematic addressal. The existence of vulnerabilities in a biometric system is largely dependent on system design and structure, the type of biometrics used, and managerial policies. Each of these areas encounters its own blend of vulnerabilities and must be analyzed to establish the appropriate countermeasures. A number of studies have analyzed potential security breaches in the biometric system and proposed methods to counter these breaches [4,34,35]. Formal methods of vulnerability analysis, such as attack trees [36], have also been used to study how biometric system security can be compromised [1].

A fishbone model (Figure 1.3) [4] can be used to summarize the various causes of biometric system vulnerability. Jain et al. [1] have

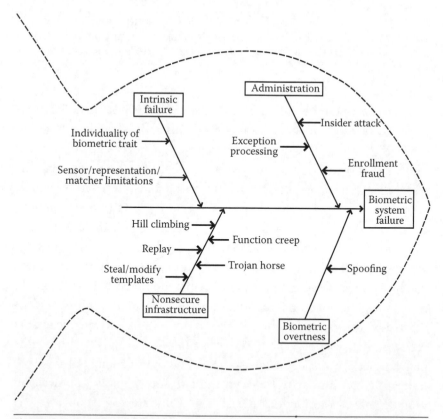

Figure 1.3 Fishbone model for categorizing biometric system vulnerabilities. (From A.K. Jain et al., *Journal on Advances in Signal Processing* 2008, 17 pp., 2008.)

categorized the failure modes of a biometric system into two classes at the highest level: intrinsic failure and failure due to an adversary attack. Intrinsic failures occur due to inherent limitations in the sensing, feature extraction, or matching technologies as well as the limited discriminability of the biometric trait. In adversary attacks, a resourceful hacker (or possibly an organized group) attempts to circumvent the biometric system for personal gains [1]. Jain et al. [1] further classified adversary attacks into three types based on factors that enable an adversary to compromise system security. These factors include system administration, nonsecure infrastructure, and biometric overtness. Jain et al. [1] describes them as follows.

1.3.1 Intrinsic Failure

Intrinsic failure is a security lapse due to an incorrect decision made by the biometric system. A biometric verification system can make two types of errors in decision making, namely, false-accept and false-reject. A genuine (legitimate) metric may be falsely rejected by the biometric system due to the large differences in the user's stored template and query biometric feature sets (Figure 1.4).

These intrauser variations may be due to incorrect interaction by the user with the biometrics (e.g., changes in pose and expression in

Figure 1.4 Illustration of biometric interclass variability. Two different impressions of the same finger obtained on different days are shown with minutiae points marked on them. Due to translation, rotation, and distortion, the number and location of minutiae in the two images are different. There are 33 and 26 minutiae in the left and right images, respectively. There are 16 common minutiae in the two images, although few of these correspondences have been indicated in the figure. (From A.K. Jain et al., *Journal on Advances in Signal Processing 2008*, 17 pp., 2008.)

a face image) or due to noise introduced at the sensor (e.g., residual prints left on a fingerprint sensor). False-accepts are usually caused by the lack of individuality or uniqueness in the biometric trait, which can lead to a large similarity between feature sets of different users (e.g., similarity in the face images of twins or siblings). Both intrauser variations and intrauser similarity may also be caused by the use of nonsalient features and nonrobust matchers. Sometimes, a sensor may fail to acquire the biometric trait of a user due to the limits of the sensing technology or adverse environmental conditions. For example, a fingerprint sensor may not be able to capture a good quality fingerprint of dry/wet fingers. This leads to failure-to-enroll (FTE) or failure-to-acquire (FTA) errors. Intrinsic failures can occur even when there is no explicit effort by an adversary to circumvent the system. Therefore, this type of failure is also known as a zero-effort attack. It poses a serious threat if the false-accept and false-reject probabilities are high.

1.3.2 Adversary Attacks

Here, an adversary intentionally stages an attack on the biometric system whose success depends on the loopholes in the system design and the availability of adequate computational and other resources to the adversary. In the study by Jain et al. [1], adversary attacks are categorized into three main classes: administration attack, nonsecure infrastructure, and biometric overtness. These are given below.

1.3.2.1 Administration Attack
This attack, also known as an insider attack, refers to all vulnerabilities introduced due to improper administration of the biometric system. These include the integrity of the enrollment process (e.g., validity of credentials presented during enrollment), collusion (or coercion) between the adversary and the system administrator or a legitimate user, and abuse of exception processing procedure.

1.3.2.2 Nonsecure Infrastructure
The infrastructure of a biometric system consists of hardware, software, and the communication channels between the various modules. There are a number of ways in which an adversary can manipulate the biometric infrastructure that can lead to

security breaches. Adversary attacks generally exploit the system vulnerability at one or more modules or interfaces. Ratha et al. [7] identified eight points of attack in a biometric system (Figure 1.5). These attacks are grouped into four categories, namely, (1) attacks at the user interface (input level), (2) attacks at the interfaces between modules, (3) attacks on the modules, and (4) attacks on the template database.

- *Attacks at the user interface:* Attack at the user interface is mostly due to the presentation of a spoof biometric trait [8–10]. If the sensor is unable to distinguish between fake and genuine biometric traits, the adversary easily intrudes the system under a false identity. A number of efforts have been made in developing hardware as well as software solutions that are capable of performing liveness detection [11–19].
- *Attacks at the interface between modules:* An adversary can either sabotage or intrude on the communication interfaces between different modules. For instance, he can place an interfering source near the communication channel (e.g., a jammer to obstruct a wireless interface). If the channel is not secured physically or cryptographically, an adversary may also intercept or modify the data being transferred. For example, Juels et al. [20] outlined the security and privacy issues introduced by insecure communication channels in an e-passport application that uses biometric authentication. Insecure communication channels also allow an adversary to

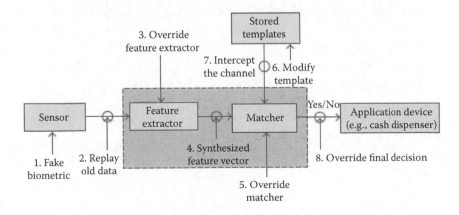

Figure 1.5 Points of attack in a generic biometric system. (From A.K. Jain et al., *Journal on Advances in Signal Processing* 2008, 17 pp., 2008.)

launch replay [21] or hill-climbing attacks [22]. A common way to secure a channel is by cryptographically encoding all the data sent through the interface, for example, using public key infrastructure. But even then, an adversary can stage a replay attack by first intercepting the encrypted data passing through the interface when a genuine user is interacting with the system and then sending this captured data to the desired module whenever he wants to break into the system. A countermeasure for this attack is to use time stamps or a challenge/response mechanism.

• *Attacks on the software modules:* The executable program at the module can be modified such that it always outputs the values desired by the adversary. Such attacks are known as Trojan horse attacks. Secure code execution practices or specialized hardware that can enforce secure execution of software should be used. Another component of software integrity relates to algorithmic integrity. Algorithmic integrity implies that the software should be able to handle any input in a desirable manner. As an example of an algorithmic loophole, consider a matching module in which a specific input value, say X_0, is not handled properly and whenever X_0 is input to the matcher, it always outputs a match (accept) decision. This vulnerability might not affect the normal functioning of the system because the probability of X_0 being generated from a real-biometric data may be negligible. However, an adversary can exploit this loophole to easily breach the security without being noticed.

• *Attacks on the template database:* One of the most potentially damaging attacks on a biometric system is against the biometric templates stored in the system database. The template of a person in the database is generated during enrollment and is often stored along with the original raw data. This has resulted in an increased need to provide privacy to the subject by providing adequate protection for the contents of the database [23].

Attacks on the template can lead to the following three vulnerabilities: (a) A template can be replaced by an imposter's template to gain unauthorized access. (b) A physical spoof can be created from the template [24,25] to gain unauthorized access to the system (as well as other systems that use the same biometric trait). (c) The stolen template can be replayed to the matcher to gain unauthorized access. A potential abuse of biometric identifiers is cross-matching or function creep [26] in which the biometric identifiers are used for purposes other than the intended purpose. As an example, a fingerprint template stolen from a bank's database may be used to search a criminal fingerprint database or cross-link to a person's health records.

The most straightforward way to secure the biometric system, including the template, is to put all the system modules and the interfaces between them on a smart card (or more generally, a secure processor). In such systems, known as match-on-card or system-on-card technology, sensor, feature extractor, matcher, and template reside on the card [27]. The advantage of this technology is that the biometric information never leaves the card. However, system-on-card solutions are not appropriate for most large-scale applications; they are expensive and users must carry the card with them all the time. Furthermore, it is possible that the template can be gleaned from a stolen card. So it is important to protect the template even in match-on-card applications. Passwords and PINs have the property that if they are compromised, the system administrator can issue a new one to the user. It is desirable to have the same property of revocability or cancelability with biometric templates.

Davida et al. [28] and Ratha et al. [29] proposed the storage of a transformed biometric template in the place of the original biometric template in the database. This was referred to as a private template [28] or a cancelable template [29]. An article by Ross and Othman [30] explores the use of visual cryptography to preserve the privacy of biometric data (the raw images). The process can be explained as follows. The original image is decomposed into two images in such a way that the original image can be revealed only when both images are simultaneously available. No information about the original image is revealed by either of the individual component images. During the enrollment process, the private biometric data is sent to a trusted third-party entity. Once the trusted entity receives the biometric data, it is decomposed into two images and the original data is discarded. The decomposed components are then transmitted and stored in two different database server locations such that the identity of the private data is not revealed to either source. For the authentication process, the trusted entity sends a request for obtaining the corresponding sheets to both servers. During the reconstruction of the private image, the sheets are overlaid (i.e., superimposed). This procedure thus avoids the complicated decryption and decoding computations that are commonly used in watermarking, steganography, or cryptosystem approaches. Once the matching score is computed, the reconstructed image is discarded. The proposed approach is applicable to a variety of biometric data, namely, fingerprint images, iris codes, and face images.

1.3.2.3 Biometric Overtness   It is possible for an adversary to covertly acquire the biometric characteristics of a genuine user (e.g., fingerprint impressions lifted from a surface) and use them to create physical artifacts (gummy fingers) of the biometric trait. Hence, if the biometric system is not capable of distinguishing between a live biometric presentation and an artificial spoof, an adversary can circumvent the system by presenting spoofed traits.

1.3.3 Effects of Biometric System Failure

When a biometric system is compromised, it can lead to two main effects: (1) denial-of-service and (2) intrusion [1].

- *Denial-of-service:* This condition refers to the scenario in which a legitimate user is prevented from obtaining the service that he is entitled to. An adversary can sabotage the infrastructure (e.g., physically damage a fingerprint sensor) thereby preventing users from accessing the system. Intrinsic failures like false-reject, failure-to-capture, and failure-to-acquire also lead to denial-of-service. Administrative abuse such as modification of templates or the operating parameters (e.g., matching threshold) of the biometric system may also result in denial-of-service.
- *Intrusion:* The term refers to an imposter gaining illegitimate access to the system, resulting in loss of privacy (e.g., unauthorized access to personal information) and security threats (e.g., terrorists crossing borders). All the four factors that cause biometric system vulnerability, namely, intrinsic failure, administrative abuse, nonsecure infrastructure, and biometric overtness can result in intrusion.

1.4 Analysis of Security Vulnerabilities

This section presents the analysis of security vulnerabilities as described in Abdullayeva et al. [5]. Vulnerability assessment is the systematic checking of systems to determine the adequacy of security measures, to determine the security weaknesses, and to obtain data for forecasting the effectiveness of proposed security measures. As mentioned in Abdullayeva et al. [5], vulnerability assessment is the sequence of the following steps:

- Search for potential vulnerabilities
- Developing intrusion tests
- Making intrusion tests
- Processing of results and reporting

Vulnerability analysis determines the imposter usage of the vulnerabilities (those that have been identified in the vulnerability assessment process) with the aim of breaking the security policy. The search for potential vulnerabilities step has two phases, one of which is searching for weaknesses and the other is the evaluation of potential attacks.

The structure, architecture, production, or implementation of a system may introduce a vulnerability to the biometric system. In some cases, a secondary system may be integrated to the biometric system that could possibly make the biometric system vulnerable. There are five points of vulnerabilities:

- Operating systems
- Database management systems (and application software)
- Biometric application software
- Software for sensor
- Hardware and drivers

The other main aspects can be categorized as follows:

- Management of operations
- Management of parameters (especially FAR/FRR parameters)
- System configuration

Wayman [31] studied the technical testing of biometric devices and divided it into five subsystems: data collection, signal processing, transmission, data storage, and decision. This makes the potential attack points more clear. Cukic and Bartlow [32] introduced three more components: administrative management, information technologies, and presentation of tokens. In total, 20 potential attack points and 22 vulnerabilities have been identified. All biometric systems require administrative supervision to some extent. The level of supervision may vary among systems but it is not difficult to imagine the related vulnerabilities. Vulnerabilities in this area may devalue even the best-planned system. A biometric system may or may not be related to an IT environment, but is usually part of a larger system. Interaction with an IT environment may introduce some new vulnerabilities not existing in the previous scheme. A token is required in some biometric systems, which makes final decisions based on the biometric characteristics and information presented on the token. A token may introduce a potential attack point to the biometric system. A smart card containing biometric information is an example of a token used in this kind of system. There are several other schemes for vulnerability classification [33]. Considering them as well, a generalized list of vulnerabilities of biometric systems is suggested [5].

- *Administration:* Intentional or unintentional administrative mistakes
- *User:* A legitimate user wants to upgrade his privileges to the administrative level
- *Enrollment:* Breaking registration procedures
- *Spoofing:* A fake biometric is used for authentication as a legitimate user
- *Mimicry:* Attacker mimics the biometric characteristics of the legitimate user
- *Undetect:* Attacks undetected by the system may encourage new attacks
- *Fail secure:* A result of abnormal utilization conditions of the biometric system or IT environment
- *Power:* Power cuts
- *Bypass:* Bypassing biometric system for access. This can be achieved by surpassing physical barriers, forcing a legitimate user to present his biometric to the sensor, or through the cooperation of a legitimate user

- *Corrupt attack:* Weakening the system by making changes in the IT environment or biometric system. Modification or replacement of system parameters is an example
- *Degrade:* Certain software in the IT environment decreases the system's security level
- *Tamper:* Counterfeiting the hardware of the system
- *Residual:* Latent fingerprints may be used to make artificial fingerprints or are accepted directly by the sensor
- *Cryptological attack:* Encryption can be broken in data transmission and this biometric data can be used for another type of attack (e.g., replay attack)
- *Brute force attack:* Attacker presents the biometric characteristic to the system repeatedly to be authenticated. This type of attack depends on FAR parameter
- *Evil twin attacks:* The biometric characteristics of an imposter are very similar to the enrolled user's biometric
- *Replay:* A stored signal is replayed into the system, ignoring the sensor. For instance, replay of an old copy of a fingerprint image or a recorded audio signal
- *Fake template:* Introducing a fake biometric template into the database or onto smart cards
- *Noise:* Access may be gained by the attacker when noise is applied to the system
- *Poor image:* Quality supervision may be utilized. If low-quality images are accepted for registration, then the attacker may hope to deceive the system, for example, in the case of noisy images
- *Weak ID:* Similar to the "poor image" weakness, and tries to fake the system by using weak templates
- *FAR/FRR:* Attacker considers FAR and FRR values to fake the system
- *Denial-of-service:* Denial of service attacks aim to prevent a user from obtaining a legitimate service

Consequently, there are many attack points and vulnerabilities in biometric systems. Using the given list, vulnerabilities for specific systems can be identified. A biometric system may not have all the vulnerabilities or attack points. The list is general enough and can be applied to any system easily. For a specific system, it is essential to consider the properties of the system to identify the vulnerabilities. The aim of vulnerability analysis is to determine the possibility of utilization of weaknesses of biometric systems in an application environment. Penetration tests are carried out to determine the vulnerability in the application environment of an imposter with a certain potential of attack. The level of potential attack can be low, medium, or high. In standard ISO/IEC 15408-3, penetration tests are considered to determine the system's resistance level [low (AVA_VLA.2), medium (AVA_VLA.3), high (AVA_VLA.4)] against penetration attacks by imposters with low, medium, or high attack potentials.

There are three categories of threat agents for biometric systems [34]:

- *Imposter:* An individual pretending to be authorized intentionally or unintentionally. An imposter may be authorized or not
- *Attacker:* Any individual or system trying to compromise the function of the biometric system. The motive could be unauthorized access or denial of service
- *Authorized users:* Authorized users of a biometric system unintentionally compromising the biometric device or the system. This category corresponds to unintentional human mistakes, for example, mistakes of administrator when configuring the system

Threat agents usually have a certain level of technical capability. At the lowest level of the risk scale, threat agents may lack specific system information and financial resources. Capable, well-informed, and well-financed threat agents can be more dangerous. It is important to develop and carry out penetration tests for each attack using certain vulnerabilities. Therefore, there is a problem of appropriate testing methodology for the determination of the resistance of biometric systems by considering countermeasures for certain attacks [5].

1.5 Biometric Institute's Vulnerability Assessment Methodology

1.5.1 Introduction

This section presents the concept of vulnerability assessment as presented by Dunstone and Poulton [6]. The main aim of the Biometric Institute's vulnerability assessment methodology is to provide a reliable level of assurance against a spoofing attack for a particular threat on a particular technology. Its other aims are to ensure that this assessment is timely and cost-effective, to incorporate the flexibility to adjust to different biometric modalities in an evolving threat landscape, and to allow it to sit as components in a wider security assessment and threat mitigation process. The vulnerability of a biometric system to a determined attack depends on three interrelated factors: a secure computing infrastructure, trust in the human operators of the system, and factors that are specific to biometrics. The first two are issues regularly dealt with for any secure computing environment. Traditional computer security has long-established standards and practices, including those to ensure the security of communication and storage, the tamperproofing of devices, protection against external infiltration, and requirements on auditing and usage policy. However, the nondeterministic nature of biometric matching opens up a number of different security issues and related vulnerabilities that must be considered to determine the vulnerability of a system to malicious attack.

The use of biometrics for identification is a probabilistic science. Every time an individual presents their biometric to a biometric system, it will be slightly different. This variation is caused by a combination of user behavior, environmental conditions, and physical changes to the biometric due to ageing and other factors. To develop a commercially useful biometric system, significant effort has gone into improving the accuracy of the biometric algorithms for the task of distinguishing between different people. Most large-scale testing results on biometrics measure false match and false non–match rates, the former focusing on the chance that a random person has biometric characteristics that are sufficiently similar to pass as that of another individual. The vulnerability of a biometric system should not be confused with its accuracy in this type of test. It is possible to have a system that is extremely accurate at distinguishing between pairs of individuals, but which is highly vulnerable to simple functions used to circumvent the security. This might be by mimicking physical biological characteristics, or by bypassing or altering the information used as part of the matching process.

The priority (or cost) of any given vulnerability is related to the value of the assets protected by the biometric multiplied by the total risk of compromise, which is the chance that these assets will be obtained through a successfully executed attack. It is this total risk factor (also called the "spoofing risk") that we are interested in when determining a system's vulnerability.

In the context of examining biometric security threats, the "known threats" are those that can be listed and defined, and each known threat that has not been investigated or evaluated fully can be categorized as a one of the "known unknowns." The threat is known but its effect or likelihood is not well understood. However, there may also be threats that are yet to be discovered and these are part of the "unknown unknowns." To discover these requires continual intelligence on the activities of attackers and also creative and knowledgeable evaluators (and system designers).

1.5.2 Methodology

The threat landscape is complex because a wide variety of factors need to be considered during the evaluation. Each biometric product will have different levels of vulnerability to a range of threats, and each threat is dependent on the attributes of an attacker. The fundamental building block of this evaluation methodology is that the spoofing risk can be broken down into two factors: the exploitation potential, which relies on the biometric system's properties, and the attack potential, which is related to the capabilities of the attacker. The spoofing risk can then be defined as

$$\text{spoofing risk} = \text{attack potential} \times \text{exploitation potential}$$

where *attack potential* is defined as the likelihood that an attacker is able to discover a vulnerability, and has the capability to exploit it, and *exploitation potential* is defined as the likelihood that a particular vulnerability exists, and that it can be exploited to breach the system. This allows a separation of components that can be deduced a priori from factors that require experimental validation. The methodology consists of four steps: determining the threats, calculating the attack potential, calculating the exploitation potential, and finally, determining the vulnerability assurance level (VAL).

1.5.2.1 Determine the Threats for Evaluation
The list of potential threats against a biometric system is diverse. It ranges from the presentation

of artifacts (such as simple pictures of a biometric) to the reconstruction of a biometric from stolen biometric templates. The protection profiles established as part of the United Kingdom's CSEG provide a baseline list of threats. However, the threat list is continually expanding as new techniques and materials become available on which to base attacks. A general threat list for a biometric system will include many methods of attack that would apply to any complex computer security environment. In this methodology, we are particularly interested in those that relate to the use of biometrics, but the line between specific biometric threats and traditional security threats can be difficult to define (Figure 1.6). However, it is where the probabilistic nature of the biometric acquisition or matching process is manifested that distinguishes specific biometric vulnerabilities from standard IT vulnerabilities. Each threat has a number of parameters that can be used to define it. These include:

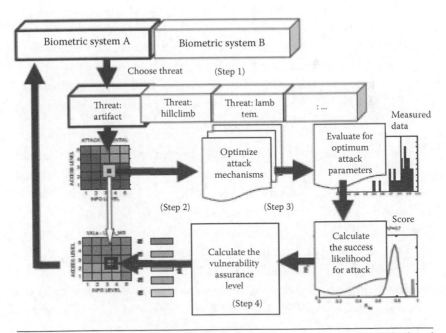

Figure 1.6 Methodology overview: threat selection, attack, potential choice, optimization of attack mechanism, evaluation for the optimum parameters, calculation of the exploitation potential, its conversion to a VAL, and finally, extrapolation across all attack potentials. (From T. Dunstone and G. Poulton, *Biometric Vulnerability: A Principled Assessment Methodology.* Biometrics Institute Ltd. With permission.)

- *Point of attack:* The points in the biometric life cycle or the part of the architecture of the system that may cause a breach. Biometric threats may be exploited at either verification or enrollment time, or on a specific part of the biometric architecture
- *Information level:* What is the effect of an attacker's knowledge or resources on their ability to exploit the threat?
- *Access level:* How does an attacker's level of access to the system (from user to administrator) affect their ability to exploit the threat? The information and access level are combined to produce an overall attack potential diagram
- *Mitigation:* What steps can be taken to prevent the threat from being exploited? These might involve new sensing mechanisms or changes to the algorithm, environment, or usage policy
- *Discovery effect:* This is the degree of effort needed to discover, characterize, and implement the vulnerability
- *Related threats:* Many threats are interrelated and this knowledge can be useful as the assessment of one threat might allow the simple simultaneous assessment of threats that share similar characteristics
- *Method of assessment:* Although the overall evaluation methodology is the same for each threat, the technique used to assess the vulnerability will vary greatly depending on the type of threat
- *Vulnerability assurance level:* The assessed maximum chance of an informed and motivated attacker exploiting the threat

We undertake this vulnerability assessment process to better understand the most serious threats and transform some of the threat list items from "known unknowns" to "known knowns." Due to the expensive nature of these measurements, we will seldom be able to investigate all known threats. Therefore, for practicality, it is necessary to rank them and evaluate only those with the highest priority. This ranking process relies heavily on the experience of the evaluator to make informed judgments about how the different threats compare. This ranking might also be different depending on the nature of the application and what is being protected.

1.5.2.2 Calculate the Attack Potential When assessing the risk of an attack being successful, it is necessary to consider the context of a particular attacker. An attacker might have no access to or knowledge about the system other than information from the Internet, or alternatively, they may be a skilled programmer with access to state sponsorship and full administrator rights. For each of these scenarios, the risk of system penetration is very difficult.

The attack potential is the likelihood that an attacker is able to discover any vulnerability, and has the capability to exploit it. In most cases, this can be estimated reasonably well by using biometric expertise and system knowledge. For instance, it can easily be seen that some attacks are impossible without higher-level access to the system to be able to change settings or to inject new information. Similarly, some attacks can be accomplished with only very few resources, whereas others require significant skill, time, and manufacturing expertise.

The two components of attack potential are the access level (Table 1.1) and the information level (Table 1.2), which correspond to the knowledge of the attacker and may also relate to the type of resources available.

Table 1.1   Different Levels of Access

A1	Simple user access (verification, enrollment, or both)
A2	Repeated access (multiple attempts at verification)
A3	Broad enrollment access (multiple and/or nonstandard enrollments)
A4	Operator level access
A5	Administrator level access, including source code and recompilation access (ability to make and substitute system changes)

Source: T. Dunstone and G. Poulton. *Biometric Vulnerability: A Principled Assessment Methodology.* Biometrics Institute Ltd., Sept. 2006.

Note: The different levels of access, in which every level includes all knowledge pertaining to the lower levels (possible collusion with system operators or administrators is also included).

Table 1.2   Levels of Information for an Attacker

I1	No knowledge
I2	Experience with similar systems (including knowledge or vulnerabilities)
I3	Experience and/or access to an identical system (including knowledge of specific weaknesses)
I4	High-level knowledge of system algorithms and architecture
I5	Detailed knowledge of software (source code level)

Source: T. Dunstone and G. Poulton. *Biometric Vulnerability: A Principled Assessment Methodology.* Biometrics Institute Ltd., Sept. 2006.

Note: The levels of information for an attacker, in which every level includes all knowledge pertaining to the lower levels.

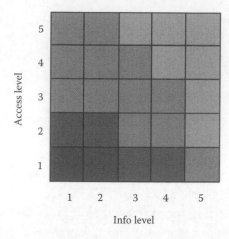

Figure 1.7 An example attack potential diagram. In this case, the system is vulnerable when the user has a high level of system access and the user is also an expert in the biometric system. (From T. Dunstone and G. Poulton, *Biometric Vulnerability: A Principled Assessment Methodology.* Biometrics Institute Ltd. With permission.)

An example attack potential diagram is shown in Figure 1.7. In this diagram, each level has been broken into five stages, the lighter the shade, the more likely that the attack will be successful.

1.5.2.3 Calculate Exploitation Potential   Once we know, in theory, how likely an attack is to be successful for a particular threat, a program of experimentation can be undertaken to determine (for a particular technology) the chance that an attacker would be successful. The result will show the chance that a motivated attacker has of breaching a system before any external mitigation has been applied.

The exploitation potential, defined previously, is a measure of the likelihood that a particular vulnerability exists and the likelihood that it can be exploited to breach the system. It is determined experimentally by first choosing the specific access level and information level of the attacker we are interested in (a point on the attack potential diagram).

An experimental program is next undertaken to determine which, among a scene of variants of a particular threat, is likely to produce the most vulnerability. For example, variants for a face recognition artifact attack could include the identity to be attacked and the type of artifact used—photograph or video of a face, or a full three-dimensional head model. Vulnerability to a threat is indicated when high match scorcs are observed during an attack. A score above the minimum threshold that could be practically set represents a potentially successful attack. The measurement process hence looks for the highest similarity scores during the experiments. Where similarity scores are not available and only the accept/reject decision is provided, the technique can still be used but requires significantly more presentations.

Each variant has many subvariants, and the process seeks to find the best of these. For example, a photograph artifact can vary with the type of paper, the lighting conditions, and several aspects of presentation to the camera. This optimization of threat variants is best achieved by experimenters that have significant creativity and experience. The attack variants must be in line with the type of attacker that it is being evaluated against. The optimization process consists of continually refining each variant to finally produce the most successful attack.

One of the challenges with biometric testing is that it often requires a large number of live subjects for it to be statistically significant. The testing is hence usually expensive and time-consuming. Vulnerability experimentation is different because it is only interested in maximizing the likelihood of a successful attack, so only one attack needs to be successful for a vulnerability to have been detected. The number of potential attackers is small, and there is seldom any need for a large and diverse number of subjects. The measurement process is relatively controlled so less variability in scores is expected. This leads to higher confidence levels for smaller test sets and allows for more sophisticated statistical methods to be used.

After the optimization process, the most successful attack technique discovered is put through a series of trials to formally determine how likely it is that an attacker, with knowledge of this best technique, could breach the system's security. Statistical measures (Bayesian or otherwise) are used to quantify this as the exploitation potential.

Finally, the exploitation potential may be discounted by the discovery effect (DE), which adjusts for the difficulty an attacker might have in characterizing and implementing the vulnerability. The factor is given in the range 0–1, and the exploitation potential is scaled by (1-DE) if a technique is used that would require significant effort for an attacker. The discovery effect is generally characterized by the

computing power that might be required to implement the attack—
for most biometric vulnerabilities, the discovery effort is sufficiently
low that it can be considered as zero.

1.5.2.4 Vulnerabilities Assurance Level   The result of the previous steps
is the measurement of the exploitation potential for one point on the
attack potential diagram. The exploitation potential is converted to a
VAL using a logarithmic measure indicating the assurance that there
will be no more than a given percentage of successes from repeated
single attacks on the system. The first five levels are shown in Table 1.3
and are computed with a confidence interval of 95%. Higher levels
are, of course, also possible.

With the assumption that the attack potential diagram is valid,
we can then set the spoofing risk at the evaluated point, and use the
relative rating of the remaining squares to set the total risk factors for
all different access and information levels. Validation of the VALs for
these other points on the attack potential diagram can be achieved, if
required, by repeating the evaluation process.

1.5.3 Example

A theoretical example will illustrate this process using two different
hypothetical face recognition systems (A and B) for the use of a video
recording of a face, which is an artifact attack. The attack potential
diagram is the same for both systems on this threat. An access level of
3 and an information level of 3 is chosen for initial experimentation
and optimization, giving an attack potential of 0.6 (Figure 1.8a).

System A has an effective liveness detection so that 300 trials failed
to breach the system. The spoofing risk is thus <0.01. Thus, system A,

Table 1.3   Vulnerability Assurance Levels

VAL4	Fewer than 1 in 100 attacks are likely to succeed
VAL3	Fewer than 1 in 30 attacks are likely to succeed
VAL2	Fewer than 1 in 10 attacks are likely to succeed
VAL1	Fewer than 1 in 3 attacks are likely to succeed
VAL0	Cannot guarantee at least VAL1

Source: T. Dunstone and G. Poulton. *Biometric Vulnerability: A Principled Assessment Methodology.*
Biometrics Institute Ltd. With permission.

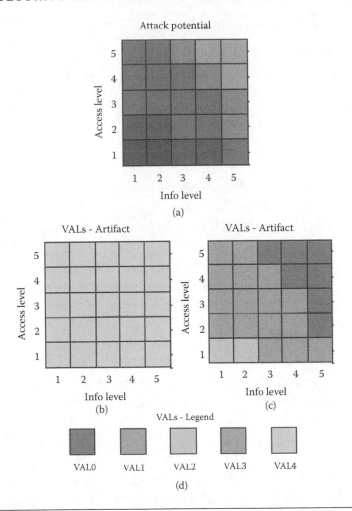

Figure 1.8 (a) Attack potential of both systems, (b) VALs for system a, (c) VALs for system b, and (d) gray scale legend for VALs. (From T. Dunstone and G. Poulton, *Biometric Vulnerability: A Principled Assessment Methodology.* Biometrics Institute Ltd. With permission.)

in this case, does not seem vulnerable to this threat regardless of the access or attack level. Hence, we estimate VAL4 for all attack potential values (Figure 1.8b).

However, 50 trials on system B gives a spoofing risk of 0.21. In practice, this means that an attacker who is familiar with these systems would have, at most, a 21% chance of fooling the system at each attack (with a confidence interval of 95%). From this the VAL is calculated at VAL1. Multiplication by the attack potential then gives system B VALs at all values of attack potential (Figure 1.8c).

1.6 Vitality Detection and Multimodal Biometrics for Increased Security

Many commercial applications could improve their personal recognition systems' security by adding required credentials or building blocks—for example, using a token or password together with biometric recognition. However, in high-security applications (such as access control to nuclear energy facilities), it is important that each component of the recognition system is secure in itself and that the many components provide additional layers of security. In many commercial applications, adding more credentials (such as passwords and tokens) can be undesirable because doing so reintroduces the problems associated with knowledge-based and possession-based systems (passwords can be forgotten or guessed, and tokens can be lost or stolen). In these applications, fake biometric attacks remain a serious concern. However, this threat can be addressed in two ways: first, by building vitality detection mechanisms in the biometric recognition system hardware and software; second, by designing multimodal-biometric systems that incorporate several different biometric characteristics (for example, face, fingerprint, and hand geometry). Fingerprint devices can incorporate vitality detection by measuring the optical, electric, or thermal properties of the human skin or other biomedical characteristics such as the pulse. Iris-recognition devices can measure the involuntary papillary hippus (constant small constrictions and dilations of the pupil caused by spontaneous movements of the iris rather than external stimulation) to ensure that the eye is alive. The resources required to defeat biometric sensors increase as they incorporate more methods of vitality detection. However, if the vitality detection method is known to the hacker, it is possible for the hacker to thwart it. For example, if the fingerprint sensor also uses finger pulse detection, the hacker can build a pulse generator into a fake finger.

Therefore, the best method for vitality detection is to use a characteristic that is distinctive to each individual, and not easily available to an adversary for copying. Such a unique characteristic is another biometric. For example, a multimodal biometric system can be built that combines a strong biometric, such as a fingerprint with another biometric (possibly, a weaker one) that is difficult to acquire covertly, such as face thermogram. Another approach might use a fingerprint system requiring each user to present several fingers in a specific order; a hacker would have to find latent fingerprints from multiple fingers from both hands and also know the order of presentation. Such a solution comes at a relatively low cost: It requires no other sensor, and an existing fingerprint verification system could be easily adapted to handle impressions from multiple fingers. Such multimodal-biometric solutions could also significantly improve recognition accuracy—at the cost of longer acquisition and processing times (with possibly extra hardware).

1.7 Conclusions

Vulnerability in biometric security results in incorrect recognition or failure to correctly recognize individuals. Furthermore, it can be seen that the existence of vulnerabilities in the biometric system is dependent mostly on system design and structure, the type of biometrics used, and managerial policies. Because each of these areas encounters its own blend of vulnerabilities, these must be analyzed to establish its own set of countermeasures. The fishbone model proposed by Jain et al. [4] summarizes the various causes of biometric system vulnerability. Abdullayeva et al. [5] present a generalized list of vulnerabilities showing the number of attack points in biometric systems. Furthermore, the aim of vulnerability analysis is to determine the possibility of utilization of weaknesses of biometrics in an application environment. The methodology developed by the Biometrics Institute is effective and can be used to access biometric systems and rate their vulnerability performance. The methodology has been designed to ensure that the evaluation is cost-effective and leads to practical outputs that can be used as part of the risk analysis process for any system using biometrics. There is much hope that such methodologies can spur developments in uncovering the vulnerabilities hampering the security of biometric systems.

References

1. A.K. Jain, K. Nandkumar, and A. Nagar. Biometric template security. *EURASIP Journal on Advances in Signal Processing* 2008, 17 pp., 2008.
2. A. Adler. Biometric system security. In *Handbook of Biometrics*, edited by A.K. Jain, P. Flynn, and A.A. Ross. Springer, 2008.

3. S. Prabhakar, S. Pankanti, and A.K. Jain. Biometric recognition: Security and privacy concerns. *IEEE Computer Society*, 33–42, 2003.

4. A.K. Jain, A. Ross, and S. Pankanti. Biometrics: A tool for information security. *IEEE Transactions on Information Forensics and Security* 1(2):125–143, 2006.

5. F. Abdullayeva, Y. Imamverdiyev, V. Musayev, and J. Wayman. Analysis of security vulnerabilities in biometric systems. *Proceedings of the Second International Conference on Problems of Cybernetics and Informatics*. Baku, Azerbaijan, Sept. 10–12, 2008. http://danishbiometrics.files.wordpress.com/2009/08/1-13.pdf.

6. T. Dunstone and G. Poulton. *Biometric Vulnerability: A Principled Assessment Methodology.* Biometrics Institute Ltd., Sept. 2006.

7. N.K. Ratha, J.H. Connell, and R.M. Bolle. An analysis of minutiae matching strength. In *Proceedings of the 3rd International Conference on Audio- and Video-Based Biometric Person Authentication (AVBPA '01)*, 223–228, Halmstad, Sweden, 2001.

8. T. Matsumoto, H. Matsumoto, K. Yamada, and S. Hoshino. Impact of artificial "gummy" fingers on fingerprint systems. In *Optical Security and Counterfeit Deterrence Techniques IV. Proceedings of SPIE* 4677, 275–289, San Jose, CA, 2002.

9. T. Matsumoto, M. Hirabayashi, and K. Sato. A vulnerability evaluation of iris matching (part 3). In *Proceedings of the Symposium on Cryptography and information Security (SCIS '04)*, 701–706, Iwate, Japan, 2004.

10. A. Eriksson and P. Wretling. How flexible is the human voice? A case study of mimicry. In *Proceedings of the European Conference on Speech Technology (Eurospeech '97)*, 1043–1046, Rhodes, Greece, 1997.

11. S.T.V. Parthasaradhi, R. Derekhshani, L.A. Hornak, and S.A.C. Schuckers. Time-series detection of perspiration as a liveness test in fingerprint devices. *IEEE Transactions on Systems, Man, and Cybernetics, Part C* 35(3):335–343, 2005.

12. A. Antonelli, R. Cappelli, D. Maio, and D. Maltoni. Fake finger detection by skin distortion analysis. *IEEE Transactions on Information Forensics and Security* 1(3):360–373, 2006.

13. D.R. Setlak. Fingerprint sensor having spoof reduction features and related methods. US Patent no. 5953441, 1999.

14. K.A. Nixon and R.K. Rowe. Multispectral fingerprint imaging for spoof detection. In *Biometric Technology for Human Identification II, Proceedings of SPIE* 5799, 214–225, Orlando, FL, 2005.

15. J. Li, Y. Wang, T. Tan, and A.K. Jain. Live face detection based on the analysis of Fourier spectra. In *Biometric Technology for Human Identification, Proceedings of SPIE*, 5404, 296–303, Orlando, FL, 2004.

16. K. Kollreider, H. Fronthaler, and J. Bigun. Evaluating liveness by face images and the structure tensor. In *Proceedings of the 4th IEEE Workshop on Automatic Identification Advanced Technologies (AUTO ID '05)*, 75–80, Buffalo, NY, 2005.

17. H.-K. Jee, S.-U. Jung, and J.-H. Yoo. Liveness detection for embedded face recognition system. *International Journal of Biomedical Sciences* 1(4):235–238, 2006.

18. J. Daugman. Recognizing persons by their iris patterns. In *Biometrics: Personal Identification in Networked Security*, edited by A.K. Jain, R. Bolle, and S. Pankanti, 103–122. Kluwer Academic Publishers, London, 1999.

19. E.C. Lee, R.K. Park, and J. Kim. Fake iris detection by using Purkinje image. In *Proceedings, International Conference on Advances in Biometrics (ICB '06), Lecture Notes in Computer Science* 3832, 397–403. Hong Kong, 2006.

20. A. Juels, D. Molnar, and D. Wagner. Security and privacy issues in E-passports. In *Proceedings 1st International Conference on Security and Privacy for Emerging Areas in Commercial Networks (Securecomm '05)*, 74–88, Athens, Greece, 2005.

21. P. Syverson. A taxonomy of replay attacks. In *Proceedings Computer Security Foundations Workshop (CSFW '97)*, 187–191, Franconia, NH, 1994.

22. A. Adler. Vulnerabilities in biometric encryption systems. In *Proceedings 5th International Conference on Audio- and Video-Based Biometric Person Authentication (AVBPA '05), Lecture Notes in Computer Science* 3546, 1100–1109, Hilton Rye Town, NY, 2005.

23. A. Ross and A. Othman. Visual cryptography for biometric security. *IEEE Transactions on Information Forensics and Security* 6(1):70–80, 2001.

24. A. Ross, J. Shah, and A.K. Jain. From template to image: Reconstructing fingerprints from minutiae points. *IEEE Transactions on Pattern Analysis and Machine Intelligence* 29(4):544–560, 2007.

25. R. Cappelli, A. Lumini, D. Maio, and D. Maltoni. Fingerprint image reconstruction from standard templates. *IEEE Transactions on Pattern Analysis and Machine Intelligence* 29(4):1489–1503, 2007.

26. A.K. Jain, R. Bolle, and S. Pankanti (eds.). *Biometrics: Personal Identification in Networked Society*. Kluwer Academic Publishers, Dordrecht, The Netherlands, 1999.

27. A.K. Jain and S. Pankanti. A touch of money. *IEEE Spectrum* 43(7):22–27, 2006.

28. G.I. Davida, Y. Frankel, and B.J. Matt. On enabling secure applications through off-line biometric identification. In *Proceedings IEEE Symposium on Security & Privacy*, 148–157, 1998.

29. N. Ratha, J. Connell, and R. Bolle. Enhancing security and privacy in biometrics-based authentication systems. *IBM Systems Journal* 40(3):614–634, 2001.

30. A. Ross and A. Othman. Visual cryptography for biometric privacy. *IEEE Transactions on Information Forensics and Security* 6(1):70–81, 2011.

31. J.L. Wayman. Technical testing and evaluation of biometric devices. In *Biometrics: Personal Identification in Networked Society*, edited by A.K. Jain et al. Kluwer Academic Publishers, Dordrecht, The Netherlands, 1999.

32. B. Cukic and N. Bartlow. The vulnerabilities of biometric systems—An integrated look at old and new ideas. Technical Report, West Virginia University, 2005.

33. C. Dimitriadis and D. Polemi. Application of multi-criteria analysis for the creation of a risk assessment knowledgebase for biometric systems. *Lecture Notes in Computer Science* 3072, Springer-Verlag, ICBA, 724–730, Hong Kong, China, 2004.

34. C. Roberts. Biometric attack vectors and defenses. *Computers and Security* 26(1):14–25, 2007.

35. A.K. Jain, A. Ross, and U. Uludag. Biometric template security: Challenges and security. In *Proceedings of the European Signal Processing Conference (EUSIPCO '05)*, Antalya, Turkey, 2005.

36. B. Cukic and N. Bartlow. Biometric system threats and countermeasures: A risk based approach. In *Proceedings of the Biometric Consortium (BCC '05)*, Crystal City, VA, 2005.

2

REVIEW OF HUMAN RECOGNITION BASED ON RETINAL IMAGES

AMIN DEHGHANI, HADI FARZIN, HANIF VAHEDIAN, POUYA NAZARI, AND MARYAM DEHGHANI

Contents

Abstract

In this chapter, we review human recognition systems based on retinal images. In addition, we also explain about the concept of a biometric recognition system. Some of the well-known retinal recognition methods are explained and comparative studies are made.

2.1 Introduction

The meaning of "biometrics" is "life measurement" but it is usually used with unique physiological characteristics to recognize an individual. For recognition, a collection of automated methods are used to recognize an individual person based on a physiological or behavioral characteristic. The application that most people think about, when it comes to biometrics, is in security. However, for biometric recognition, a number of biometric traits have been developed and are used for recognition. A biometric system is like a pattern recognition system that makes a personal identification or verification by determining the authenticity of a specific physiological or behavioral characteristic possessed by the user. Biometric technologies are thus defined as the "automated methods of identifying or verifying of a living person based on a physiological or behavioral characteristic" [1,2]. Biometric traits are used for both identification and verification. Depending on the application context, a biometric system may operate in verification or identification mode. In the verification mode, the system confirms or denies a person's claimed identity by comparing the captured biometric features with the biometric template(s) stored in the system's database. In the identification mode, the system recognizes an individual by searching the templates of all the users in the database for a match [3]. Some biometric characteristics of a person for identification and recognition are fingerprint, hand geometry, face, handwriting, voice, ear, DNA, hand thermogram, hand vein, palmprint, iris, and retina. Each biometric pattern has its strengths and weaknesses, and the choice depends on the application. In Figure 2.1, some of the well-known biometric patterns are illustrated.

The use of specific biometric characters involves a weighting of several factors. In the book by Jain et al. [15], some factors that affect the

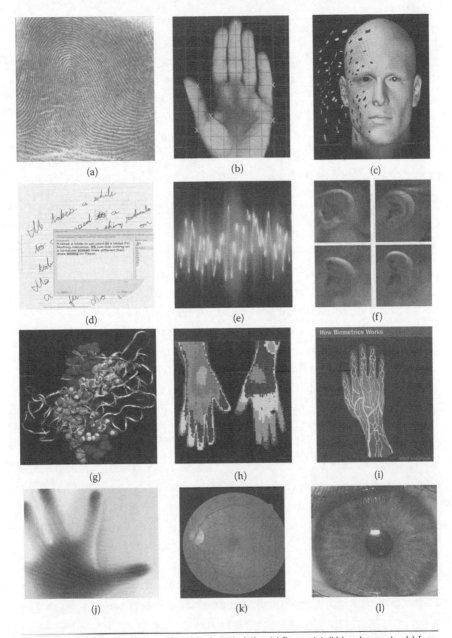

Figure 2.1 Examples of various biometric characteristics: (a) fingerprint, (b) hand geometry, (c) face, (d) handwriting, (e) voice, (f) ear, (g) DNA, (h) hand thermogram, (i) hand vein, (j) palmprint, (k) retina, and (l) iris. (From en.wikipedia.org, www.lconnica.com, www.cosmosmagazine.com, www.netdip.com, www.findbiometrics.com, www.ece.vt.edu, www.ks.uiuc.edu, www.apmsurgery.com, www.science. howstuffworks.com, www.advancedsourcecode.com, and www.en.wikipedia.org.)

selection of suitable traits for biometric authentication were mentioned. Here, we briefly discuss the factors, such as universality, uniqueness, permanence, measurability, performance, and acceptability, which could have an effect on biometric authentication. Universality means that every person using a system should possess the trait. Uniqueness means that the trait should be sufficiently different for individuals in the relevant population such that they can be distinguished from one another. Permanence relates to the manner in which a trait varies over time. More specifically, a trait with "good" permanence will be reasonably invariant over time with respect to the specific matching algorithm. Measurability (collectability) relates to the ease of acquisition or measurement of the trait. In addition, acquired data should be in a form that permits subsequent processing and extraction of the relevant feature sets. Performance relates to the accuracy, speed, and robustness of the technology used. Acceptability relates to how well individuals in the relevant population accept the technology such that they are willing to have their biometric trait captured and assessed. Circumvention relates to the ease with which a trait might be imitated using an artifact or substitute [16]. In Table 2.1, the characteristics of different biometric methods are shown.

None of the single biometric traits satisfy all factors for each application. Before both identification and verification, there is a step called enrollment.

During enrollment, biometric characteristics from an individual are captured and stored. In subsequent uses, biometric information is detected and compared with the information stored at the time of enrollment. In Figure 2.2, the procedure of a recognition system is shown. The first block (sensor) refers to the capture process. Therefore, the raw biometric, which is the interface between the real world and the system, is captured by a sensing device such as a fingerprint scanner or video camera, and it has to acquire all the necessary data. Most of the time, it is an image acquisition system, but it can change according to the characteristics desired. The second block performs the preprocessing: it has to remove artifacts from the sensor, enhance the input (e.g., removing background noise), use some kind of normalization, etc. In the third block, the necessary features are extracted. These features are important characteristics of an image used for recognition. Then, these features are stored as templates and will be used in the matching phase [15–17].

Table 2.1 Characteristics of Different Biometric Methods

BIOMETRIC METHOD	UNIVERSALITY	DISTINCTIVENESS	PERMANENCE	COLLECTABILITY	PERFORMANCE	ACCEPTABILITY	CIRCUMVENTION
DNA	H	H	H	L	H	L	L
Ear	M	M	H	M	M	H	M
Face	H	L	M	H	L	H	H
Fingerprint	M	H	H	M	H	M	M
Gait	M	L	L	H	L	H	M
Hand geometry	M	M	M	H	M	M	M
Hand vein	M	M	M	M	M	M	L
Iris	H	H	H	M	H	L	L
Palmprint	M	H	H	M	H	M	M
Retina	H	H	M	L	H	L	L
Signature	L	L	L	H	L	H	H
Voice	M	L	L	M	L	H	H

Source: A. Jain et al., *Biometrics: Personal Identification in a Networked Society.* Kluwer Academic Publishers, Dordrecht, the Netherlands, 1999; http://en.wikipedia.org/wiki/Biometrics; With kind permission from Springer Science+Business Media: *Handbook of Biometrics*, edited by Jain, A.K., Flynn, P., Ross, A., Introduction to biometrics, 2008, 1–22, A.K. Jain, and A. Ross.

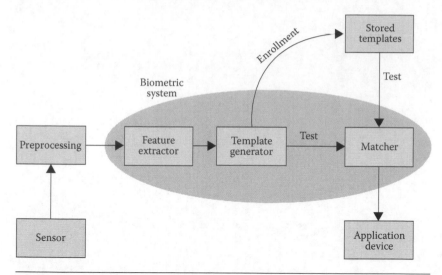

Figure 2.2 Block diagram of the recognition system. (From http://en.wikipedia.org/wiki/Biometrics.)

2.2 Performance

The performance of the recognition method is evaluated using the following parameters:

- False accept rate or false match rate (FAR or FMR): the probability that the system incorrectly matches the input pattern to a nonmatching template in the database. It measures the percentage of invalid inputs that are incorrectly accepted.
- False reject rate or false non–match rate (FRR or FNMR): the probability that the system fails to detect a match between the input pattern and the templates in the database. It measures the percentage of valid inputs that are incorrectly rejected.
- Receiver operating characteristic or relative operating characteristic (ROC): The ROC plot is a visual characterization of the trade-off between the FAR and the FRR. In general, the matching algorithm performs a decision based on a threshold which determines how close to a template the input needs to be for it to be considered a match. If the threshold is reduced, there will be fewer false nonmatches but more false accepts. Correspondingly, a higher threshold will reduce the FAR but increase the FRR. A common variation is the detection error

trade-off (DET), which is obtained using normal deviate scales on both axes. This more linear graph illuminates the differences for higher performances (rarer errors) [17].

Up to now, we have explained the concept of biometrics, recognition, and the characteristics of each biometric trait. In the next section, we explain the anatomy of the eye and the retina, and then we explain some of the well-known retinal recognition methods.

2.3 Anatomy of the Eye

The human eye is a complex anatomical device that remarkably demonstrates the architectural wonders of the human body. Like a camera, the eye is able to refract light and produce a focused image that can stimulate neural responses and enable the ability to see. The eye is essentially an opaque eyeball filled with a water-like fluid. In the front of the eyeball is a transparent opening known as the cornea. The cornea is a thin membrane that has an index of refraction of approximately 1.38. The cornea has the dual purpose of protecting the eye and refracting light as it enters the eye. After light passes through the cornea, a portion of it passes through an opening known as the pupil. Rather than being an actual part of the eye's anatomy, the pupil is merely an opening. The pupil is the black portion in the middle of the eyeball. Its black appearance is attributed to the fact that the light that the pupil allows to enter the eye is absorbed on the retina (and elsewhere) and does not exit the eye. Thus, as you look into another person's pupil opening, no light is exiting their pupil and coming to your eye; subsequently, the pupil appears black. Like the aperture of a camera, the size of the pupil opening can be adjusted by the dilation of the iris. The iris is the colored part of the eye—being blue for some people and brown for others (and so forth); it is a diaphragm that is capable of stretching and reducing the size of the opening. In bright-light situations, the iris adjusts its size to reduce the pupil opening and limit the amount of light that enters the eye and in dim-light situations, the iris adjusts so as to maximize the size of the pupil opening and increase the amount of light that enters the eye. Light that passes through the pupil opening will enter the crystalline lens. The crystalline lens is made of layers of a fibrous material that has an index of refraction of roughly 1.40. Unlike the lens on a camera, the lens of the eye is able to change its shape and thus serves to fine-tune the vision process. The lens is attached to the ciliary muscles. These muscles relax and contract to change the shape of the lens. By carefully adjusting the lenses' shape, the ciliary muscles assist the eye in the critical task of producing an image on the back of the eyeball. The inner surface of the eye is known as the retina. The retina contains the rods and cones that serve the task of detecting the intensity and the frequency of the incoming light. An adult eye is typically equipped with up to 120 million rods that detect the intensity of light and about six million cones that detect the frequency of light. These rods and cones send nerve impulses to the brain. The nerve impulses travel through a network of nerve cells. There are as many as one million neural pathways from the rods and cones to the brain. This network of nerve cells is bundled together to form the optic nerve on the very back of the eyeball [18]. In Figure 2.3, the components of the human eye are shown.

When an ophthalmologist uses an ophthalmoscope to look into your eye, the following view of the retina (as shown in Figure 2.4) can be seen. In the center of the retina is the optic nerve, a circular to oval white area measuring approximately 2 × 1.5 mm across. From the center of the optic nerve radiates the major blood vessels of the retina. Approximately 17 degrees (4.5–5 mm), or two and a half disk

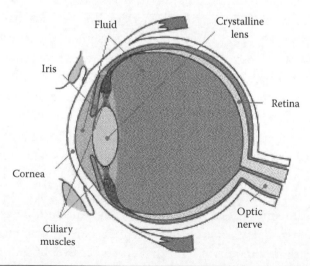

Figure 2.3 All components of the human eye. (From http://www.physicsclassroom.com/class/refrn/u14l6a.cfm.)

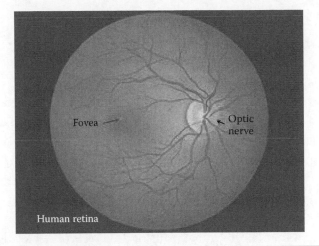

Figure 2.4   Retina as seen through an ophthalmoscope. (From http://webvision.med.utah.edu/book/part-i-foundations/simple-anatomy-of-the-retina/.)

diameters to the left of the disk, can be seen the slightly oval-shaped, blood vessel–free reddish spot, the fovea, which is at the center of the area known by ophthalmologists as the macula.

A circular field of approximately 6 mm around the fovea is considered the central retina, whereas beyond this is the peripheral retina stretching to the oraserrata, 21 mm from the center of the retina (fovea). The total retina is a circular disk that is between 30 and 40 mm in diameter.

The retina is approximately 0.5 mm thick and lines the back of the eye. The optic nerve contains the ganglion cell axons running to the brain and, additionally, incoming blood vessels that open into the retina to vascularize the retinal layers and neurons. A radial section of a portion of the retina reveals that the ganglion cells (the output neurons of the retina) lie innermost in the retina closest to the lens and front of the eye, and the photosensors (the rods and cones) lie outermost in the retina against the pigment epithelium and choroid. Light must, therefore, travel through the thickness of the retina before striking and activating the rods and cones. Subsequently, the absorption of photons by the visual pigment of the photoreceptors is first translated into a biochemical message and then into an electrical message that can stimulate all the succeeding neurons of the retina. The retinal message concerning the photic input and some preliminary organization of the visual image into several forms of sensation are transmitted to the brain from the spiking discharge pattern of the ganglion cells [19].

2.4 Retinal Scanners

The first idea for retinal recognition came from Dr. Carleton Simon and Dr. Isadore Goldstein and was published in the *New York State Journal of Medicine* in 1935. The first technology for a retinal scanning device emerged in 1975. In 1976, Robert "Buzz" Hill formed a corporation named EyeDentify, Inc., and made a full-time effort to research and develop such a device. In 1978, the specific means for a retinal scanner was patented, followed by a commercial model in 1981 [20,21].

The first types of devices used to obtain images of the retina were called "fundus cameras." These were instruments created for ophthalmologists but were adapted to obtain images of the retina. However, there were a number of problems using this type of device. First, the equipment was considered to be very expensive and difficult to operate. Second, the light used to illuminate the retina was considered to be far too bright and discomforting to the user. As a result, further research and development were conducted, which subsequently yielded the first true prototype of a retinal scanning device in 1981. This time, infrared light was used to illuminate the blood vessel pattern of the retina. Infrared light has been primarily used in retinal recognition because the blood vessel pattern in the retina can absorb infrared light at a much quicker rate than the rest of the tissue in the eye. The infrared light is reflected back to the retinal scanning device for processing. This retinal scanning device utilized a complex system of scanning optics, mirrors, and targeting systems to capture the blood vessel pattern of the retina. However, later research and development created devices with much simpler designs. For example, these newer devices consisted of integrated retinal scanning optics, which sharply reduced the costs of production, in comparison with the production costs of the EyeDentification System 7.5. The last known retinal scanning device to be manufactured by EyeDentify was the ICAM 2001. This device could store data from up to 3,000 enrollees, with a storage capacity of up to 3,300 history transactions. However, this product was eventually taken off the market because of user acceptance and public adoption issues and its high price. It is believed that some companies, like Retica Systems, Inc., are working on a prototype retinal scanning device that will be much easier to implement for commercial applications and will be much more user-friendly. In summary, given

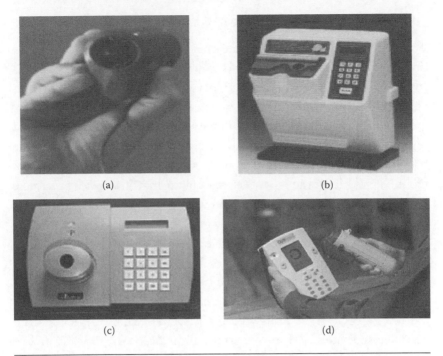

(a)

(b)

(c)

(d)

Figure 2.5 Some retinal scanners, (a) a human retinal scanner, (b) and (c) human retinal recognition scanners, and (d) a cow retinal scanner.

its strong and weak points, retinal recognition has the potential to be a very powerful biometric identification technology. In Figure 2.5, you can see four types of retinal scanners: (a), (b), and (c) correspond to human retinal scanners, and (d) corresponds to an animal retinal scanner [22–24].

2.5 Applications of Retinal Recognition

The primary applications for retinal recognition have been for physical access entry for high-security facilities. This includes military installations, nuclear facilities, and laboratories. One of the best-documented applications of the use of retinal recognition was conducted by the State of Illinois, in an effort to reduce welfare fraud. The primary purpose was to identify welfare recipients, so that benefits could not be claimed more than once. Iris recognition is also used in conjunction with this project [24]. Retinal imaging is a form of recognition that can be used in both animals and humans.

2.6 Retinal Recognition Methodology

This section will introduce some major techniques that have been proposed for retinal recognition during the recent decade. The retina may provide a higher level of security due to its inherent robustness against imposture. On the other hand, the retinal blood vessels of each subject, which are the main characters for recognition, undergo fewer modifications during life. Despite these properties, the retina has not been used frequently in biometric systems mainly because of technological limitations in the manufacturing of low-cost scanners [15,25–29]. This is the reason why few works have been published for human recognition using retinal images. Nowadays, with the progress in retinal scanner technology, relatively low-cost retinal scanners have been introduced to the market [30–34].

As discussed previously, it is the blood vessel pattern in the retina that forms the foundation for the science and technology of retinal recognition. There are two famous studies which confirmed the uniqueness of the blood vessel pattern of the retina. In 1935, an article was published by Simon and Goldstein [30], in which they discovered that every retina possesses a unique and deferent blood vessel pattern. They even later published an article that suggested the use of photographs of these blood vessel patterns of the retina as a means to identify people. The second study was conducted in the 1950s by Dr. Paul Tower. He discovered that even among identical twins, the blood vessel patterns of the retina were unique and deferent [35].

The proposed methods for retinal recognition are divided into two different parts. The first part uses the results of vessel segmentation of retinal images. Therefore, at the first step, segmentation methods are used to obtain retinal blood vessels. Therefore, these methods take a large amount of computational time. The second part extracts features from retinal images without using blood vessel segmentation methods. In the following subsections, we review some previous methods.

2.6.1 Farzin's Method

Farzin et al. [24] proposed a novel method based on the features obtained from human retinal images. Blood vessel segmentation is essential for some retinal recognition methods. The automatic extraction and analysis of the retinal vessel's pattern is a difficult task because images taken at standard examinations are sometimes poorly contrasted and contain artifacts. Nonuniformity of illumination increases the intensity (brightness) levels in some regions of an image, whereas other regions farther away from the optic disc (OD) may suffer from a reduction of brightness. Many algorithms have been proposed for extracting retinal vessels but a few of them are suitable for identification purposes. Local contrast enhancement and gradient orientation analysis (GOA) are the most two suitable approaches that will be discussed here.

2.6.1.1 Local Contrast Enhancement This method includes the following steps: (i) using a template matching technique, the OD is localized in the retinal image; (ii) the original image is divided by the correlation image obtained in the previous step to achieve an image in which the undesired brightness effect of OD is suppressed; (iii) the vessel/background contrast is enhanced using a local processing operation based on the statistical properties of the resulting image (discussed above); and (iv) finally, a binary image containing the blood vessels is produced by histogram thresholding of the contrast-enhanced image [36,37].

2.6.1.2 Reducing the Effect of the Optical Disk Here, a template-matching technique was used to localize the OD [38]. For this purpose, the original green plane image was correlated with a template. The template was generated by averaging rectangular regions of interest (ROIs) containing OD in the retinal image database. After correlating each retinal image with the template, the OD was localized as a bright region in the correlated image with a high density of vessels. Figure 2.6 shows the template and the resulting correlated image. As illustrated, the bright region in the correlated image corresponds to the OD in the original image.

Afterward, the original image is divided (pixel by pixel) using the correlation image obtained in the previous step to achieve a new image in which the undesired brightness effect of OD is suppressed. In local processing operations, a sliding window of size $M \times M$ (M is at least 50 times smaller than the dimensions of the

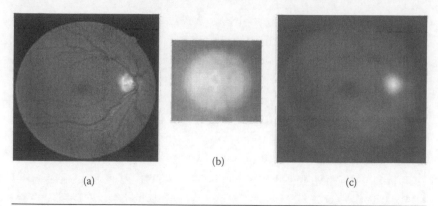

(b)

(a)

(c)

Figure 2.6 Optical disk localization: (a) original image, (b) template, and (c) correlated image. (From H. Farzin et al., A novel retinal identification system. *EURASIP J. Adv. Signal Process 2008*, article ID 280635, 2008. doi:10.1155/2008/280635.)

original image) was used to obtain a contrast-enhanced image. In each pixel, the new value was computed using the mean/variance of window values and global maximum/minimum values of the pixels in the original image [36].

Let $f(i, j)$ be the value of the pixel (i, j) in the original image. The enhanced image $g(i, j)$ was computed according to Equations 2.1 through 2.4:

$$f(i, j) \rightarrow g(i, j) = \frac{H - w_{min}}{w_{max} - w_{min}} \tag{2.1}$$

$$H = \frac{1}{\text{mean} + \left(\frac{1}{\sqrt{\text{var}}} \right) \exp\left(\frac{-[\text{mean} - f(i, j)]^{0.98}}{\sqrt{\text{var}}} \right)} \tag{2.2}$$

$$w_{min} = \frac{\text{mean}}{1 + \exp\left(\frac{-(\text{mean} - f\,\text{min})}{\sqrt{\text{var}}} \right)} \tag{2.3}$$

$$w_{max} = \frac{\text{mean}}{1 + \exp\left(\frac{-(f\,\text{mean} - f\,\text{max})}{\sqrt{\text{var}}} \right)} \tag{2.4}$$

where var and mean are variance and mean of values inside the window and $f$min and $f$max are global minimum and maximum of the original green plan image. It is clear that H is a mapping function from f to g. Figure 2.6 shows the results of vessel segmentation after thresholding [36].

2.6.1.3 Retinal Identification Process   The identification process via retinal images started with vessel segmenting and will be continued by feature generation and, finally, feature matching as the last stage.

2.6.1.4 Feature Generation   Features of blood vessel patterns including their diameters and their relative locations and angles were used in the feature generation vectors. For generating these features, the algorithm used four submodules, and detailed descriptions of these submodules are given in the following subsections.

2.6.1.4.1 Vessel Masking in the Vicinity of the Optical Disk   Vessels around the OD are more important for identification purposes because their distribution pattern around the OD has less randomness within a subject. In other words, as the vessels are farther from the OD, they become thinner and their distribution is more random, such that it has less discriminative property. Hence, the OD's location can be used as a reference point for positioning the human eye with respect to the scanner system. This means that the OD should be placed at the central region of the scanned image to allow the system to perform the identification. After extracting the vessels and localizing the OD with a vessel segmentation algorithm, vessels in the vicinity of the OD were considered. A ring mask centered at the OD's location, with radii r_1 and r_2 ($r_1 < r_2$), was used to select a ROI in the vessel segmented binary image (Figure 2.4a). This binary ROI was used for feature generation in the next stages [24,36].

2.6.1.4.2 Polar Transformation and Rotation Invariance   Eye and head movements in front of the scanner may result in some degrees of rotation in retinal images acquired from the same subject. Therefore, rotation-invariant features were essential for preventing identification errors caused by image rotation. This is the reason why polar transformation was used to obtain a rotation-invariant binary image containing retinal vessels in the proximity of the OD. The polar image can be constructed by the following transformations from Cartesian coordinates.

The point (x, y) in Cartesian coordinates was transformed to the point $\left[\rho = \sqrt{x^2 + y^2}, \theta = \arctan(y/x) \right]$ in the polar coordinates. The polar image created from the ROI image is shown in Figure 2.7. The polar image size is 30 × 360, in which the second dimension refers to the view angle of ROI [24].

2.6.1.4.3 Multiresolution Analysis of the Polar Image   Vessels in the vicinity of the OD have different diameter sizes. This property was used as the first feature in the feature generation module. In other words, one can recognize large, medium, and small vessels that originate from the OD and their distribution pattern is unique for each individual. For this purpose, three scale analyses using discrete stationary bi-orthogonal wavelet transforms were used. Figure 2.8a shows residual coefficients resulting from the application of wavelet transforms to the polar image in Figure 2.8b in the first three scales. To extract large vessels from the polar image, they applied threshold residual coefficients in the third scale of the wavelet transform. For extracting medium-sized vessels, large vessels were removed from the polar image and the same procedure was repeated on residual

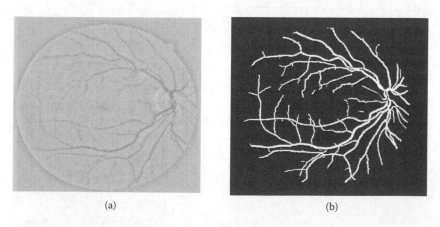

(a)   (b)

Figure 2.7   Blood segmentation and masking: (a) original image with OD effect suppressed, and (b) vessel pattern. (From H. Farzin et al., A new method for blood vessels segmentation in retinal images. In *Proceedings of the 13th Iranian Conference on Biomedical Engineering (ICBME '07)*, Tehran, Iran, February 2007.)

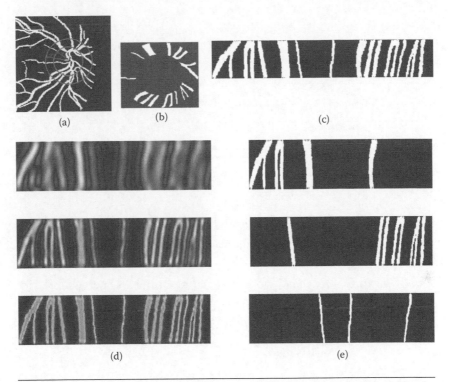

Figure 2.8 Polar image created from ROI image: (a) ROI of vessels images around OD polar transformation; (b) ROI in Cartesian coordinates; and (c) polar image. Multiresolution analysis of polar image. (d) Wavelet transform: approximations of scale 3 (top), scale 2 (middle), and scale 1 (bottom). (e) Vessel separation results: large (top), medium (middle), and small (bottom) vessels. (From H. Farzin et al., A novel retinal identification system. *EURASIP J. Adv. Signal Process 2008*, article ID 280635, 2008. doi:10.1155/2008/280635.)

coefficients of the wavelet transform in the second scale. Finally, large-sized and medium-sized vessels were removed from the polar image to obtain small vessels. The results of the vessel separation procedure are illustrated in Figure 2.8b [24].

2.6.1.4.4 Feature Vector Construction For constructing the feature vector, vessels in each scale were localized and replaced with rectangular pulses. The duration of each pulse was experimentally fixed to three points and its amplitude was equal to the angle between the corresponding vessel orientation and the horizontal axis. Therefore, the final feature vector was composed of three vectors (one per scale), each containing 360 values. Evidently, zero values in each vector

Figure 2.9   Construction of feature vector in the second scale (medium-sized vessels). (From H. Farzin et al., A novel retinal identification system. *EURASIP J. Adv. Signal Process 2008*, article ID 280635, 2008. doi:10.1155/2008/280635.)

corresponded to nonvessel positions in polar coordinates. Figure 2.9 shows the feature vector construction in detail [24].

2.6.1.5 Feature Matching   For feature matching, a new similarity index (SI) based on a modified correlation (MC) between the feature vectors was introduced. For computing MC between two feature vectors (at the ith scale), they used the following equation:

$$MC_i(\phi) = \sum_{\tau=1}^{N} sgn\{\theta_i(\tau) \times \theta q_i(\tau+\phi)\} * cos[\theta_i(\tau) - \theta q_i(\tau+\phi)], \, i = 1, 2, 3$$

$$(2.5)$$

where θ is a feature vector corresponding to the enrolled image and θq is a feature vector corresponding to the entered image, i represent three images of different sizes, sgn is sign function, τ is the rotation of the correlation process, and N is the length of the vector (e.g., 360). Because the generated feature vector does not get a negative value, the first term of the sigma has only 0, 1 values. In this equation, if two images are the same, the cosine term gets values of 1 or near 1. On the other hand, if they are different, this term gets small values (zero or near zero). The similarity index, by choosing the maximum value of the MC function, was as follows [24].

$$SI_i = \underset{\phi}{maximum}\{MC_i(\phi)\}, \, i = 1, 2, 3 \qquad (2.6)$$

Then, a scale-weighted summation of SIs was used to obtain a total SI for every matching that was defined in Equation 2.7. Large vessels are more effective in identification; therefore, $w_1 = 2$, $w_2 = 1.5$, and $w_3 = 0.5$. Choosing a suitable threshold from the FRR/FAR diagram and applying it on SI was the end stage of the proposed method.

$$SI = w_1^* SI_1 + w_2^* SI_2 + w_3^* SI_3 \qquad (2.7)$$

2.6.2 Dehghani's Method

Dehghani et al. [39] proposed a new identification method based on retinal images. In this algorithm, they used rotation-invariant features extracted from the retinal images. One of the most important features that can be used in pattern recognition is statistical features. Statistical features can help us to generate new sets of patterns with less difficulty. They used Hu's moments, which are invariant under translation, rotation, orthogonal transformations, and under general linear transformations. Let $I(x, y)$ be a continuous image function. The geometric moment of order $p + q$ is defined as

$$m_{pq} = \int \int_{-\alpha}^{\alpha} x^p y^q I(x, y)\, dx\, dy \qquad (2.8)$$

Then the central moment can be expressed as

$$\mu_{pq} = \int \int_{-\alpha}^{\alpha} (x - \bar{x})^p (y - \bar{y})^q I(x, y)\, dx\, dy \qquad (2.9)$$

In the last equation, $\bar{x}$ and $\bar{y}$ are given by

$$\bar{x} = \frac{m_{10}}{m_{00}}$$
$$\bar{y} = \frac{m_{01}}{m_{00}} \qquad (2.10)$$

The normalized central moments can be expressed as

$$\eta_{pq} = \frac{\mu_{pq}}{\mu_{00}^{\gamma}} \qquad (2.11)$$

$$\gamma = \frac{p + q}{2} + 1 \qquad (2.12)$$

These moments are rotation invariant. Based on the last equations, the Hu moments are defined as a set of seven moments that are invariant under the actions of translation, scaling, and rotation. These are

$$p+q = 2$$
$$\phi_1 = \eta_{20} + \eta_{02}$$
$$\phi_2 = (\eta_{20} - \eta_{02})^2 + 4\eta_{11}^2$$
$$p+q = 3$$
$$\phi_3 = (\eta_{30} - 3\eta_{12})^2 + (\eta_{03} - 3\eta_{21})^2$$
$$\phi_4 = (\eta_{30} + \eta_{12})^2 + (\eta_{03} + \eta_{21})^2$$
$$\phi_5 = (\eta_{30} - 3\eta_{12})(\eta_{30} + \eta_{12})[(\eta_{30} + \eta_{12})^2 - 3(\eta_{03} + \eta_{21})^2] \quad (2.13)$$
$$\quad\quad + (\eta_{03} - 3\eta_{21})(\eta_{03} + \eta_{21})[(\eta_{03} + \eta_{21})^2 - 3(\eta_{30} + \eta_{12})^2]$$
$$\phi_6 = (\eta_{20} - \eta_{02})[(\eta_{30} + \eta_{12})^2 - (\eta_{03} + \eta_{21})^2]$$
$$\quad\quad + 4\eta_{11}(\eta_{30} + \eta_{12})(\eta_{03} + \eta_{21})$$
$$\phi_7 = (3\eta_{21} - \eta_{03})(\eta_{30} + \eta_{12})[(\eta_{30} + \eta_{12})^2 - 3(\eta_{03} + \eta_{21})^2]$$
$$\quad\quad + (\eta_{30} - 3\eta_{12})(\eta_{03} + \eta_{21})[(\eta_{03} + \eta_{21})^2 - 3(\eta_{03} + \eta_{21})^2$$

Only ϕ_1 and ϕ_2 were used for human identification using retinal images because their invariance under the actions of rotation and translation are less compared with the others. These features have values in the range of [0–1]; therefore, for increasing the distance between the features and finally improving the efficiency of identification algorithm, they mapped these features to a large scale. Therefore,

$$c = \log\phi_1$$
$$d = \log\phi_2 \quad\quad (2.14)$$

Then they are mapped to a large scale as follows:

$$e = \text{map}(c)$$
$$f = \text{map}(d) \quad\quad (2.15)$$

Then, for assigning each of the extracted features to a special person and finally classifying these features, they used Euclidean distance between the features of the testing and data set images, and by applying thresholding on the distance, they could classify testing features and, finally, the identity of the testing images (query images) was determined. The security system first checked if the person was already enrolled in the database; then it identified the testing person. For this purpose, they used the difference between f of testing person and f of each data set image and then they applied thresholding to accept or reject the existence of that testing person in the data set. Therefore,

$$\text{dist}_i = \text{abs}(f_i - f_{\text{test}})$$

$$\text{if dist}_i < \text{thresholding} \qquad (2.16)$$

$$\Rightarrow \text{the test person is in the data set}$$

In the next step, the identity of the person (testing image) must be determined. For this purpose, the minimum difference between e of the testing image and e of each data set image was obtained and the person producing the minimum value was identified as the subject in the test image [39].

2.6.3 Shahnazi's Method

Shahnazi et al. [40] proposed a new method based on the wavelet energy feature (WEF), which is a powerful tool for multiresolution analysis. WEF can reflect the wavelet energy distribution of the vessels with different thicknesses and widths in several directions at different wavelet decomposition levels (scales), so its ability to discriminate retinas is very strong. Simple computation was another virtue of WEF. Using semiconductors and various environmental temperatures in electronic imaging systems cause noisy images, so they used noisy retinal images for recognition. This method is based on the segmentation results of retinal images.

A GOA and orientation compensation of blood vessels was proposed in the study by Kondo [41] and was used by Shahnazi et al. [40] in a retinal recognition system.

The gradient vectors of the image were obtained and then they were normalized into the unit gradient vectors because only gradient orientation was required. The unit vectors converge on (or diverge from) anatomical features as long as the features are brighter (or darker) than the background. Therefore, the unit vectors are highly discontinuous where there are features—especially with radially and bilaterally symmetrical structures. Features in retinal images can be detected by finding discontinuities in gradient orientation. It should be emphasized that this technique is effective irrespective of image contrast and intensity because the magnitude of the gradient vectors is not used. Summarizing the GOA procedure, let $g(x, y)$, $g_x(x, y)$, and $g_y(x, y)$ denote a retinal image and partial derivatives of $g(x, y)$ in x (horizontal) and y (vertical) directions, respectively. The unit gradient vectors are obtained by Equation 2.17

$$\begin{cases} n_x(x, y) = g_x(x, y) / \sqrt{g_x^2(x, y) + g_y^2(x, y)} \\ n_y(x, y) = g_y(x, y) / \sqrt{g_x^2(x, y) + g_y^2(x, y)} \end{cases} \tag{2.17}$$

To find discontinuities in gradient orientation, the first derivatives of the unit vectors was computed as

$$\begin{cases} d_{xx}(x, y) = n_x^* k_x & d_{yx}(x, y) = n_y^* k_x \\ d_{xy}(x, y) = n_x^* k_y & d_{yy}(x, y) = n_y^* k_y \end{cases} \tag{2.18}$$

in which the same first-derivative operators were once again used. The discontinuity magnitude of gradient orientation $D(x, y)$ was expressed as

$$D^2(x, y) = d_{xx}^2(x, y) + d_{yx}^2(x, y) + d_{xy}^2(x, y) + d_{yy}^2(x, y) \tag{2.19}$$

The width of the vessel varies widely as it travels radially from the OD. With the aim of detecting various sizes of features, we apply GOA at three different scales. The Sobel operator was first used as k_x and k_y to detect very fine features. To detect larger features, the Sobel operator was modified as

$$k_x' = \begin{pmatrix} 1 & 0 & 0 & 0 & -1 \\ 0 & 0 & 0 & 0 & 0 \\ 2 & 0 & 0 & 0 & -2 \\ 0 & 0 & 0 & 0 & 0 \\ 1 & 0 & 0 & 0 & -1 \end{pmatrix}, \quad k_y' = \begin{pmatrix} 1 & 0 & 2 & 0 & 1 \\ 0 & 0 & 0 & 0 & 0 \\ 0 & 0 & 0 & 0 & 0 \\ 0 & 0 & 0 & 0 & 0 \\ -1 & 0 & -2 & 0 & -1 \end{pmatrix}$$

$$\tag{2.20}$$

The above equation was applied to the original image as well as to its half-sized subimage (equivalent to the low-pass filtered subimage of the Haar wavelet transform).

Denoting the discontinuity magnitude of gradient orientation at each scale $D_1(x, y)$, $D_2(x, y)$, and $D_3(x, y)$, respectively, a response of GOA was defined, $D_{GOA}(x, y)$, as Equation 2.21

$$D_{GOV}^2(x, y) = D_1^2(x, y) + D_2^2(x, y) + D_3^2(x, y) \qquad (2.21)$$

where $D_3(x, y)$ was resized to the original image size by upsampling. It is important to note that GOA responds to both valley and ridge structures in the same manner, as they are equally discontinuous in gradient orientation. In the case of extracting blood vessels (i.e., valleys), high GOA responses owing to ridges need to be excluded. This can be achieved by the sign of $\nabla^2 g(x, y)$ according to Equation 2.22

$$D_{valley}^2(x, y) = \begin{cases} D_{GOV}^2(x, y), & \text{sgn } [\nabla^2 g(x, y)] \geq 0 \\ 0 & \text{otherwise} \end{cases} \qquad (2.22)$$

where ∇^2 denotes the Laplacian operator. Figure 2.10 shows the result of gradient analysis orientation vessel detection.

Feature extraction was done after blood vessel detection in retinal images. In the retina, different vessels have different resolutions, main and thick vessels broke into branches and spread all over the retina. Thick and thin vessels could be analyzed in low and high resolution,

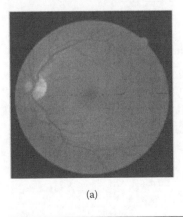
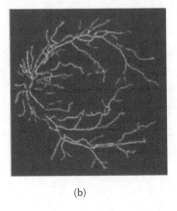

(a)   (b)

Figure 2.10 Results of gradient analysis orientation vessel detection: (a) retinal image and (b) blood vessel extraction using GOA.

respectively. Therefore, a multiresolution method was used to analyze the retina. Directional property was another important character of these features. Two-dimensional wavelet transformations could decompose the image in several directions at different resolutions. Therefore, discrete wavelet transform (DWT) shown in Figure 2.11 was used.

A_{k-1} is the approximation coefficients of the (K-1)th level decomposition, A_k, H_k, V_k, and D_k are the approximation, horizontal, vertical, and diagonal detail coefficients of the Kth level decomposition, respectively. A_0 is the original image I. So, after decomposition on the Jth level, the original image I is represented by $3J + 1$ subimages containing $\{H_i, V_i, D_i\}i = 1,\ldots,J$. The wavelet energy in the horizontal, vertical, and diagonal directions, respectively, at the ith level can be defined as

$$E_i^{\mathrm{h}} = \sum_{x=1}^{M}\sum_{y=1}^{N} H_i(x, y)^2$$

$$E_i^{\mathrm{v}} = \sum_{x=1}^{M}\sum_{y=1}^{N} V_i(x, y)^2 \tag{2.23}$$

$$E_i^{\mathrm{d}} = \sum_{x=1}^{M}\sum_{y=1}^{N} D_i(x, y)^2$$

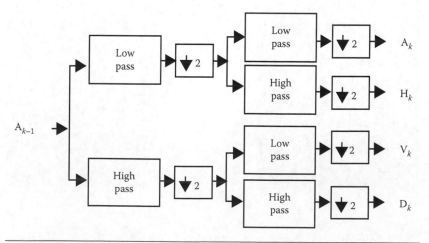

Figure 2.11 One-level DWT decomposition.

These energies reflect the strength of the images' details in different directions at the ith wavelet decomposed level. The details of the retinal images are in the blood vessels. Hence, Equation 2.23 could describe the intensity of these features in different orientations at the ith wavelet decomposition level (scale). In addition, because the amplitudes of wavelet coefficients of nonoscillating pattern increased with the extension of wavelet decomposition scale whereas that of the high-frequency oscillating pattern at the large scale are much smaller than at fine scale, which matches the spatial frequency of the oscillations, the energy of the thick vessels, which were nonoscillating patterns, were concentrated at the large wavelet decomposition scales and most of the energy of the thin vessels, which are oscillating pattern, are focused at the small scales. Therefore, the feature vector

$$\left\{ E_i^{\mathrm{h}}, E_i^{\mathrm{v}}, E_i^{\mathrm{d}} \right\}_{i=1,\dots M} \tag{2.24}$$

where M is the total wavelet decomposition level, can describe the global detail features of blood vessels effectively. The features extracted from the whole images were not suitable and did not contain important information. Therefore, the retina image was divided to $S \times S$ nonoverlap blocks and the energy of each block was computed. Retina recognition included two stages: the training stage and the recognition stage. In the training stage, WEFs of all training samples were captured, and the template of a retina was obtained by averaging the WEFs of all training samples captured from the same retina. In the recognition stages, WEF of the input retina was computed first, and then compared with all the registered templates; finally, find the most similar template and take it as the recognition result.

2.6.4 Xu's Method

Xu et al. [42] proposed a new method for recognition. They used the green grayscale ocular fundus image. The skeleton feature of optic fundus blood vessel using contrast-limited adaptive histogram equalization was extracted at the first step. After filtering treatment and extracting shape feature, shape curve of blood vessels was obtained. Shape curve matching was later carried out with reference point matching. In their method for recognition, feature matching consisted of finding affine transformation parameters, which relates the query image and its best corresponding enrolled image. The computational time of this algorithm is high because a number of rigid motion parameters should be computed for all possible correspondences between the query and enrolled images in the data set.

2.6.5 Ortega's Method

Ortega et al. [43–44] used a verification based on some features used in fingerprint recognition like crossovers (between two different vessels) and bifurcation points (one vessel coming out of another one). Therefore, the biometric pattern can be considered as a set of feature points and the proposed method contains three steps:

- Retinal vessel pattern extraction
- Feature points extraction
- Biometric pattern matching

According to the essential belief that vessels can be determined as creases (ridges and valleys), curvature level was used to calculate the creases to achieve the main purpose of this step. One of the most practical usages of crease, which was employed in this work, was level set extrinsic curvature or LSEC. Negative minima of the level curve curvature κ, level by level, formed valley curves whereas positive maxima formed ridge curves:

$$\kappa = (2L_x L_y L_{xy} - L_y^2 L_{xx} - L_x^2 L_{yy})(L_x^2 + L_y^2)^{-3/2} \qquad (2.25)$$

L can be considered as a topographic relief or landscape and the level sets as its level curves when two-dimensional images were used. The creaseness measure κ had been improved by prefiltering the image gradient vector using a Gaussian function. Figure 2.12 shows the result of the crease extraction algorithm for an input digital retinal image [43].

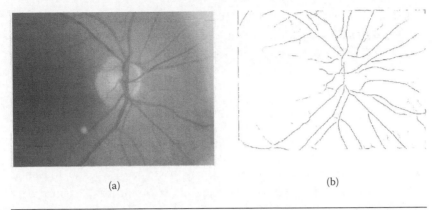

(a)   (b)

Figure 2.12 Example of digital retinal images showing the vessel tree. (a) Input retinal image. (b) Images of creases from the input representing the main vessels in the retina. (From M. Ortega et al., Retinal verification using a feature points-based biometric pattern. *EURASIP J. Adv. Signal Process* 2009, 1–13, 2009.)

Because of different illumination in retinal images, there are discontinuities in some creases. Therefore, the process of joining segments is needed to build whole vessels before the bifurcation/crossover analysis.

Removing some possible spurious feature points was considered as the final stage. Therefore, four of the main stages in the feature point extraction process were:

- Labeling of the vessels segments
- Establishing the joint or union relationships between vessels
- Establishing crossover and bifurcation relationships between vessels
- Filtering of the crossovers and bifurcations

2.6.5.1 Biometric Pattern Matching If M is the total number of feature points in the reference pattern and N the total number of points in the candidate pattern, the size of the set T of possible transformations is computed:

$$T = \frac{(M^2 - M)(N^2 - N)}{2} \qquad (2.26)$$

where M and N represent the cardinality of v and $\dot{v}$, respectively. Because T represents a high number of transformations, some restrictions must be applied to decrease it. To decrease the amount of T, two different thresholds S_{min} and S_{max} were used to bound the scale factor (T). Therefore, the formulation for restriction was:

$$S_{min} < \frac{\text{distance} (p,q)}{\text{distance } \dot{p},(\dot{q})} < S_{max} \qquad (2.27)$$

where p, q are points from v pattern, and $\dot{p}$, $\dot{q}$ are the matched points from the v pattern. To check feature points, a similarity value between points (SIM) was defined, which indicates how similar two points were. The distance between these two points will be used to compute that value. For two points A and B, their similarity value is defined by

$$\text{SIM}(A,B) = 1 - \frac{\text{distance}(A,B)}{D_{max}} \qquad (2.28)$$

where D_{max} is a threshold that stands for the maximum distance allowed for those points to be considered a possible match. If distance $(A, B) > D_{max}$, then SIM(A, B) = 0. D_{max} is a threshold introduced to consider the quality loss and discontinuities during the crease's extraction process leading to mislocation of feature points by some pixels.

In some cases, two points B_1, B_2 could have both a good value of similarity with one point A in the reference pattern. This happens because B_1 and B_2 are close to each other in the candidate pattern. To identify the most suitable matching pair, the possibility of correspondence is defined comparing the similarity value between those points to the rest of similarity values of each one of them:

$$P(A_i, B_j) = \frac{\text{SIM}(A_i B_j)^2}{\left(\sum\nolimits_{i'=1}^{M} \text{SIM} (A_{i'}, B_j) + \sum\nolimits_{j'=1}^{N} \text{SIM} (A_i, B_{j'}) - \text{SIM} (A_i B_j) \right)} \qquad (2.29)$$

An $M \times N$ matrix Q was constructed such that position (i, j) holds $P(A_i, B_j)$. Note that if the similarity value was 0, the possibility value was also 0. This meant that only valid matching will have a nonzero value in Q. The desired set C of matching feature points was obtained from P using a greedy algorithm. The element (i, j) inserted in C was the position in Q where the maximum value was stored. Then, to prevent the selection of the same point in one of the images again, the row (i) and the column (j) associated with that pair was set to 0. The algorithm finished when no more non-zero elements could be selected from Q. The final set of matched points between patterns was C. Using this information, a similarity metric must be established to obtain a final criterion of comparison between patterns. The similarity measure (S) between two patterns was defined as

$$S = \frac{C}{f(M,N)} \tag{2.30}$$

where C is the number of matched points between patterns, and M and N are the matching pattern sizes. The first f function defined and tested was:

$$f(M, N) = \min (M, N) \tag{2.31}$$

To improve the class separability, a new normalization function f was defined:

$$f(M,N) = \sqrt{MN} \tag{2.32}$$

Also, some other functions were applied to improve the proposed method.

2.6.6 Tabatabaee's Method

Tabatabaee et al. [45] presented a new algorithm based on the fuzzy C-means clustering algorithm. They used Haar wavelet and snakes model for OD localization. The Fourier–Mellin transform coefficients and simplified moments of the retinal image have been used as extracted features for the system. The computational cost and implementation time of this algorithm were high and the performance of the algorithm was evaluated using a small data set.

2.6.7 Oinonen's Method

Oinonen et al. [46] proposed a novel method for verification based on minutiae features. The proposed method consisted of three steps: blood vessel segmentation, feature extraction, and feature matching. In practice, vessel segmentation can be viewed as a preprocessing phase for feature extraction. After segmentation, the next step was to extract the vessel crossings together with their orientation information. These data were then matched with the corresponding ones from the comparison image. The method used vessel direction information for improved matching robustness. The computational time of this method for segmentation, feature extraction, and matching was high and this method was used in the verification mode.

2.7 Comparison between Different Methods

To evaluate the proposed methods, these methods were applied on public data sets. The data sets used in most of methods are DRIVE [24], STARE [39], and VARIA [43]. The images in the DRIVE database were obtained from a control program on diabetic retinopathy in Holland. The population consisted of 400 controlled diabetic subjects between 5 and 90 years old. Forty retinal images were selected randomly, 33 retinal images didn't show any trace of diabetic retinopathy whereas 7 retinal images showed the disease at an early stage. The STARE data set contains 81 retina images and were captured using a Topcon TRV-50 fundus camera. This data set contains 31 images of normal retinas and 50 of diseased retinas. The VARIA database is a set of retinal images used for authentication purposes. The database currently includes 233 images from 139 different individuals. The images were acquired with a TopCon nonmydriatic camera NW-100 model and are OD-centered with a resolution of 768×584. In Table 2.2, the results of applying different retinal recognition methods are shown.

Table 2.2 Comparison of Different Retinal Recognition Methods

METHOD	NUMBER OF IMAGES	NUMBER OF SUBJECTS	IDENTIFICATION OR VERIFICATION MODE	RUNNING TIME (S)		ACCURACY (%)
				IDENTIFICATION	VERIFICATION	
Farzin et al. [24]	300	60	Identification	>120	—	99
Dehghani et al. [39]	300	60	Identification	0.06	—	99.75
	3600					99.78
Shahnazi et al. [40]	400	40	Identification	3.34	—	100
Xu et al. [42]	—		Identification	277.8	—	98.5
Ortega et al. [44]	90		Verification	—	—	100
Tabatabaee et al. [45]	108	27	Identification	—	—	—
Islam et al. [47]	18	6	Identification	—	—	100
Sukumaran et al. [48]	40	40	Identification	—	—	96
Barkhoda et al. [49]	360	60	Identification	—	—	98

2.8 Conclusion

In this chapter, we review the latest methods of human recognition using retinal images and compared these different methods. Retina recognition provides higher level of security due to its inherent robustness against imposture. On the other hand, the retinal blood vessels of each subject, which are the main characters for recognition, undergo fewer modifications during life. Despite these properties, the retina has not been used frequently in biometric systems, mainly because of the technological limitations in manufacturing low-cost scanners. These problems result in the lack of existing reliable data sets for retinal images and therefore there are few works on recognition using retinal image. However, developments in the manufacture of retinal scanners make it possible to use retinal recognition instead of other recognition methods such as face, fingerprint, and so on. Retinal recognition methods are divided into two parts. The first part uses the vessel segmentation results of retinal images, and in some of them, OD localization methods such as the methods proposed in studies by Dehghani et al. [50,51]. Therefore, at the first step, in these methods segmentation methods are used to obtain retina blood vessels. Therefore, these methods take high computational time. The second part extracts features from retinal images without using blood vessel segmentation methods and the computational time of these methods are very low.

References

1. R. Parashar and S. Joshi. Proportional study of human recognition methods. *International Journal of Advanced Research in Computer Science and Software Engineering* 2, 2012.
2. K. Delac and M. Grgic. A survey of biometric recognition methods. *46th International Symposium Electronics in Marine*, 2004.
3. A.K. Jain, A. Ross, and S. Prabhakar. An introduction to biometric recognition. *IEEE Transactions Circuits and Systems for Video Technology* 14(1):4–20, January 2004.
4. en.wikipedia.org.
5. www.Iconnica.com.
6. www.cosmosmagazine.com.
7. www.netdip.com.
8. www.findbiometrics.com.
9. www.ece.vt.edu.

10. www.ks.uiuc.edu.
11. www.apmsurgery.com.
12. www.science.howstuffworks.com.
13. www.advancedsourcecode.com.
14. www.en.wikipedia.org.
15. A. Jain, R. Bolle, and S. Pankanti. *Biometrics: Personal Identification in a Networked Society.* Kluwer Academic Publishers, Dordrecht, the Netherlands, 1999.
16. http://en.wikipedia.org/wiki/Biometrics.
17. A.K. Jain and A. Ross. Introduction to biometrics. In *Handbook of Biometrics*, edited by Jain, A.K., Flynn, P., Ross, A. 1–22, 2008. Springer. ISBN 978-0-387-71040-2.
18. http://www.physicsclassroom.com/class/refrn/u14l6a.cfm.
19. http://webvision.med.utah.edu/book/part-i-foundations/simple-anatomy-of-the-retina/.
20. EyePrints. *TIME Magazine*, Dec. 16, 1935. Retrieved on 2008-04-10.
21. Hill, Robert. Retina Identification. Msu.Edu. Retrieved on 2007-04-02.
22. http://www.retica.com/index.html.
23. http://www.raycosecurity.com/biometrics/EyeDentify.html.
24. H. Farzin, H. Abrishami Moghaddam, and M.-S. Moin. A novel retinal identification system. *EURASIP J. Adv. Signal Process 2008*, article ID 280635, 2008. doi:10.1155/2008/280635.
25. D. Zhang. *Automated Biometrics: Technologies and Systems.* Kluwer Academic Publishers, Dordrecht, the Netherlands, 2000.
26. R.B. Hill. Rotating beam ocular identification apparatus and method. 1983, U.S. patent no. 4393366.
27. R.B. Hill. Fovea-centered eye fundus scanner. 1986, U.S. Patent no. 4620318.
28. J.C. Johnson and R.B. Hill. Eye fundus optical scanner system and method. 1990, U.S. patent no. 5532771.
29. R.B. Hill. Retinal identification. In *Biometrics: Personal Identification in Networked Society*, edited by A. Jain, R. Bolle, and S. Pankati, 126, Springer, Berlin, Germany, 1999.
30. C. Simon and I. Goldstein. A new scientific method of identification. *New York State Journal of Medicine* 35(18):901–906, 1935.
31. H. Tabatabaee, A. Milani Fard, and H. Jafariani. A novel human identifier system using retina image and fuzzy clustering approach. In *Proceedings of the 2nd IEEE International Conference on Information and Communication Technologies (ICTTA '06)*, 1031–1036, Damascus, Syria, April 2006.
32. X. Meng, Y. Yin, G. Yang, and X. Xi. Retinal Identification Based on an Improved Circular Gabor Filter and Scale Invariant Feature Transform. Sensors, 13, No. 7, 2013, doi:10.3390/s130709248.
33. M. Ortega, C. Marino, M.G. Penedo, M. Blanco, and F. Gonzalez. Biometric authentication using digital retinal images. In *Proceedings of the 5th WSEAS International Conference on Applied Computer Science (ACOS '06)*, 422–427, Hangzhou, China, April 2006.
34. http://www.retica.com/index.html.

35. P. Tower. The fundus oculi in monozygotic twins: report of six pairs of identical twins. *Archives of Ophthalmology* 54(2):225–239, 1955.
36. H. Farzin, H. Abrisham Moghaddam, and M. Sh. Moin. A new method for blood vessels segmentation in retinal images. In *Proceedings of the 13th Iranian Conference on Biomedical Engineering (ICBME '07)*, Tehran, Iran, February 2007.
37. K.G. Goh, W. Hsu, and M.L. Lee. An automatic diabetic retinal image screening system. In *Medical Data Mining and Knowledge Discovery*, 181–210, Springer, Berlin, Germany, 2000.
38. A. Osareh, M. Mirmehdi, B. Thomas, and R. Markham. Comparison of colour spaces for optic disc localization in retinal images. *Proc. 16th International Conference on Pattern Recognition*, 743–746, 2002.
39. A. Dehghani, H. Abrishami Moghaddam, and M.-S. Moin. Retinal identification based on rotation invariant moments. *IntConfBioinform Biomed Eng.* 2011, 1–4.
40. M. Shahnazi, M. Pahlevanzadeh, and M. Vafadoost. Wavelet based retinal recognition. In *Proceedings of the 9th IEEE International Symposium on Signal Processing and Its Applications*, 1–4, 2007.
41. T. Kondo. Detection of anatomical features in retinal images using a gradient orientation. *IEEE Transactions on Medical Imaging* 23(3):350–362, 2004.
42. Z.-W. Xu, X.-X. Guo, X.-Y. Hu, and X. Cheng. The blood vessel recognition of ocular fundus. In *Proceedings of the 4th International Conference on Machine Learning and Cybernetics (ICMLC '05)*, 4493–4498, Guangzhou, China, August 2005.
43. M. Ortega, M.G. Penedo, J. Rouco, N. Barreira, and M.J. Carreira. Retinal verification using a feature points-based biometric pattern. *EURASIP J. Adv. Signal Process* 2009, 1–13, 2009.
44. M. Ortega, C. Marino, M.G. Penedo, M. Blanco, and F. Gonzalez. Biometric authentication using digital retinal images. In *Proceedings of the 5th WSEAS International Conference on Applied Computer Science (ACOS '06)*, 422–427, Hangzhou, China, April 2006.
45. H. Tabatabaee, A. Milani-Fard, and H. Jafariani. A novel human identifier system using retina image and fuzzy clustering approach. In *Proceedings of the 2nd IEEE International Conference on Information and Communication Technologies (ICTTA 06)*, 1031–1036, Damascus, Syria, April 2006.
46. H. Oinonen, H. Forsvik, P. Ruusuvuori, O. Yli-Harja, V. Voipio and H. Huttunen. Identity Verification Based on Vessel Matching from Fundus Images. *17th International Conference on Image Processing*, 4089–4092, 2010.
47. M.N. Islam, Md. A. Siddiqui, S. Paul. An efficient retina pattern recognition algorithm (RPRA) towards human identification. *2nd International Conference on Computer, Control and Communication, IC4 2009*, 1–6, 2009.
48. S. Sukumaran and M. Punithavalli. Retina recognition based on fractal dimension. *IJCSNS International Journal of Computer Science and Network Security* 9(10):66–67, 2009.

49. W. Barkhoda, F. Akhlaqian Tab, and M. Deljavan Amiri. Rotation invariant retina identification based on the sketch of vessels using angular partitioning. *Proceedings of the International Multiconference on Computer Science and Information Technology*, 3–6, 2009.

50. A. Dehghani, A. Abrishami Moghaddam, and M.-S. Moin. Optic disc localization in retinal images using histogram matching. *EURASIP Journal on Image and Video Processing* 2012(1):1–11, 2012.

51. A. Dehghani, M.-S. Moin, and M. Saghafi. Localization of the optic disc center in retinal images based on the Harris corner detector. *Biomedical Engineering Letters* 2(3):198–206, 2012.

PART II
ADVANCED TOPICS IN BIOMETRICS

3

VISUAL SPEECH AS BEHAVIORAL BIOMETRIC

PREETY SINGH, VIJAY LAXMI, AND MANOJ SINGH GAUR

Contents

Abstract

For information-sensitive systems, multimodal biometrics is employed for person identification. This article explores the use of the dynamic information contained in the speech of a person as an alternative biometric. Individuals have specific manners of speaking and distinct lip shapes. This article shows how specific patterns formed by the utterance of speech by a person can be used for the task of speaker identification. We extract visual features from lip contour in successive images forming the speech sample of a speaker. We apply feature selection to determine a small number of features that are relevant toward the task of speaker identification. Minimizing the feature set gives an added advantage of reducing the system response time in a real-time implementation. Experiments also prove that our minimized feature set is robust to different words in the vocabulary. It is also demonstrated that static lip features, representing the lip shape, do not provide the same recognition performance as achieved by visual speech.

3.1 Introduction

Biometrics is increasingly gaining importance as security requirements become more demanding. Over the years, multiple fraudulent cases have come to the fore, making it imperative for information-sensitive systems to look for alternative protective measures. Accurate verification or identification of a person can be a major deterrent to crime. Physiological and behavioral characteristics are commonly used nowadays for establishing the identity of a person. For improved performance of an identification system relying on biometrics, multiple modalities are often used (Gudavalli et al. 2012). These may include fingerprints, palm prints, hand geometry, facial features, iris, voice, signature, etc. (Ross and Jain 2003). Each biometric has its strengths and drawbacks and no single biometric satisfies all the requirements of an application.

"Voice" is an individualistic behavioral characteristic that can be employed for the identification of an individual (Furui 1997). It is based on the differences arising due to the shape of individual vocal tracts and speaking habits. It is an acceptable biometric in almost all societies. Moreover, voice capture is nonintrusive and user-friendly. Applications requiring person authentication over the telephone have to consider voice as it may be the only feasible biometric. Voice-biometric is also popular because of the low cost factor of hardware devices. Common sound cards and microphones can easily be used for data acquisition.

A voice-biometric system may employ either a text-dependent verification or a text-independent one. In a text-dependent approach, the speaker is identified on the basis of utterance of a predetermined phrase. In a text-independent system, the speaker has to be identified irrespective of the phrase that is spoken. This is comparatively difficult. Another more challenging approach is a language-independent system in which the speaker has to be identified based on a phrase, which might be spoken in any language (Jain et al. 2004).

For using the voice signal as a biometric, the amplitude of the recorded signal is normalized. It is then broken into several bandpass frequency channels for the purpose of feature extraction. The features determined from each band may be either in time-domain or frequency-domain. Cepstral features are commonly used. These are defined as the logarithm of the Fourier transform of the voice signal in each band. These features are mapped to a preexisting set of features using vector quantization, hidden Markov model, or dynamic time warping.

In a database containing many identities, voice alone may not be unique enough to permit identification. Moreover, the audio signal may be degraded by the quality of the microphone, disturbances in the communication channel, or characteristics of the digitizer. It might also be corrupted by background noise (Jain et al. 2006). The voice signal may also be affected by the physical health or emotional state of a person. Mimicry or the use of a previously recorded voice are other challenges faced by this biometric. Although voice recognition is a fairly acceptable modality, it can be aided by *visual speech*, or *lipreading*, which is known to supplement the audio information (Potamianos et al. 2003). The challenges faced by audio signals can be countered using the information provided by the movement of the lips while speaking.

3.2 Visual Speech as a Biometric

It is known that visual cues from the speech articulators along with audio speech enhance speaker recognition (Dieckmann et al. 1997) compared with unimodal systems. Lipreading can also play an important role where the audio signal is degraded or missing. Visual speech systems deal with the video sequence of an individual's mouth while that person is speaking at the time of enrollment. Processing this visual input to a sequence of images, features are extracted from these images of the lip in successive frames. These features form the biometric template. At the time of identification, the visual input presented by the speaker through the cameras is again processed for features. These are then matched with the stored template for a match. Visual speech is emerging as a fairly acceptable biometric because it possesses most of the characteristics desirable of a biometric:

- *Universality*, because every individual has it. Although speech-impaired people might not be able to provide an appropriate audio signal, visual inputs from their mouths can compensate for it.
- *Uniqueness*, because individuals have specific manners of speaking. Although some are fast talkers, and some are slow. The mouth shapes, *visemes*, formed during their utterance of speech also differ. Moreover, each person has a distinguishing set of static features defining their lip shape.
- *Permanence*, is present because an individual can speak lifelong under normal circumstances. However, it may be affected by a person's health and age.
- *Collectability*, because it is feasible to obtain mouth images using a camera focused on the speaker's mouth. These images can be processed to derive further information from them regarding the identity of the speaker.

Although visual speech may be a fairly acceptable biometric possessing a few desirable qualities, it may not be suitable in applications requiring high security levels. This is because the lip shape is not an absolutely unique feature (e.g., in the case of identical twins) and the manner of speech may also be acquired through intensive training. Visual speech may then be used as an additional modality in a multimodal system. Multimodal biometric systems utilize more than one physiological or behavioral biometric for enrollment or verification. Doing this enhances the security of a sensitive system as the verification does not depend on a single biometric that may be circumvented. Customer acceptance is another reason for having a multimodal system because some biometrics might not be acceptable in certain societies. The modalities can be combined to conform to a desired security level or may be adaptive to varying levels of security requirements (Kumar et al. 2012).

Ichino et al. (2006) have used both lip movements and voice in a multimodal system. They extract Fourier descriptors from images of the lips. For the audio signal, they use linear predictive coefficients (LPC) as features. The two feature vectors are concatenated and kernel Fisher discriminant analysis (KFDA) is used for classification. The performance of KFDA is also compared with other algorithms like Linear Discriminant Analysis (LDA), median, AND, and OR. The experiments are performed on the audiovisual data of 62 subjects from the XM2VTS database. It has been observed that the recognition rate using KFDA is better than single modalities and other fusion methods.

Brunelli and Falavigna (1995) have described a multibiometric system in which they use facial and voice features for identification. For the voice signal, a system based on vector quantization (VQ) is used. Each speaker is represented by two sets of vectors describing his or her acoustic characteristics. During identification, static and dynamic acoustic features are computed from the short-time spectral analysis of the input speech sample. These are classified using their distances from the prototype vectors stored in the speaker codebook couples. Thus, the audio modality sends two scores to the integration module. For facial recognition, a pixel-level comparison of a set of regions is done. These include the eye, nose, and mouth of the person. These regions are matched with corresponding regions of the individual stored in the database. The audio and visual scores are normalized and combined using weighted geometric averages. The correct identification rate of the system is reported to be 98%, compared with 88% and 91% rates provided by the stand-alone speaker and face recognition systems, respectively.

Frischholz and Dieckmann's commercial product, BioID takes into account three modalities, that is, voice, lip motion, and facial features of a user for verification (Frischholz and Dieckmann 2000). The system records and classifies each feature separately. During the enrollment process, each feature template is generated and stored. The face is located using Hausdorff distance. Appropriate normalization and scaling is done to ensure that relevant facial features are analyzed. For lip movement, it considers the optical flow of identifiable points on the lip. This gives the movement of the lip from frame to frame. The audio feature vector consists of cepstral coefficients derived from the speech signal. A synergetic computer classifies the optical features and a vector quantifier is used for the audio features. Various sensor fusion options are available and a choice can be made depending on the security level.

Aravabhumi et al. (2010) represent the lip shape by a set of points. For each boundary pixel, its distance and angle from the centroid are computed. These are used as visual features for the task of speaker identification. A recognition rate of 96% has been reported.

In this chapter, we propose an efficient text-dependent lipreading system that identifies a person from a given database of speakers using a minimal set of input visual features. This system accepts visual inputs from a speaker's mouth as he or she utters a given word. The features contained in the images of the mouth are representative of the typical way a person speaks. The extracted features are stored as a template and used to identify a person when he or she provides an input feature set at the time of identification.

In any real-time implementation system, it is imperative that the response time should be as minimal as possible. This can be achieved only when the input data to be processed by the system is of low-dimensionality. To achieve this goal, we explore feature selection to extract a meaningful set of attributes from the lip parameters determined from images of the mouth. This is done so as to remove redundancy from the input feature vector, making it more compact. If prominent features are identified, only those features need to be extracted during the feature extraction process. A reduced feature set will also minimize the processing time and ensure a prompt response from the identification system apart from decreasing the computational complexities and storage overheads. This will lead to an overall improvement in the efficiency of the system.

We perform experiments to show how this set of features is able to achieve a high speaker identification rate. We also demonstrate that the static features conforming to an individual's lip shape are not able to give the same performance. It is the dynamic nature of the manner of speaking that leads to improved speaker recognition system efficiency. We use the reduced set of visual features to check their robustness for different words of the vocabulary.

3.3 Proposed Methodology

Our proposed methodology is shown in Figure 3.1. The first step is acquiring the visual speech database. The database should contain a number of utterances per speaker to take into account the speaker variability. The manner of speech of a speaker may differ from instance-to-instance, depending on that speaker's mood, physical health, and mental health. This may change the way the speaker's lips move in each different utterance of speech. Increasing the number of recorded visual speech samples for the database makes the system more robust and makes identification more accurate.

Visual speech data is acquired and features are extracted from the region-of-interest (ROI), in this case, the lips. For this, lip contour detection has to be done using edge detection techniques. As the person speaks, the lip's boundaries change. The changes in the lip boundary can be represented by features. Here, we have extracted geometric visual features representing the lip boundary and the area contained within it.

The visual features extracted from the lip boundary may contain redundant features. This redundancy not only increases computational efforts but might also cause a negative effect on recognition accuracy. Processing of additional features will decrease response time of the identification system. Storage overheads also increase with the increase in visual data. To extract meaningful information from the set of input visual features, we apply a feature selection method, minimum redundancy maximum relevance (mRMR; Peng et al. 2005), to select the most prominent features.

Based on the ranking of features, as determined by application of mRMR, we form feature subsets using the geometric features. These feature subsets are then used for the task of speaker recognition. Using certain evaluation metrics, we determine an optimal feature subset,

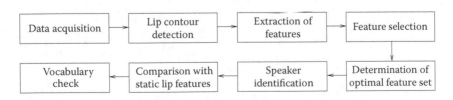

Figure 3.1   Proposed methodology for speaker identification using visual speech.

which yields the most prominent features. The geometric and shape features are combined to form a hybrid model of features to be used for the identification of a speaker.

Each person has a specific lip shape. To validate that it is not the static features describing the lip shape of a speaker, but the dynamic information contained in the lip movement, we perform experiments to compare the two. We prove that it is indeed the typical way in which a person moves his lips while speaking which results in a higher identification rate. We also test the efficacy of our computed optimal visual feature set for different words of the vocabulary to check the robustness of the system.

3.4 Minimum Redundancy Maximum Relevance

The feature selection method of mRMR, introduced by Peng et al. (2005), is based on the concept of mutual information. It computes the mutual information between various features as well as between the features and the class. It selects a subset of features that exhibits maximum relevance toward the target class but in which the features are not highly correlated, so as to minimize redundancy.

The mutual information I between two variables x and y can be given by their marginal probabilities $p(x)$ and $p(y)$, respectively, and their joint probability $p(x, y)$.

$$I(x, y) = \sum_{i,j} p(x_i, y_j) \log \frac{p(x_i, y_j)}{p(x_i) p(y_j)} \tag{3.1}$$

Let $F = \{f_1, f_2, \ldots f_n\}$ represent the complete set of n features. Let the target subset of features, containing k relevant features (where, $k \leq n$), be represented by S and $S \subset F$.

According to the condition of minimal redundancy, min W_I, features are so selected that they are mutually exclusive.

$$\min W_I, \quad W_I = \frac{1}{k^2} \sum_{i,j \in S} I(f_i, f_j) \tag{3.2}$$

Let the target classes be denoted by $C = \{C_1, C_2, \ldots C_m\}$. Then, the relevance between feature and class, represented by $I_{C,fi}$ should be at a maximum. According to the condition of maximum relevance, max V_I, the relevance of all features in target subset S should be maximized.

$$\max V_I, \quad V_I = \frac{1}{k} \sum_{i \in S} I(C, f_i) \quad \quad (3.3)$$

The criterion of combining Equations 3.2 and 3.3 gives us features that exhibit minimum redundancy and maximum relevance. This can be done using two approaches:

- Mutual information difference (MID): MID = $\max(V_I - W_I)$
- Mutual information quotient (MIQ): MIQ = $\max(V_I/W_I)$

An incremental algorithm can then be employed to rank features in the feature subset S. We have used the MID approach.

3.5 Experiments

To develop a speaker-verification system based on visual cues from lip movements, we recorded an audiovisual database, *Vaani*, in our laboratory. *Vaani*, a Hindi word, translates to *speech* in English. Twenty speakers participated in the recording. To make our database more text-varied, we recorded ten English digits, *zero* to *nine*. This was done to ensure that the visual features we computed were robust to different words.

To incorporate variability that can occur in a speaker's manner of speech, we recorded five utterances of each digit per speaker in two separate recording sessions. The first three speech samples were recorded in the first session whereas two samples were recorded in the second session after two months. The recording was done in our laboratory in moderate illumination. The camera was focused on the lower part of the speaker's face. Although the database consists of audio as well as visual recording of the speech samples, only the visual modality has been used for this set of experiments. The audio can be used in future research while developing a multimodal speaker identification system.

Each speech sample is frame-grabbed at 30 frames/s to obtain its image frames. The lip contour is detected in each image frame and visual features are extracted from it. It consists of geometric parameters, defining the lip width, height, area segments within the lip contour, and number of visible teeth and oral cavity pixels. The method of detection of the lip boundary and extraction of features is described in the following subsections.

3.5.1 Detection of Lip Contour

Lip contour detection is done using a method based on point distribution model (PDM), which describes an object by a set of points (Cootes et al. 2001). We take a set of ten training images. These RGB images are converted into HSV (hue-saturation-value) space. Thresholding is applied to separate the lip region from the rest of the face. Suitable morphological operators are used for erosion and dilation to remove the effects of noise. Sobel edge detector is now applied, which yields the edges in the image. Connectivity analysis is then done to obtain the largest connected component, which is the outer lip boundary. However, this is not an accurate contour (due to erosion and dilation) and is used only to build a template of the lips. This process is shown in Figure 3.2.

Horizontal and vertical intensity analysis of the binary image of the lip contour is done to determine six key-points on the lip contour. These are the two lip corners, the bottommost point on

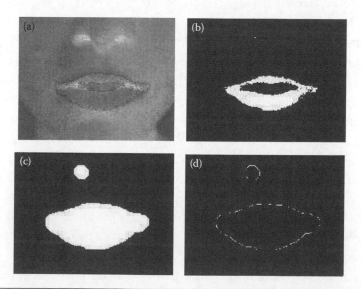

Figure 3.2 Detection of lip contour. (a) RGB image into HSV space, (b) thresholding, (c) erosion and dilation, and (d) edge detection.

Figure 3.3 Six keypoints on the lip contour.

the lower lip, and the three points on the arch of the upper lip, as shown in Figure 3.3.

Between each pair of key-points, 20 points are interpolated, giving a total of 120 points describing each lip contour. Thus, the lip contour in each of the 10 images is defined by a set of points, S, given by

$$S = \{x_1, y_1, x_2, y_2 \ldots x_{120}, y_{120}\} \qquad (3.4)$$

The mean of the $\{xy\}$ coordinates over the 10 images is taken to give a statistical shape of the lip, which is taken as the lip template. This lip template is placed over each input RGB image and allowed to deform. As soon as the template senses a change in the pixel-intensity, it converges and yields the outer lip boundary in the input image.

3.5.2 Extraction of Visual Features

We extract a set of geometric visual features from the detected lip boundary. The feature set, G, consists of 16 parameters (Singh et al. 2012a). These include the lip height (h) and width (w). The line joining the two lip corners is divided into six equal parts. Vertical lines through these equidistant points and bounded by the lip boundary, divide the area within the lip contour into 12 area segments given by ($A_1 \ldots A_{12}$). Intensity analysis is done within the lip boundary to determine the number of visible teeth pixels (TP) and visible oral cavity pixels (OP). Thus, the geometric visual feature set is given by

$$G = \{h \; w \; A_1 \ldots A_{12} \; \text{TP} \; \text{OP}\} \qquad (3.5)$$

As the lips move during the utterance of speech, these parameters change and form a specific visual pattern of the spoken phrase, which is typical to each speaker. The extracted geometrical features are shown in Figure 3.4.

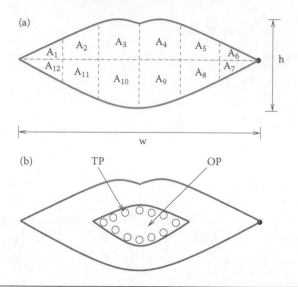

Figure 3.4 Extracted geometric visual features. (a) Lip height, width and area segments and (b) teeth pixels and oral pixels.

To ensure that the task of speaker identification is not affected by the static lip shape, typical to an individual, we normalize the features speaker-wise. This is done by dividing the feature value by the maximum absolute value contained in that feature set. This is done for all features, for all speakers.

3.5.3 Reduction of Visual Features

The efficiency of a real-time identification system is dependent on the input feature set. Not only should it be small in size but it should also contain relevant features. Redundant features not only increase computation time but may also cause a negative effect on recognition accuracy. A smaller number of attributes may also give us a better knowledge of the data set. Thus, reducing the dimensionality of the input feature set is of utmost importance.

Dimensionality reduction of features may be done either by feature selection or feature extraction. Feature selection removes the irrelevant and redundant features. Feature extraction transforms the information contained in the existing feature set into a new feature space in which they lose their physical meaning. Because apart from reducing data dimensionality, we are also interested in determining prominent features in the physical space, we use the feature selection method of mRMR (Peng et al. 2005).

To reduce the number of features, we apply a feature selection technique, mRMR, which is based on the concept of mutual information. Application of mRMR on our feature sets ranks the features in order of their prominence. We form feature subsets using these ranked features. The feature subsets are used for the task of speaker identification using classification algorithms. Based on certain evaluation criteria, we determine most optimal geometric features.

3.5.4 Formation of Feature Subsets

Using the features ranked by mRMR, we form feature subsets. Starting with the feature ranked first by mRMR, to form the first subset, we keep on adding subsequently ranked features. These feature subsets are denoted by G_k, indicating that this feature subset contains k top-ranking features. Thus, G_1 stands for the feature subset containing the first, top-ranked feature. G_2 represents the feature set containing the top two features, and so on till G_{15}. Adding one more feature will result in the original feature set, G, which contains 16 features.

3.5.5 Computing of Optimal Feature Set

An optimal feature subset should be such that it contains a minimum number of relevant features so that the response time in a real-time implementation system is as small as possible. This can be achieved only when the number of features to be processed is small. To this end, we want our optimal feature set to be small in size compared with G, but not to compromise on the recognition accuracy.

To determine an optimal feature subset, we classify them with respect to the speaker class (Singh et al. 2012b). The feature subsets are evaluated for speaker recognition using the k-fold cross-validation method, with $k = 10$ (Kohavi 1995). The classifiers used are k-nearest neighbor (kNN) and random forest (RF). We have employed these classification algorithms with the help of the data-mining toolkit, WEKA (Hall et al. 2009).

The accuracy of a set of features can be indicated by its F-measure. This is the harmonic mean of precision and recall and defined by

$$F - measure = \frac{2 * precision * recall}{precision + recall} \tag{3.6}$$

where *precision* is given by

$$Precision = \frac{true\ positives}{true\ positives + false\ positives} \tag{3.7}$$

and *recall* is defined as

$$Recall = \frac{True\ Positives}{True\ Positives + False\ Negatives} \tag{3.8}$$

To ensure that the performance of the identification system is not compromised, we define a few terms that will help us compute the optimal feature set. We take into account F_k, which is the F-measure value of a feature subset when used to identify the speaker class. The difference of F_k with respect to F_n, which is the F-measure value using the complete set G, should not be large. The change in these values is computed using ξ, which is given by

$$\xi = \frac{F_n - F_k}{F_n} \tag{3.9}$$

For an enhanced performance of the feature subset (considering that redundancy has been removed), $\xi < 0$ and $|\xi| \rightarrow \infty$. This will be possible when $F_k > F_n$. Positive values of ξ will indicate $F_k < F_n$, showing degraded performance of feature subset w.r.t. G. However, they may be considered if they do not exceed a certain threshold. We have taken this threshold as 0.1. Thus, subsets having positive ξ values less than 0.1 are also considered to be qualifying for computation of optimality (Singh et al. 2012b).

We also define η, which gives us the change in size of the feature subset G_k with respect to G. If G contains n number of features and G_k contains k features, then η is defined as

$$\eta = \frac{n - k}{n} \tag{3.10}$$

It is desired that η should be as large as possible, that is, η → 1. This indicates that the size of the feature subset is considerably reduced as compared with G. To compute the optimal feature vector, we perform the following:

- Short-list feature subsets that satisfy F_k threshold values
- Compute optimality factor, OF, which is given by

$$OF = \eta^* P^* A \qquad (3.11)$$

where P is the precision and A is the area under the receiver operator characteristic (ROC) curve. As can be seen, the feature subset with the largest value of optimality factor can be considered to be containing the most optimal set of features. The most optimal feature subset is now considered for the task of speaker identification.

3.5.6 Recognition with Static Features

Every person has a typical lip shape. The geometric parameters defining the lip contour may vary from person to person, although we might not presume that it is unique. To validate that it is not the static lip features of an individual that are differentiating the speaker, but the typical manner in which they speak and move their lips during the course of utterance of a word, we compare the performance of the static features with the results using dynamic features.

3.6 Results

The feature set, G, is subjected to feature selection. The ranking of features, as determined by mRMR, in descending order of relevance is shown below:

$$G = \{w\ \text{TP OP}\ A_{11}\ A_5\ A_1\ A_{12}\ A_7\ A_6\ A_2\ A_4\ h\ A_3\ A_8\ A_9\ A_{10}\}$$

As can be seen, lip width is shown to be the most prominent feature. Intuitively, we know that lip protrusion plays an important role in visual speech and changes in lip width are a subtle reflection of the protrusion. It is also observed that the teeth and visible oral cavity pixels are also important contributors to the recognition of a speaker.

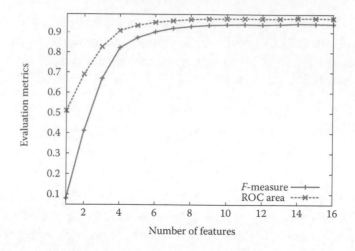

Figure 3.5 Evaluation metrics for feature subsets $G_1 \ldots G_{15}$.

The feature subsets, $G_1 \ldots G_{15}$, formed using ranked features of mRMR, are used for speaker identification and their F-measure values are noted for short-listing subsets for computing optimality factor. These F-measure values along with ROC area for the different subsets are shown in Figure 3.5.

3.6.1 Optimal Feature Subset

For each feature subset, the change in F-measure values, ξ, and change in feature length, η, with respect to the base vector, G, are computed. These are shown in Table 3.1. As can be seen, feature subsets G_1 to G_4 are not considered suitable for computation of the optimality factor by both kNN and RF classifiers. This is because the ξ values do not satisfy the threshold values (being >0.1).

For appropriate feature subsets, comparing the values of the optimality factors, we find that G_5 shows the largest values of OF, being 0.561 (computed from kNN results) and 0.569 (computed using RF results). It is also observed that only two feature subsets (G_{14} and G_{15}) are able to show better F-measure values (negative values of ξ) compared with the complete feature vector, G. However, because their feature length is almost similar to G, their optimality factors are not

Table 3.1 Evaluation Metrics of Short-Listed Feature Subsets

Feature Subset		KNN				RF			
	η	ξ	P	A	OF	ξ	P	A	OF
G_1	0.938	0.915	0.080	0.510	0.038	0.681	0.297	0.772	0.215
G_2	0.875	0.562	0.414	0.690	0.250	0.400	0.560	0.900	0.441
G_3	0.813	0.290	0.670	0.827	0.450	0.242	0.708	0.949	0.546
G_4	0.750	0.127	0.823	0.908	0.560	0.138	0.804	0.972	0.586
G_5	0.688	0.073	0.874	0.934	0.561	0.095	0.844	0.980	0.568
G_6	0.625	0.042	0.902	0.950	0.536	0.070	0.867	0.984	0.533
G_7	0.563	0.023	0.920	0.958	0.496	0.056	0.880	0.986	0.488
G_8	0.500	0.014	0.930	0.964	0.448	0.045	0.890	0.988	0.439
G_9	0.438	0.007	0.936	0.967	0.396	0.040	0.895	0.990	0.387
G_{10}	0.375	0.004	0.938	0.968	0.340	0.028	0.906	0.990	0.336
G_{11}	0.313	0.002	0.940	0.969	0.285	0.028	0.906	0.992	0.281
G_{12}	0.250	0.003	0.940	0.968	0.227	0.025	0.909	0.991	0.225
G_{13}	0.188	0.001	0.941	0.969	0.171	0.010	0.923	0.993	0.171
G_{14}	0.125	0.002	0.944	0.971	0.115	0.004	0.928	0.994	0.115
G_{15}	0.063	0.001	0.944	0.971	0.057	0.001	0.931	0.994	0.058
G	0	0	0.943	0.970	0	0	0.932	0.994	0

large. Thus, we can assume that G_5 is the most optimal feature subset. The features contained in feature subset G_5 are:

$$G_5 = \{w \ \mathrm{TP} \ \mathrm{OP} \ A_{11} \ A_5\}$$

Reducing the feature length from 16 features to just 5 features reduces the computational complexities and improves the real-time response of a system. It is seen that lip width, teeth pixels, and oral cavity pixels are major contributors in the recognition of a speaker. It is also observed that lip height does not figure in the set of optimal features.

3.6.2 Speaker Identification

The reduced set of features is used for the task of speaker identification. The word chosen for testing is "zero." A few random images of

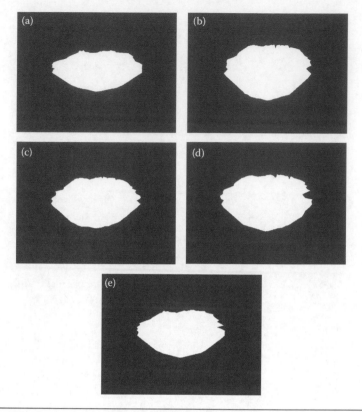

Figure 3.6   Random images from a visual speech sequence of *"zero."*

a speaker uttering the digit *zero* are shown in Figure 3.6. We take visual speech templates of this particular word and use it to identify the speaker from a database of 20 speakers. Using the *k*NN method, cross-validation results show that the false positive rate (FPR) is 0.5%. The FPR can be taken to denote the false acceptance rate (FAR). The true positive rate (TPR) is shown to be 90.6%. From the TPR, an estimate of the false rejection rate (FRR) gives a value of 9.4%. This is comparable with the results shown by using other biometric modalities.

Aravabhumi et al. (2010) have reported a recognition rate of 96%. However, multiple speech samples of the same person have not been taken into account to make the system more robust to speaker variability. The recognition rate achieved by Mehra et al. (2010) is 91.07% on applying principal component analysis on the visual speech images and using radial basis function network for recognition. This performance uses a vocabulary of four digits spoken by 12 subjects, each digit spoken twice. Speaker identification using a single digit has not been mentioned.

3.6.3 Speaker Identification with Static Features

To ensure that it is indeed the dynamic nature of lips during speech that is giving us good results, we compare it with results using static lip features. The closed lip visual features of an individual are now considered. These are representative of the shape of the lip of a person. Using these features, results show an average FAR of 56.23% and FRR of 5.95%. As can be seen, the FAR is very high and this will greatly compromise the security of any system. Comparing the results of speaker identification using visual speech and static lip features, it can be argued that the shape of the lip is not a major contributor to the task at hand. Thus, it is indeed the manner in which an individual utters speech that can be utilized for the recognition of the speaker.

3.6.4 Vocabulary Test

The reduced set of visual features is also tested for various digits (the results are shown in Table 3.2). It can be seen that the average FRR is 11.9% and the average FAR is 0.62%, which are reasonable results. Thus, we can argue that the set of visual inputs, containing only five features, is robust to different words of the vocabulary.

Table 3.2   Vocabulary Test

DIGIT	FRR (%)	FAR (%)
Zero	9.4	0.5
One	11.6	0.6
Two	10.0	0.5
Three	12.4	0.7
Four	10.2	0.5
Five	14.2	0.7
Six	11.1	0.6
Seven	15.8	0.8
Eight	11.0	0.6
Nine	13.3	0.7

3.7 Conclusions

In this chapter, we present a biometric system that uses the visual inputs from the lip of a person as he or she utters a word. The manner of speech of an individual is used to identify a person from a given database. To improve response time in a real-time implementation system, we employ feature selection to reduce the number of input features. It has been observed that a small set of features is sufficient as a biometric input using visual speech. It gives fairly high recognition rates. It is also seen that our feature set is independent of vocabulary and maintains an almost constant result. Thus, the choice of vocabulary can be left to the system designer. We also observe that static lip features show degraded results, thus proving that it is the dynamic information contained in the manner of movement of a person's mouth that leads to enhanced system performance.

Although movements of the lip aid in person verification, it may give better performance if used as an additional modality in a multimodal system. As part of future work, the computed optimal feature set can be used in conjunction with other modalities to develop a more secure and robust identification system.

References

Aravabhumi, V.R., Chenna, R.R., and Reddy, K.U. 2010. Robust method to identify the speaker using lip motion features. In *2010 International Conference on Mechanical and Electrical Technology (ICMET 2010)*. 125–129.

Brunelli, R., and Falavigna, D. 1995. Person identification using multiple cues. *IEEE Transactions on Pattern Analysis and Machine Intelligence* 12(10):955–966.

Cootes, T.F., Edwards, G.J., and Taylor, C.J. 2001. Active appearance models. *IEEE Transactions on Pattern Analysis and Machine Intelligence* 23(6):681–685.

Dieckmann, U., Plankensteiner, P., Schamburger, R., Froeba, B., and Meller, S. 1997. SESAM: a biometric person identification system using sensor fusion. *Pattern Recognition Letters* 18(9):827–833.

Frischholz, R.W., and Dieckmann, U. 2000. BioID: a multimodal biometric identification system. *IEEE Computer* 33(2):64–68.

Furui, S. 1997. Recent advances in speaker recognition. *Pattern Recognition Letters* 18(9):859–872.

Gudavalli, M., Raju, S.V., Babu, A.V., and Kumar, D.S. 2012. Multimodal biometrics—Sources, architecture and fusion techniques: an overview. In *2012 International Symposium on Biometrics and Security Technologies*. 27–34.

Hall, M., Frank, E., Holmes, G., Pfahringer, B., Reutemann, P., and Witten, I.H. 2009. The WEKA data mining software: an update. *SIGKDD Explorations* 11(1):10–18.

Ichino, M., Sakano, H., and Komatsu, N. 2006. Multimodal biometrics of lip movements and voice using Kernel Fisher discriminant analysis. In *9th International Conference on Control, Automation, Robotics and Vision.* 1–6.

Jain, A., Ross, A., and Prabhakar, S. 2004. An introduction to biometric recognition. *IEEE Transactions on Circuits and Systems for Video Technology* 14:4–20.

Jain, A., Ross, A., and Pankanti, S. 2006. Biometrics: a tool for information security. *IEEE Transactions on Information Forensics and Security* 1(2):125–143.

Kohavi, R. 1995. A study of cross-validation and bootstrap for accuracy estimation and model selection. In *14th International Joint Conference on Artificial Intelligence.* Morgan Kaufmann Publishers Inc., San Francisco, 1137–1143.

Kumar, A., Kanhangad, V., and Zhang, D. 2010. A new framework for adaptive multimodal biometrics management. *IEEE Transactions on Information Forensics and Security* 5(1):92–102.

Mehra, A., Kumawat, M., Ranjan, R., Pandey, B., Ranjan, S., Shukla, A., and Tiwari, R. 2010. Expert system for speaker identification using lip features with PCA. In *2010 2nd International Workshop on Intelligent Systems and Applications.* 1–4.

Peng, H., Long, F., and Ding, C. 2005. Feature selection based on mutual information: criteria of max-dependency, max-relevance, and min-redundancy. *IEEE Transactions on Pattern Analysis and Machine Intelligence* 27:1226–1238.

Potamianos, G., Neti, C., Gravier, G., Garg, A., and Senior, A.W. 2003. Recent advances in the automatic recognition of audio-visual speech. *Proceedings of the IEEE* 91:1306–1326.

Ross, A., and Jain, A. 2003. Information fusion in biometrics. *Pattern Recognition Letters, Special Issue in Multimodal Biometrics* 24(13):2115–2125.

Singh, P., Laxmi, V., and Gaur, M.S. 2012a. *n*-Gram modeling of relevant features for lip-reading. In *Proceedings of the International Conference on Advances in Computing, Communications and Informatics.* 1199–1204.

Singh, P., Laxmi, V., and Gaur, M.S. 2012b. Lip peripheral motion for visual surveillance. In *Proceedings of the Fifth International Conference on Security of Information and Networks.* 173–177.

4

HUMAN GAIT SIGNATURE FOR BIOMETRIC AUTHENTICATION

VIJAY JOHN

Contents

Abstract

With the increased interest in security and surveillance, the effective authentication of people has assumed great significance in recent years. Consequently, the development of highly accurate biometric authentication systems has received prominent attention in the research community. Biometric authentication is defined as the process of utilizing unique personal or biometric features to identify a person. Popular biometric features used for person authentication include the face, fingerprint, DNA, retina, etc. However, the use of these features in biometric authentication systems requires the active cooperation of the subject involved, which is often difficult and inconvenient. To avoid the need for active user cooperation, without compromising on the authentication accuracy of the biometric authentication system, researchers have investigated the use of human gait, or walk, as a biometric feature. Specifically, the property of human gait or walk being unique to each individual has been utilized in biometric authentication systems to identify or verify individuals. In this chapter, we present a detailed overview of a gait-based biometric authentication system and present a discussion on the various components of the system. Additionally, we categorize the literature on gait-based biometric authentication systems into three classes: camera-based systems, floor sensor–based systems, and wearable sensor–based systems, and present a detailed comparative study. Finally, we present a short discussion on the susceptibility of gait to mimicking attacks, thus motivating the need for gait-based multimodal biometric authentication systems.

4.1 Introduction

Effective authentication of humans assumes significance owing to the recent interest in security and surveillance. In this regard, several physiological features like face, fingerprint, DNA, retina, etc., have been utilized by researchers as biometric signatures within biometric authentication systems for effective authentication. Biometric authentication is defined as the technique of utilizing unique physiological or behavioral features to identify a person, and it has been observed that certain features such as the face, fingerprint, DNA, and retina require active subject cooperation. The need for active subject cooperation is a significant disadvantage in biometric systems. To circumvent this problem, researchers have been actively investigating alternative biometric features, and one such feature is the human gait. Human gait is a biometric feature that encodes a person's walk, considered to be a unique biometric trait, thus facilitating the use of human gait as an effective biometric signature. As discussed previously, gait has the important advantage of being independent of subject involvement, unlike features such as fingerprint, DNA, etc. Moreover, gait features can also be estimated from people available at larger distances. Consequently, gait has been the subject of extensive research in the biometric authentication community.

In this chapter, we present a detailed study of the gait-based biometric authentication system and categorize the existing literature into three classes: camera based, floor sensor based, and wearable sensor based. Additionally, we present a brief introduction into the problem of forgery on biometric authentication systems with single features (unimodal systems), thus, motivating the need for multimodal biometric authentication systems. Finally, a short introduction to key gait-based multimodal biometric authentication is presented with special emphasis on the biometric tunnel developed at the University of Southampton (Figure 4.1; Seely et al. 2008).

Our chapter is structured as follows: we first present an overview of a standard biometric authentication system in Section 4.2. Next, we introduce gait from a biomechanical perspective in Section 4.3, before introducing the standard gait-based human authentication system in Section 4.4. Apart from presenting an introduction to the system, we also review the key literature in the field. We also briefly review recent studies on the susceptibility of gait-based authentication systems to mimicking attacks; thus, motivating the need for gait-based multimodal biometric authentication systems. Finally, in Section 4.5, we present our summary of the research area, and conclude with our observations.

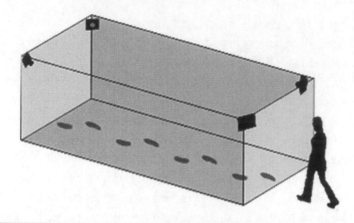

Figure 4.1 Illustration of step and stride. (From Seely 2008.)

4.2 Biometric Authentication System

Miller (1988) defines biometric authentication systems as "automated methods of verifying or recognizing the identity of a living person based on a physiological or behavioral characteristic." Specifically, given a database of human biometric signatures, a biometric authentication system is used to, first, verify if a query person is present in the database and, if present, identify the individual.

The standard biometric authentication system model has three components. The authentication system begins with the acquisition of a person's biometric data using relevant sensors (data acquisition module). Given the acquired biometric data, biometric features are extracted and stored (feature extraction and storage module). The extracted features are then used for person identification using a matching framework. The matching framework measures the similarity between the test person's extracted feature and the stored feature database to verify the person's authenticity (feature-matching module). The operating phases of the biometric authentication system consist of the learning phase and the testing phase. Although the testing phase includes all three components of the biometric authentication system, the learning or enrolling phase comprises only the data acquisition and feature extraction modules. An overview of the biometric authentication system is presented in Figure 4.2.

Before the deployment of the biometric authentication system, the authentication accuracy of the system is measured. Researchers,

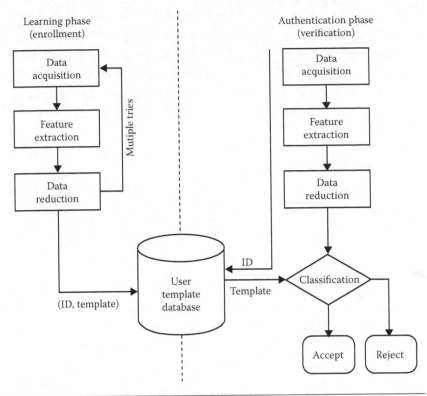

Figure 4.2   Overview of the biometric authentication system comprising the learning phase and authentication phase. (From Cattin, P., Biometric Authentication Using Human Gait. PhD diss. ETH, 2002.)

typically evaluate the system using measures such as the false acceptance rate (FAR), false rejection rate (FRR) (Gafurov 2007a,b), failure to enroll rate (FER), and failure to capture rate (FCR). These error measures are defined as *false acceptance rate*, the probability of wrongly accepting an impostor; *false rejection rate*, the probability of wrongly rejecting a person in the database; *failure to enroll rate*, the failure rate associated with enrolling a new person into the existing database; and *failure to capture rate*, the failure rate associated with acquiring the biometric signature from an available person. An additional measure used to evaluate the system is known as the decision error trade-off curve (DET), which is the plot between the FAR and FRR. The abovementioned error measures validate the system's ability to accept the correct individual, while simultaneously rejecting the wrong individual.

To minimize the errors within a biometric authentication system, researchers typically pay significant attention to the feature extraction module. Essentially, the extracted features should reduce the intra-person variations, whereas simultaneously enhancing the interperson variations. Popular biometric features, which include face, fingerprint, voice, retina, etc., have demonstrated good performance. However, as discussed previously, the major drawback of such feature-based systems is the requirement of active user participation, which is addressed by the use of human gait as a biometric feature. An introduction to human gait and its role within the biometric authentication system is presented in the subsequent sections.

4.3 Biometric Feature: Human Gait

Human gait refers to human motion pertaining to the way people walk. We can observe that every person has a unique gait signature, thus facilitating the use of human gait as a biometric signature. In terms of their characteristics, we observe that the human gait is a periodic motion and is typically expressed using the gait cycle or stride. A gait cycle corresponds to one complete cycle between feet on ground, right foot forward, feet on ground, left foot forward, and rest (Kale et al. 2004). The various events during the gait cycle or stride is represented using two phases, the *stance phase* and the *swing phase* (Vaughan et al. 1992) as seen in Figure 4.3. The stance phase includes intervals of gait cycle when both feet are in contact with the ground, and include subphases comprising the intervals between ground heel strike to foot flat, foot flat through midstance, midstance through heel off, heel off to toe off (Cuccurullo 2004). On the other hand, the swing phase is composed of intervals of gait cycle when both feet are not in contact with the ground and in the air (Vaughan et al. 1992). The stance phase represents 60% of the gait cycle, whereas the swing phase represents 40% of the gait cycle (Vaughan et al. 1992). It can be seen that the periodic gait cycle encompasses the motion of various body parts including the head, feet, and hands during the two phases. Consequently, researchers have exploited the embedded motion within the gait cycle, and have managed to extract discriminative gait features. These motion-based gait features have been utilized in camera-based and wearable sensor–based biometric authentication

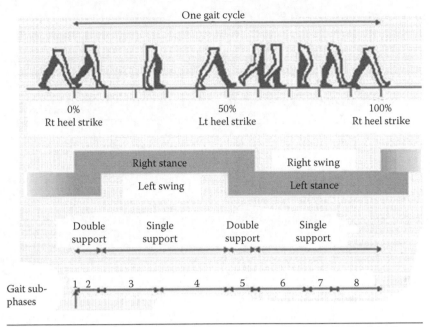

Figure 4.3   Illustration of the gait cycle. (From Cattin, P., Biometric Authentication Using Human Gait. PhD diss. ETH, 2002.)

systems. Apart from motion-based gait features, researchers have also observed that the ground force exerted by people during walking is unique, resulting in the use of force-based gait features within floor sensor–based biometric authentication systems, in which floor sensors are used to measure the exerted ground force. Given an introduction to the standard biometric authentication system in Section 4.2, and a brief overview of the characteristics of human gait in Section 4.3, we next present a detailed review of gait-based biometric authentication.

4.4 Gait-Based Biometric Authentication System

Gait-based biometric authentications have been investigated for an extensive period by researchers, owing to the aforementioned advantages, with applications in surveillance and security. The standard gait-based biometric authentication system model has three components: the data acquisition module, the feature extraction module, and the feature-matching module. We next briefly review the three system components, before reviewing the important biometric authentication systems in the literature.

4.4.1 Gait Biometric Authentication System Overview

4.4.1.1 Data Acquisition Module An important consideration for the gait-based biometric authentication system is the type of sensor used for data acquisition. The choice of sensors depends entirely on the environment or applications for which the gait-based biometric authentication system is designed. Based on our survey of literature, we identify three sensors that are used for data acquisition, which include the camera, the floor sensor, and the wearable sensor (Gafurov 2007a,b). Comparing the above sensor-based biometric systems, we observe that the camera-based biometric authentication system is comparatively cheaper and easier to install, while being easily available. On the other hand, the floor sensors are expensive and tedious to set up. As a result, the camera-based systems are widely used. Recently, researchers have utilized wearable sensors within biometric authentication system to extract the gait feature (Boyle et al. 2011).

In terms of the type of sensors used within the three sensor classes, we observe that researchers and system designers typically use the monocular or stereo camera in camera-based gait authentication systems, pressure sensors in floor sensor–based systems, and accelerometers and gyroscopes in wearable sensor–based systems.

4.4.1.2 Feature Extraction Module Given the acquired data from the various sensors, the next step in the biometric authentication system is the extraction of gait features. A primary consideration for feature extraction is the selection of features that enhance interperson discrimination and reduce intraperson discrimination. As briefly discussed previously in Section 4.3, one of the methods in gait-based feature extraction involves the identification of discriminative motion patterns from the periodic gait cycle. The periodic gait cycle encodes the movements of various body joints that occur during a person's walk. We term the gait features extracted from the periodic gait cycle as *motion–based* gait features. Popular features extracted from the gait cycle include: *gait period*, defined as the time per gait cycle; *distance travelled*, defined as the distance per gait cycle; and *cadence*, defined as the number of steps per minute (BenAbdelkader et al. 2002). Apart from motion-based features, the gait-based features can also be extracted from the ground force exerted by a person on pressure sensors while walking. We term such gait-based features as the *ground reaction force* (GRF)–based features, which are used predominantly in floor sensor–based biometric authentication system. Typically, camera-based systems and wearable sensor–based systems utilize motion-based features, whereas the floor sensor–based systems utilize the GRF-based features. In camera-based biometric authentication systems, the extracted gait features correspond to the periodic spatiotemporal variations of the human foreground during walking, whereas the extracted gait features in the wearable sensor–based biometric authentication system correspond to the periodic spatiotemporal variations of the human foreground and the anthropometric features. The anthropometric features refer to the human body proportion in relation to shape and size. On the other hand, in the floor sensor–based biometric authentication system, the gait-based features are based on the GRFs obtained from the pressure sensors.

4.4.1.3 Feature-Matching Module   In the gait-based biometric authentication system, to authenticate a test person, given the extracted features, a matching framework is adopted. Two popular matching frameworks can be identified in the literature: the probabilistic matching framework and the distance measure-based matching framework.

Given an overview of the system components, we next categorize the gait-based biometric authentication systems according to the type of data acquisition sensors and review the key features extracted and matching frameworks in each class.

4.4.2 Camera-Based Gait Biometric Authentication System

With the easy availability of low-cost cameras, camera-based biometric authentication systems have gained prominence in recent years, and have been the focus of extensive research in the field of computer vision. Among the vast array of camera-based biometric literature, we identify the important gait features and matching algorithms used in camera-based biometric authentication systems.

4.4.2.1 Camera-Based Gait Biometric Authentication System: Gait Features   The main advantage of a camera-based system is the ease of installation and the acquisition of gait data at large distances.

Consequently, the gait features extracted correspond to the spatio-temporal variations of the acquired human walk in the video sequence. Based on the nature of the camera used, the gait features captured can be categorized as monocular camera–based gait features or stereo camera–based gait features.

4.4.2.1.1 Monocular Gait Features   Several researchers have sought to extract discriminative features corresponding to the human gait from the monocular camera. The monocular gait features can be broadly classified as two-dimensional (2-D) spatiotemporal gait features, three-dimensional (3-D) spatiotemporal gait volume, and 2-D gait templates. The 2-D spatiotemporal gait feature corresponds to a feature vector that combines the anthropometric feature along with the gait-based dynamics, in which the gait-based dynamics refers to the gait feature time series. In the 2-D spatiotemporal gait feature, the anthropometric features, corresponding to a person's body structure, are extracted using tracking algorithms (Jean et al. 2009), motion capture data (Tanawongsuwan and Bobick 2001), or models such as wavelet transform, radon transform, Fourier descriptors, etc. Given the extracted anthropometric features, the gait-based dynamics are then extracted from a sequence of human walk using methods such as optical flow (Lu et al. 2006) and Fourier transform.

The 2-D spatiotemporal gait features are popular gait features. In 1998, Little and Boyd explored the use of optical flow to derive the gait dynamics from a sequence of background subtracted subjects, the authors calculated the time series for human width and human height, and used optical flow to represent the frequency components (Little and Boyd 1998). The authors demonstrated good identification accuracy with their proposed gait feature, especially with the limited training population. Ho et al. (2011) also adopted optical flow to extract gait dynamics. However, unlike the earlier work by Little and Boyd (1998), Ho et al. (2011) quantized the magnitude and orientation of the optical flow vectors and represent the features using a 2-D histogram. Additionally, the authors also extract the anthropometric features using Fourier descriptors. Cunado et al. (2003) propose a more detailed feature vector in which a technique termed the *velocity Hough transform* is used to extract the horizontal, vertical, and rotational angles of the thigh. A Fourier analysis of the hip rotation time series represents the detailed gait signature. The abovementioned gait features are shown to be discriminative features in the literature. In the work by Collins et al. (2002), the authors address an important issue associated with the extraction of gait features, that is, computational complexity. Specifically, to reduce the computational complexity during query matching, the authors extract several key-frames from the human foreground width and height time series corresponding to the most discriminative instants of the walk cycle. The authors demonstrated a significant reduction in computational complexity with their novel representation of gait features. Another popular 2-D spatiotemporal gait feature involves the use of human tracking algorithms. Specifically, in the works of Wang et al. (2004) and Tanawongsuwan and Bobick (2001), the anthropometric features and the gait dynamics are derived from a human tracking algorithm and motion capture data, respectively. The tracker-based gait features have the advantage of being more descriptive and detailed, with the authentication accuracy greatly depending on the accuracy of the tracker.

3-D spatiotemporal gait volume is another popular gait feature extracted in monocular literature. The 3-D spatiotemporal volume refers to the accumulation of human foreground across time in a walking sequence, representing a dense and descriptive feature. Several researchers have investigated the use of such spatiotemporal gait volume as features within the gait-based biometric authentication system. Mowbray and Nixon (2003), in their work, derive the silhouette volume from the gait period, or walk cycle, and represent the derived volume using the 2-D Fourier descriptor. The 2-D Fourier descriptor is used to encode the deformation of the spatiotemporal gait volume, and function as rich descriptors. In the work by Makihara et al. (2006), the 2-D Fourier transform is applied to the gait volume and the corresponding frequency components are extracted. Additionally, the authors also propose a view transformation model to ensure that the gait features are view-invariant. Specifically, the Fourier transform–based frequency domain features extracted from several camera views are normalized using a view transformation model. The use of Fourier transform to encode the spatiotemporal volume deformations was also observed in the work of Ohara et al. (2004), in which the authors utilize a 3-D Fourier to represent the spatiotemporal deformations. Additionally, the authors also incorporate anthropometric features such as torso distance within their feature vector. Based on the above literature, we can observe that the 3-D spatiotemporal gait volume functions as a rich feature vector that encodes the spatiotemporal variations in great detail, at the cost of increased computational complexity and storage size. Consequently, researchers have focused on encoding the gait volume deformation using a single template, which we discuss next.

2-D gait feature template encodes the detailed spatial–temporal deformation of the gait volume within a single template or image. The gait template represents a dense and discriminative feature vector, with reduced storage size. Consequently, template-based gait features have been widely used in gait-based biometric authentication systems wherein high authentication accuracies have been reported. In 1996, Bobick and Davis (1996a) proposed the motion energy image (MEI) template, which describes the spatial distribution of motion for an action. Specifically, the MEI represents the cumulative binary motion energy for a silhouette sequence in a single image. In their subsequent work, Bobick and Davis (1996b) proposed a simple decay operator on the cumulative binary motion energy, such that the recent motion has a brighter value, resulting in the motion history image (MHI). In the work by Han and Bhanu (2006), the authors had proposed a novel gait-based template feature known as the gait energy image (GEI). The GEI is represented by a single template or image, in which each pixel value corresponds to the mean intensity value of that particular pixel across a gait period. An example of GEI is shown in Figure 4.4. The GEI is a popular gait-based feature that is often used in biometric authentication systems as a baseline feature. Recently, in the work by Wang et al. (2010), the authors propose a novel template termed the *chrono-gait image* (CGI) to describe the spatiotemporal gait pattern. The CGI template encodes the temporal and spatial information in the silhouette gait using color mapping. The authors report that incorporating color mapping within the GEI

Figure 4.4   Illustration of gait energy image. (From Seely 2010.)

significantly improves the recognition performance because color has higher variance than grayscale intensity and can better represent the gait sequence variations.

Among the different monocular gait features, we observe that the 2-D gait-based template is the most discriminative and widely used feature in monocular systems.

4.4.2.1.2 Stereo Camera Gait Features With the recent advent of commercial color-depth cameras, and the availability of low-cost stereo cameras, many researchers have started to focus on extending 2-D gait techniques to the 3-D space. Based on our survey of the 3-D camera literature, we identify two categories of stereo features: 3-D spatiotemporal gait features and 3-D gait feature templates.

3-D spatiotemporal gait features are important gait features in which the depth value obtained from the stereo camera or depth sensors are incorporated within the 2-D spatiotemporal gait features. For example, in the work of Uddin et al. (2010), depth values are incorporated within the extracted human foreground, and the 3-D gait dynamics are modeled using the hidden Markov model (HMM). Similarly, in Ning et al. (2013) the 3-D gait dynamics are also modeled using the HMM. However, the authors represent each depth frame using a histogram. The authors report good authentication accuracies with their histogram-based model. In the recent work by Ar and Akgul (2012), the authors use a histogram and 3-D Haar-like features to represent the gait dynamics of the entire sequence. Similar to 2-D spatiotemporal gait features, we observe that a few 3-D spatiotemporal gait features are also based on the use of human tracking algorithms. Examples include the work by Xia et al. (2012). Recently, Munsell et al. (2012) used the Kinect sensor to derive the anthropometric features from which the dynamic features are derived using the discrete Fourier transform.

3-D gait feature templates encode the deformation of the four-dimensional spatiotemporal gait volume within a single 3-D template. A few researchers have been involved in extending the 2-D gait features template to the 3-D space. Rigoll et al. (2012), in their work, integrate the 2-D GEI with the histogram of oriented gradients to generate depth gradient histogram energy image (DGHEI). Similarly, in the recent work by Ning et al. (2013), the authors extend the MHI (Bobick and Davis 1996a,b) to the 3-D space, generating the 3-D MHI. Both studies demonstrate the great effectiveness of the 3-D gait feature template, which can be attributed to their rich description of human gait.

An important factor to consider in gait feature extraction is the use of background subtraction to localize people. Background subtraction helps in localizing the gait feature extraction algorithm to relevant regions in the image, thus, reducing the computational complexity and increasing the feature extraction accuracy. Typically, the background is removed using methods like background subtraction or background modeling using computer vision models like the Gaussian mixture model (Zivkovic 2004). An example of a background subtracted human silhouette is shown in Figure 4.5. Note that background subtraction is not a trivial problem, and has been addressed as a separate research problem in computer vision. The challenges in accurate background subtraction include background noise and illumination noise. An example of poor background segmentation is shown in Figure 4.6.

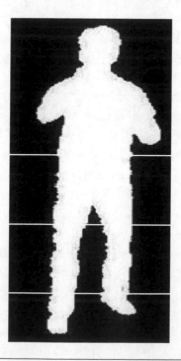

Figure 4.5   Example of foreground human silhouette after background subtraction.

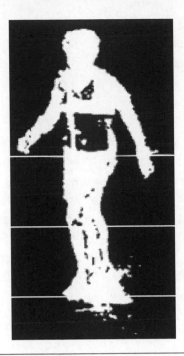

Figure 4.6 Example of noisy foreground human silhouette.

4.4.2.2 Camera-Based Gait Biometric Authentication System: Feature-Matching We next review the popular feature-matching algorithms deployed in camera-based biometric authentication systems. The goal of the matching framework in a biometric authentication system is to identify a test feature vector or person by performing feature-matching with the training database. Based on our survey of literature, we identify two feature-matching formulations that are adopted to identify the test person: the probabilistic matching formulation and the nearest neighbor matching formulation.

4.4.2.2.1 Probabilistic Matching Formulation Several probabilistic matching formulations have been utilized in the gait-based biometric authentication system, and one of the most popular approaches is the maximum likelihood identification scheme. A person is identified using the maximum likelihood identification by the assignment of the label of the person distribution in the training data set with the highest likelihood. Typically, the distribution over each person in the training data set is learned during the training phase (BenAbdelkader et al. 2002). Another popular probabilistic matching framework used in gait-based biometric systems is the naïve Bayesian classification. A naïve Bayesian classifier is a probabilistic classification model that is based on Bayes' theorem and a naïve independence assumption between multiple gait features.

4.4.2.2.2 Nearest Neighbor–Based Matching Formulation Another popular approach used to identify people is the nearest neighbor–based matching scheme. In the nearest neighbor matching formulation, the test person is identified by assigning the label of the person in the training data set with the shortest distance. In the *k*-nearest neighbor matching formulation, the test person is assigned the label of the *k*-nearest neighbors. The key component of the nearest neighbor matching formulation is the distance measures used to calculate the distance between the query and the training data set. The popular distance measures used in the nearest neighbor–based matching formulation include: *the Euclidean distance measure*, which is the distance measured between two points in the feature space based on the Pythagorean formula (Wang et al. 2010; Mowbray and Nixon 2003); *the Mahalonabis distance measure*, which is based on the correlation between the test and training variables (Bobick and Davis 1996a,b); *dynamic time warping* (DTW), which aligns two temporal sequences varying in time and speed (Kale et al. 2002; Tanawongsuwan and Bobick 2001; Ioannidis et al. 2007). In the case of speed-varying or time-varying signals, DTW is used to warp the sequences nonlinearly to match each other, and the training sequence with the least warping is used to identify the test person; and finally, the *Bhattacharya coefficient*, which is used to compare histogram-based features (Ho and Huang 2011).

4.4.2.3 Discussion Based on our survey of the literature, we observe that the camera-based system has the advantage of negating the need for subject cooperation. Additionally, the gait signature can be extracted from large distances. More importantly, with the recent advent of cost-effective cameras, the camera-based systems are comparatively cheaper and can be deployed in a wide range of environments. On the other hand, the major drawbacks of camera-based systems are the sensor and illumination noises, which degrade the acquired gait data. Additionally, the system is prone to self-occlusion and occlusion from other people and background objects.

4.4.3 Floor Sensor–Based Gait Biometric Authentication System

In this section, we review the literature on floor sensor–based gait biometric authentication systems. Typically, when humans walk, they exert a certain force on the ground and it has been reported in the literature that features extracted from the ground forces are unique to each individual. The force exerted on the ground by both feet during walking is termed as the GRF, and represents the gait features of the floor sensor–based biometric authentication. To acquire the GRF, researchers have typically used floor sensors, which are essentially force plates that measure the GRF while people walk over it.

In this section, we discuss the following aspects of the floor sensor–based gait biometric authentication system: the setup of the floor sensors, the different components of the acquired GRF, and an overview of the gait features that are extracted from the GRF.

4.4.3.1 Floor Sensor–Based Gait Biometric Authentication System

4.4.3.1.1 Force Plate Sensors Researchers typically use pressure-based sensors such as piezoelectric sensors to measure the GRF of humans walking. During the installation of the floor sensors, great care is taken to ensure that the subjects are unaware of the installation. This is essentially done to permit the subjects to walk naturally because it has been reported that subjects who are aware of the sensors walk unnaturally (Cattin et al. 2002). Consequently, the floor sensors or force plates are integrated into the floor, and do not rise above the floor level, as illustrated in Figure 4.7.

4.4.3.1.2 Ground Reaction Force The installed floor sensors measure the GRF when humans walk over them. The measured GRF is a 3-D vector corresponding to three ground force components that are perpendicular to each other and are called anterior, vertical, and lateral force components (Cattin 2001). The force applied on the floor sensor is measured using two methods: the gait cycle method and the

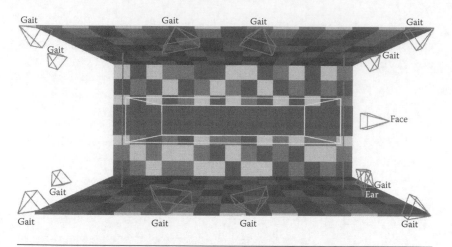

Figure 4.7   Detailed layout of the biometric tunnel. (From Seely et al. 2008.)

steady method. In the gait cycle method, the force applied during walking is assumed to be uniform for each walk period, and the force observed for several walk periods is averaged. On the other hand, the steady state method assumes that the force generated during walking achieves a steady state over the course of time, after which the force-based features are extracted (Jenkins and Ellis 2007).

4.4.3.1.3 Floor Sensor–Based Gait Features   Among the various GRF components, we observe that the vertical component of GRF, or vertical GRF, forms the basis for several force-based features. Features derived from the vertical GRF include area under the curve, average body mass, amplitude and time between feet placement, the spatial position of the GRF loop, curve gradient, etc. (Cattin 2001). Among the above discussed features, we observe that the average body mass is most frequently used (Jenkins and Ellis 2007), and is defined as the average GRF force divided by the gravity. A detailed study of several force plate–based features is presented by Suutala and Roning (2008), in which they investigate 31 varied features. Examples of the GRF are illustrated in Figure 4.8. In Figures 4.9, 4.10, and 4.11, the discriminative property of GRF-based features for three persons is illustrated. Apart from GRF-based gait features, other features have also been explored in floor sensor–based biometric authentication systems. Example features include footstep profiles (Orr and Abowd 2000), stride length, and stride cadence (Middleton et al. 2005).

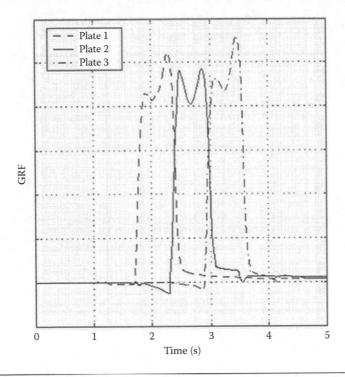

Figure 4.8 Plot of the GRF versus time, which forms the basis for the floor sensor–based gait feature. (From Cattin, P., Biometric Authentication Using Human Gait. PhD diss. ETH, 2002.)

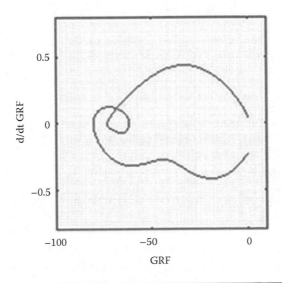

Figure 4.9 Discriminative ability of GRF derivative—subject 1. (From Cattin, P., Biometric Authentication Using Human Gait. PhD diss. ETH, 2002.)

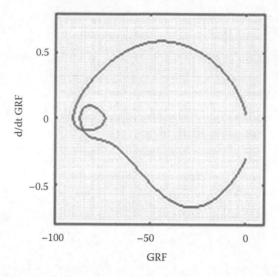

Figure 4.10 Discriminative ability of GRF derivative—subject 2. (From Cattin, P., Biometric Authentication Using Human Gait. PhD diss. ETH, 2002.)

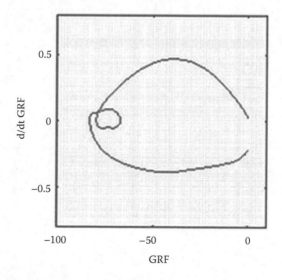

Figure 4.11 Discriminative ability of GRF derivative—subject 3. (From Cattin, P., Biometric Authentication Using Human Gait. PhD diss. ETH, 2002.)

4.4.3.2 Discussion   Because the floor sensor–based biometric authentication system is generally designed to be unobtrusive and hidden, it helps to acquire data without the knowledge of the subject, thus, eliminating the necessity for subject cooperation. Moreover, because the subject is unaware of the presence of floor-based sensors, it allows the user to walk naturally. Note that the same advantages are also observed in the camera-based biometric authentication system. However, unlike the camera-based system features, the floor sensor–based system's features are considered as weakly discriminative features because the GRF measured depends on the body mass of the person, which is a weak identification feature and is subject to many variations. As a proposed solution, researchers have sought to use supplementary biometric authentication systems, such as the wearable sensor–based biometric authentication system to increase the authentication accuracy.

4.4.4 Wearable Sensor–Based Biometric Authentication System

In this section, we present an overview of the wearable sensor–based gait biometric authentication system. In recent years, researchers have focused on utilizing wearable sensors, such as the accelerometer and the motion capture system, to acquire data for gait-based biometric authentication systems. We first discuss the different types of wearable sensors that are used in gait biometric authentication systems, before providing a summary of the extracted gait features.

4.4.4.1 Wearable Sensor–Based Biometric Authentication System: Wearable Sensors In the literature, we identify two popular sensors that are used in gait biometric authentication systems, the accelerometer and the motion capture system. The motion capture systems involve the placement of markers at various locations in the body to capture joint information in the form of 3-D joint angles and positions. Several types of motion capture systems exist, namely, magnetic, optical, and mechanical motion capture (John 2011). Whereas the motion capture system is used to measure 3-D joint information, the accelerometer is used to measure joint acceleration along the 3-D axis. An accelerometer can be placed at various locations on the body, including the shoes, breast, waist, legs, hips, and ankle, or can even be carried in the pocket or attached to the belt (Derawi 2010). With the recent advances in technology, accelerometers embedded in smartphones and GPS have been used as sensors to extract gait signatures (Boyle et al. 2011). The joint information acquired by these sensors during a person's walk forms the basis for the gait features that are used within the biometric authentication system.

4.4.4.2 Wearable Sensor–Based Biometric Authentication System: Gait Features   In the survey by Derawi (2010), the author summarizes the different gait features that are extracted from wearable sensors, and categorize them as either time domain features or frequency domain features. Here, we briefly review a few important gait features. First, the authors define the time domain features as gait features that are derived from the time series data of the 3-D joints. The time series of the acquired 3-D joints encodes the unique gait signature of each person and, hence, can be exploited for discriminative feature extraction. An important feature extracted from the time series is known as *the average cycle time interval,* which represents the time interval between one foot hitting the ground and the same foot hitting the ground again (Derawi 2010). The frequency domain features represent the gait features that are extracted from the transformed frequency domain of the 3-D joint time series. The frequency domain features encode the periodicity of human gait, and are obtained using techniques such as the Fourier transform, the cosine transform, and the wavelet transform (Derawi 2010; Boyle et al. 2011).

4.4.4.3 Discussion   Based on our survey of the literature, we observe that the performance of the wearable sensor–based biometric authentication system is inferior to that of the floor sensor–based biometric authentication system (Hanlon et al. 2009). Consequently, researchers have proposed to use the wearable sensors as supplemental or additional sensors for other sensor–based biometric authentication systems (Derawi 2010). Note that owing to the requirement of sensor attachment, the wearable sensor–based biometric system is greatly restricted to very specific applications, such as biomechanical laboratories, motion capture studios, and patient or elderly care in smart homes.

4.4.5 Gait-Based Biometric Authentication System: Forging

Thus far, we have discussed the various components present in a gait-based biometric authentication system in great detail. Next, we will present a brief introduction to an important factor that has to be considered when designing a biometric authentication system—the ability of the system to withstand forging.

Typically, biometric features are difficult to forge because they are unique to each individual. For example, it is not possible to change one's fingerprint or facial features. However, it is possible for an imposter to steal a given person's fingerprint or take the person's picture, without that person's knowledge, to fool the authentication system. Thus, it is fairly important to review a biometric feature's ability to withstand forging. Consequently, we present a discussion based on two detailed studies presented by Gafurov (2007a,b) and Stang (2007). In the study by Gafurov (2007a,b), the author designed an experiment to test the gait acceleration-based biometric system's ability to withstand forging. During the forging test, an individual imposter mimics the gait of a person in the database and the authentication system's response is measured. Based on their study, the authors report that it is difficult to mimic gait, with the observation that trying to mimic gait makes it unnatural and uneven. On the other hand, in the study by Stang (2007), the authors report that when imposters are given live feedback of how their gait varies from the target gait during an attack, they are able to breach security. To provide the live feedback, during the attack testing, the authors conduct the testing indoors with a projector displaying the dynamic update of difference between the attacker's gait and the test gait.

From the above studies, we can infer that—with sufficient and rigorous practice—it is possible to mimic gait. This is similar to a person's signature, which can be forged with sufficient and rigorous practice. To overcome this problem, researchers have proposed to incorporate multiple biometric features to strengthen a single biometric authentication system. We next review the literature on gait-based multimodal features.

4.4.6 Gait-Based Multimodal Biometric Authentication System

A unimodal biometric system, apart from being susceptible to forgery, is subject to challenges like noisy data and intraperson variations. It can be seen that these limitations can be addressed by the deployment of a multimodal biometric system. A multimodal biometric authentication system is obtained by the integration of biometric features from multiple sensors. In the case of gait-based multimodal biometric authentication systems, researchers take considerable care to select physiologically discriminative features to supplement gait. In this regard, the face has been investigated as a suitable biometric feature for multimodal fusion (Hossain and Chetty 2011). In the proposed multimodal biometric system, the authors combine a face classifier and a gait classifier at the matching stage. Recently, researchers at the University of Southampton have constructed a gait-based multimodal biometric authentication system known as the *biometric tunnel* (Seely et al. 2010). The biometric tunnel has been designed keeping in mind the environment at airport security. Thus, people walking through the tunnel are captured by multiple synchronous cameras of lower resolution, and their 3-D volumes are reconstructed from the silhouettes for gait feature extraction. In addition to gait extraction, two high-resolution cameras are set up to capture the face and ear, which function as additional biometric features. In the biometric tunnel, gait, face, and ear-based features are combined together to form a novel multimodal feature. Researchers report nearly 100% accuracy with their proposed setup. An illustration of the setup is shown in Figure 4.7, in which the room is painted with a rectangular color pattern to aid automatic camera calibration. Thus, we can conclude that a gait-based multimodal biometric authentication system holds great promise for biometric authentication, and has the potential to be researched extensively in the coming years.

4.5 Conclusion

In this chapter, we have presented a detailed overview of the gait-based biometric authentication system. We observe that human gait is an effective biometric signature and, unlike other biometric features, has the advantage of being extracted at larger distances without the knowledge or cooperation of the subject. This has resulted in gait-based biometric authentication systems receiving significant attention in the literature for important applications utilizing gait-based authentication including video surveillance, law enforcement, airport security, etc. Additionally, we have reported a detailed survey of the literature and categorized the literature based on the type of acquisition sensors, that is, camera-based, floor sensor–based, and wearable sensor–based. We observed that among the different sensor-based authentication systems, the camera-based system is the most cost-effective and widely used. On the downside, camera-based systems are prone to sensor noise and occlusion. On the other hand, the wearable sensor–based and floor sensor–based biometric systems are comparatively less susceptible to noise and occlusion, but are limited to specific applications and environments because of the difficulty in their installation and setup. With the advent of technology, and need for foolproof systems, current research is focused on developing gait-based multimodal biometric authentication systems by fusing different biometric features. In the future, the technology derived from gait-based biometric authentication has the potential to be extensively used for identifying people in varied environments.

References

Ar, I., and Akgul, Y. 2012. A framework for combined recognition of actions and objects. In *ICCVG*.

Aravind, S., Amit, R., and Rama, C. 2003. A hidden Markov model based framework for recognition of humans from gait sequences. In *Proceedings of the IEEE International Conference on Image Processing*.

Bashir, K., Xiang, T., and Gong, S. 2010. Gait recognition without subject cooperation. *Pattern Recognition Letters* 31(13):2052–2060.

BenAbdelkader, C., Cuttler, R., and Davis, L. 2002. Stride and cadence for gait recognition. In *Proceedings of Conference on Face and Gesture Recognition*.

Bisacco, A., Chiuso, A., Ma, Y., and Soatto, S. 2001. Recognition of human gaits. *CVPR*.

Bobick, A., and Davis, J. 1996a. An appearance-based representation of action. *Proceedings 13th International Conference on Pattern Recognition*.

Bobick, A., and Davis, J. 1996b. Real-time recognition of activity using temporal templates. *IEEE Workshop on Applications of Computer Vision*.

Boyle, M., Klausner, A., Starobinski, D., Trachtengburg, A., and Wu, H. 2011. Gait-based user classification using phone sensor. *Proceedings of Conference on Mobile Systems, Applications and Services*.

Cattin, P. 2002. Biometric Authentication Using Human Gait. PhD diss. ETH.

Collins, R., Gross, R., and Shi, J. 2002. Silhouette-based human identification from body shape and gait. In *Proceedings of the Fifth IEEE International Conference on Automatic Face and Gesture Recognition*.

Cuccurullo, S. 2004. *Physical Medicine and Rehabilitation Board Review*. Demos Medical Publishing, New York, USA.

Cunado, D., Nixon, M., and Carter, J. 2003. Automatic extraction and description of human gait models for recognition purposes. *Computer Vision and Image Understanding* 1(90):1–41.

Derawi, M. 2010. Accelerometer-based gait analysis, a survey. In *Norwegian Information Security Conference*.

Gafurov, D. 2007a. A survey of biometric gait recognition: Approaches, security and challenges. *In Proceedings of NIK*.

Gafurov, D. 2007b. Security analysis of impostor attempts with respect to gender in gait biometrics. *In IEEE International Conference on Biometrics: Theory, Applications and System*.

Han, J., and Bhanu, B. 2006. Individual recognition using gait energy image. *IEEE Transactions on Pattern Analysis and Machine Intelligence* 28(2):316–322.

Hanlon, M., and Anderson, R. 2009. Real-time gait event detection using wearable sensors. *Gait & Posture* 30(4):523–527.

Ho, M., and Huang, C. 2011. Gait analysis for walking paths determination and human identification. *Hsiuping Journal* 23:1–16.

Hossain, S., and Chetty, G. 2011. Next generation identification based on face-gait biometric. In *IPCBEE*.

Ioannidis, D., Tzovaras, D., Damousis, I., Argyropoulos, S., and Moustakas, K. 2007. Gait recognition using compact feature extraction transforms and depth. *Transactions on Information Forensics and Security* 2(3): 623–630.

Jean, F., Albu, A., and Bergevin, R. 2009. Towards view-invariant gait modeling using spatio-temporal features. In *Pattern Recognition* 42(11):2936–2949.

Jenkins, J., and Ellis, C. 2007. Using ground reaction forces from gait analysis: Body mass as a weak biometric. In *Proceedings of the 5th International Conference on Pervasive Computing*.

John, V. 2011. Markerless Multiple-View Human Motion Analysis Using Swarm Optimisation and Subspace Learning. PhD Thesis. University of Dundee.

Kale, A., Rajagopalan, A., Cuntoor, A., and, Krüger, V. 2002. Gait-based recognition of humans using continuous HMMs. In *Proceedings of the Fifth IEEE International Conference on Automatic Face and Gesture Recognition*.

Kale, A., Sundaresan, S., Rajagopalan, A., Cuntoor, A., Roy-Chowdhury, A., Krüger, V., and Chellappa, R. 2004. Human identification using gait. *Transactions of Image Processing* 13(9):1163–1173.

Little, J., and Boyd, J. 1998. Recognizing People by Their Gait: the Shape of Motion. Videre: Journal of Computer Vision Research, MIT Press 1(2):2–36.

Lu, J., Zhang, E., and Jing, C. 2008. Gait recognition using wavelet descriptor and ICA. *Advances in Neural Networks*.

Makihara, Y., Sagawa, R., Mukaigawa, Y., Echigo, T., and Yagi, Y. 2006. Gait recognition using view transform in frequency domain. In *Proceedings of European Conference of Computer Vision*.

Middleton, L., Buss, A., Bazin, A., and Nixon, M. 2005. A floor sensor system for gait recognition. In *Fourth IEEE Workshop on Automatic Identification Advanced Technologies*.

Miller, B. Everything you need to know about biometric identification. *Personal Identification News 1988 Biometric Industry Directory*. Warfel & Miller, Inc., Washington DC.

Mowbray, S., and Nixon, M. 2003. Automatic gait recognition via Fourier descriptors of deformable objects. *Audio- and Video-Based Biometric Person Authentication* 566–573.

Munsell, B., Temlyakov, A., Qu, C., and Wang, S. 2012. Person identification using full-body motion and anthropometric biometrics from kinect videos. In *ECCV Workshops*.

Ning, B., Wang, G., and Moulin, P. 2013. RGB-D Huda Act: a color-depth video database for human daily activity recognition. *CVPR Workshop*.

Ohara, Y., Sagawa, R., Echigo, T., and Yagi, Y. 2004. Gait volume: Spatiotemporal analysis of walking. *OMNIVIS*.

Orr, R., and Abowd, G. 2000. The smart floor: A mechanism for natural user identification and tracking. In *Proceedings of the Conference on Human Factors in Computing Systems*.

Ran, Y., Weiss, I., Zheng, Q., and Davis, L. 2006. Pedestrian detection via periodic motion analysis. *International Journal of Computer Vision* 71(2): 143–160.

Rigoll, G., Hofmann, M., and Bachmann, S. 2012. 2.5d gait biometrics using the depth gradient histogram energy image. In *IEEE Fifth International Conference on Biometrics: Theory, Applications and Systems*.

Seely, R., Samangooei, S., Middleton, L., Carter, J., and Nixon, M. 2008. The University of Southampton multi-biometric tunnel and introducing a novel 3D gait dataset. In *Proceedings of the 2nd IEEE International Conference on Biometrics: Theory, Applications and Systems*.

Stang, O. 2007. Gait Analysis: Is It Easy to Learn to Walk Like Someone Else? Master's Thesis, Gjøvik University College—Department of Computer Science and Media Technology.

Stone, E. 2012. Capturing habitual, in-home gait parameter trend. *EMBS*.

Suutala, J., and Roning, J. 2008. Methods for person identification on a pressure-sensitive floor: Experiments with multiple classifiers and reject option. *Information Fusion* 9(1):21–40.

Tanawongsuwan, R., and Bobick, A. 2001. Gait recognition from time-normalized joint-angle trajectories in the walking plane. In *Proceedings of Conference of Computer Vision and Pattern Recognition*.

Teixeria, T., Jung, D., Dublon, G., and Savvides, A. 2009. PEM-ID: Identifying people by gait-matching using cameras and wearable accelerometers, *ICDSC*.

Uddin, M., Kim, T., and Kim, J. 2010. Video-based human gait recognition using depth imaging and hidden Markov model: A smart system for smart home. *Indoor and Built Environment* 20(1):120–128.

Vaughan, C., Davis, B., and Connor, J. 1992. *Dynamics of Human Gait*. Kiboho Publishers.

Wang, C., Zhang, J., Pu, J., Yuan, X., and Wang, L. 2010. Chrono-gait image: A novel temporal template for gait recognition. In *Proceedings of the 11th European Conference on Computer Vision*.

Wang, L., Ning, H., Tan, T., and Hu, W. 2004. Silhouette-based human identification from body shape and gait. *IEEE Transactions on Circuits and Systems for Video Technology* 14:4–19.

Xia, L., Chen, C., and Aggarwal. 2012. View invariant human action recognition using histograms of 3D joints. *The 2nd International Workshop on Human Activity Understanding from 3D Data (HAU3D) in Conjunction with IEEE CVPR.*

Zivkovic, Z. 2004. Improved adaptive gaussian mixture model for background subtraction. In *Proceedings of International Conference of Pattern Recognition.*

5

HAND-BASED BIOMETRIC FOR PERSONAL IDENTIFICATION USING CORRELATION FILTER CLASSIFIER

MOHAMMED SAIGAA,
ABDALLAH MERAOUMIA,
SALIM CHITROUB, AND
AHMED BOURIDANE

Contents

Abstract

Biometrics technology has been attracting extensive attention
from researchers and engineers of personal authentication due
to the ever-growing demands on access control, public security,
forensics, and e-banking. With the fast development of biometric data acquisition sensors and data-processing algorithms,
diverse biometric systems have now been widely used in various
applications. Among these biometric technologies, the hand-
based biometrics, including fingerprint, two-dimensional and
three-dimensional palmprints, hand geometry or hand shape,
hand vein, finger–knuckle-print, etc., are the most popular and
have the largest shares in the biometrics market. This is due to
the advantages of these traits, such as low cost, low-resolution
imaging, and stable features. However, there are still many challenging problems in improving the accuracy, robustness, efficiency, and user-friendliness of hand-based biometric systems,
and new problems are also emerging with new applications,
for example, personal authentication on mobile devices and the
Internet. Many types of unimodal biometric systems have been
developed. However, these systems are only capable of providing

low to middle range security features. Thus, for higher security features, the combination of two or more unimodal biometrics is required. In this chapter, we propose a multimodal biometric system for person identification using palmprint, finger–knuckle-print, and fingerprint modalities. This work describes the development of a multibiometric personal identification system based on minimum average correlation energy filter method (for matching). Therefore, a fusion process is proposed for fusing these traits. Comprehensive reviews on unimodal and multimodal biometric systems are given. We report on our latest results and findings in hand-based biometrics authentication, and we propose new ideas and directions for future development.

5.1 Introduction

Nowadays, we are frequently being asked for verification of our identity. Normally, this is done through the use of passwords when pursuing activities like public security, access control and surveillance, application log-on, etc. The problem of traditional system security entails the protection of system elements (passwords, ID cards); therefore, this security can be easily breached when a password is divulged or a card is stolen. Furthermore, most people use the same password across different applications; an impostor, upon determining a single password, can now access multiple applications. Simple passwords can be easily guessed whereas difficult passwords may be hard to recall, and passwords can also be broken by simple dictionary attacks [1]. The need for reliable user authentication techniques has increased in the wake of heightened concerns about security and rapid advancements in networking, communication, and mobility. These limitations associated with the use of passwords can be ameliorated by the incorporation of better methods for user authentication. Biometrics technology has proven to be an accurate and efficient answer to the problem. Biometrics is an emerging field of research in recent years and has been devoted to the identification of individuals using one or more intrinsic physical or behavioral traits (also known as traits or identifiers). Among these biometric technologies, hand-based biometrics, including fingerprint, two-dimensional and three-dimensional palmprints, hand geometry or hand shape, hand vein, finger–knuckle-print

(FKP), etc., are the most popular and have the largest share in the biometrics market. This is due to the advantages of these traits, such as low cost, low-resolution imaging, and stable features [1,2].

Depending on the application context, a biometric system may operate in two modes [3,4]: verification or identification. Biometric verification is the task of authenticating that a test biometric sample match is the pattern or model of a specific user. Biometric identification is the task of associating a test biometric sample with one of N patterns or models that are available from a set of known or registered individuals.

Unimodal biometrics systems (based on a single biometric trait) are often not able to meet the desired performance requirements for large user population applications due to problems such as noisy sensor data, nonuniversality or lack of distinctiveness of the biometric trait, unacceptable error rates, and spoof attacks. Therefore, multimodal biometric methods have been developed to overcome those problems, which combine multiple biometric samples or characteristics derived from samples. Several studies [5–10] have suggested consolidating information from multiple biometric traits, in the hope that the supplementary information between different biometrics, might improve the identification performance.

The design of a multimodal biometric system is strongly dependent on the application scenario. A number of multimodal biometric systems have been proposed in the literature that differ from one another in terms of their architecture [11], the number and choice of biometric modalities, the level at which the evidence is accumulated, and the methods used for the integration or fusion of information. In this chapter, palmprint, FKP, and fingerprint are integrated to construct an efficient multimodal biometric identification. In this system, we propose to use an (unconstrained) minimum average correlation energy (U)MACE method for matching. The palmprint, FKP, and fingerprint images are used as inputs from the matcher modules. The outputs from the matcher modules [Max peak size or peak-to-side lobe ratio (PSR)] are combined using the concept of data fusion at matching score level and decision level.

5.2 Hand Biometric

Various measurable characteristics can be found in the human hand, which can be used by biometrics systems. From the image of the hand, four types of biometric features can be extracted: hand geometry features, palmprint features, fingerprint features, and, most recently, FKP features. These modalities of the human hand are relatively stable and the hand image from which they are extracted can be acquired relatively easily.

Today, many biometric technologies, such as face, iris, voice print, and hand-based biometric traits (palmprint, FKP, and fingerprint), can be used to identify persons. Each biometric has its advantages and defects, no single biometric can effectively meet all requirements (e.g., accuracy, practicality, cost) of all applications.

5.2.1 Palmprint Biometric

The palmprint is the kind of biometric indicator that can be extracted from low-resolution images; palmprint features, are composed of principal lines, wrinkles, and ridges. This modality can be easily used for authentication systems to provide an enhanced level of confidence in personal authentication.

5.2.2 Fingerprint Biometric

Among all hand-based biometric traits, fingerprints have one of the highest levels of reliability and have been extensively used by forensic experts in criminal investigations [2]. A fingerprint refers to the flow of ridge patterns at the tip of the finger. The ridge flow exhibits anomalies in local regions of the fingertip, and it is the position and orientation of these anomalies that are used to represent and match fingerprints [12].

5.2.3 Finger-Knuckle Print

Recently, another new hand-based biometrics modality, FKP, has attracted an increasing amount of attention. The image pattern formation of a FKP contains information that is capable of identifying the identity of an individual. The FKP trait recognizes a person based on the knuckle lines and the textures in the outer finger surface. These line structures and finger textures are stable and remain unchanged throughout the life of an individual [13].

5.3 Related Work

The human hand has attracted several studies on its individuality and uniqueness. Most biometric systems are based on a grayscale image of the human hand using a palmprint, fingerprint, or FKP.

We found three approaches based on the type of extracted features for palmprint authentication: (i) texture-based approaches [14], (ii) line-based approaches [15], and (iii) appearance-based approaches [16].

Fingerprint recognition is extensively described in the work by Lu et al. [17]. Most fingerprint-based biometric systems follow the minutiae-based approach [18]. However, the fingerprint-based biometric systems, by using ridge-based approaches [19], as well as hybrid systems making use of more than one basic approach [20], have also been proposed because of the sensitivity of minutiae-based approaches to the noise of the sensor and distortion during the acquisition of the fingerprint. Recently, fingerprint-recognition systems that follow appearance-based approaches [21] have been developed.

The finger–knuckle feature is a new biometric authentication system and has great potential to be widely accepted as a biometric identifier. In the work of Ross et al. [22], they proposed a two-dimensional finger-back surface–based personal authentication system. With respect to the feature extraction, they resorted to some subspace analysis methods such as principal component analysis (PCA), linear discriminant analysis (LDA), and independent component analysis (ICA).

Multimodal biometric systems are more robust than unimodal systems. They take advantage of multiple biometric traits to improve performance in many aspects including accuracy, noise resistance, universality, resistance against spoof attacks, and reduced performance degradation in huge database applications. Many works [23,24] have proposed a multimodal biometric system that decreases the recognition error rate using different modes of fusion.

5.4 Proposed System

The proposed system is composed of two different subsystems exchanging information at the decision or matching score levels. Each subsystem exploits different modalities (palmprint, fingerprint, or FKP). Each unimodal biometric system (for example, Figure 5.1 shows a

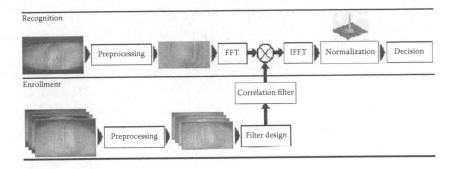

Figure 5.1 The block-diagram of the proposed unibiometric identification system based on MACE.

unimodal biometric identification system based on FKP modality) consists of preprocessing, matching (correlation process), normalization, and decision processes. Modality (palmprint, fingerprint, or FKP) identification with correlation filters is performed by correlating a test image [transformed into the frequency domain via a discrete fast Fourier transform (FFT)] with the designed filter (enrollment) also in the frequency domain. The output correlation is subjected to an inverse fast Fourier transform (IFFT) and reordered into the dimensions of the original training image before being phase-shifted to the center of the frequency square. The resulting correlation plane is then quantified using performance measures (PSR) or max peak size ratio. Based on this unique measure, a final decision is made.

5.4.1 Preprocessing Process

From the whole image (palmprint, fingerprint, or FKP), only some characteristics are useful. Therefore, each image may have variable size and orientation. Moreover, the region of nonuseful interest may affect accurate processing and thus degrade the identification performance. Therefore, image preprocessing [region of interest (ROI) extraction] is a crucial and necessary part before feature extraction.

5.4.1.1 Palmprint Preprocessing The palmprint ROI is extracted from the original palmprint image. To extract the center part of the palmprint, we employ the method described by Hanmandlu et al. [25]. In this technique, the tangent of these two holes are computed and used to align the palmprint. The central part of the image, which is 128 × 128, is then cropped to represent the whole palmprint. The preprocessing steps are shown in Figure 5.2. The basic steps to extract the ROI are summarized as follows: first, apply a low-pass filter, such as Gaussian smoothing, to the original palmprint image. A threshold, T_p, is used to convert the filtered image to a binary image; then, a boundary tracking algorithm is used to obtain the boundaries of the binary image. This boundary is processed to determine the points F_1 and F_2 for locating the ROI pattern and, based on the relevant points (F_1 and F_2), the ROI pattern is located on the original image. Finally, the ROI is extracted.

5.4.1.2 FKP Preprocessing   After the image is captured, it is necessary and critical to align FKP images by adaptively constructing a local coordinate system for each image. With such a coordinate system, an ROI can be cropped from the original image for reliable feature extraction and matching. The detailed steps for preprocessing process are as follows [16]: First, apply a Gaussian smoothing operation to the original image. Second, determine the x axis of the coordinate system fitted from the bottom boundary of the finger; the bottom boundary of the finger can be easily extracted by a Canny edge detector. Third, determine the y axis of the coordinate system by applying a Canny edge detector on the cropped subimage extracted from the original image based on the x axis; then, find the convex direction coding scheme. Finally, extract the ROI coordinate system, in which the rectangle indicates the area of the ROI subimage that will be extracted. The preprocessing steps are shown in Figure 5.3.

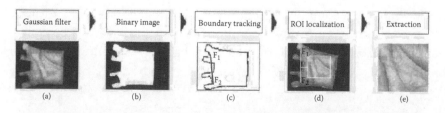

Figure 5.2   Various steps in a typical ROI extraction algorithm: (a) the filtered image; (b) the binary image; (c) the boundaries of the binary image and the points for locating the ROI pattern; (d) the central portion localization; and (e) the preprocessed result (ROI).

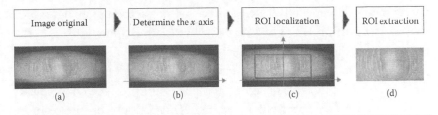

(a)   (b)   (c)   (d)

Figure 5.3   Illustration for the ROI extraction process: (a) original image; (b) *x* axis of the coordinate system; (c) ROI coordinate system; and (d) ROI.

5.4.1.3 Fingerprint Processing   The input fingerprint–containing images need to be processed so that the characteristic fingerprint features can be extracted for comparison. During the preprocessing steps, the actual fingerprint region in a digital fingerprint image is isolated. Generally, the technique of fingerprint ROI extraction consists of foreground/background separation before extracting the ROI and its features. Then, to perform a comparison between fingerprints, the segmented fingerprint region needs to be aligned to a fixed size. The normalization process is performed by mapping the segmented region to a rectangular area. Figure 5.4 shows a fingerprint extraction process.

5.4.2 Recognition Process

Correlation filters have been successfully applied to a variety of pattern recognition applications, including object detection, biometric recognition, and image registration. Attractive properties such as shift-invariance, noise robustness, and distortion tolerance make

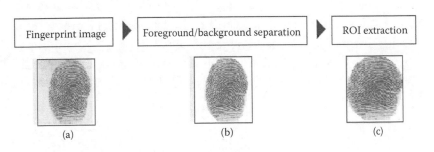

(a)   (b)   (c)

Figure 5.4   Illustration for the ROI extraction process: (a) original image; (b) foreground/background separation; (c) ROI extraction.

these methods especially well-suited for applications such as biometric recognition. In the simplest sense, correlation filtering is the process of computing the cross-correlation between an input image and a template [26]. This process can be carried out efficiently using a FFT algorithm. A well-designed template will produce sharp peaks in the correlation output when the input image contains one or more instances of the target pattern, and the peak locations will correspond to the target coordinates in the input.

5.4.2.1 MACE Filter Formulation   MACE filters function to increase the peak sharpness by minimizing the average correlation energy over a set of training images while constraining the correlation peak height at the origin to a user-defined value. This in turn produces sharp peaks at the origin of the correlation plane while producing values close to zero over the rest of the plane. The optimal solution to the MACE filter H is found using Lagrange multipliers in the frequency domain and is given by [27]:

$$H = D^{-1} X(X^*D^{-1}X)^{-1}u \qquad (5.1)$$

D is a diagonal matrix of size $d \times d$ (d is the number of pixels in the image) containing the average correlation energies of the training images across its diagonals. X is a matrix of size $N \times d$, where N is the number of training images and * is the complex conjugate. The columns of the matrix X represent the discrete Fourier coefficients for a particular training image X_n. The column vector (u) of size N contains the correlation peak constraint values for a series of training images. These values are normally set to 1.0 for images of the same class.

5.4.2.2 UMACE Filter Formulation   The UMACE filter, like the MACE filter, minimizes the average correlation energy over a set of training images, but does so without constraint (u), thereby maximizing the peak height at the origin of the correlation plane. The UMACE filter expression H is given by [28]:

$$H = D^{-1} X \qquad (5.2)$$

D is a diagonal matrix containing the average correlation energy of the training images. X is a column vector of size d, containing the average Fourier coefficients of the training images. Computationally,

UMACE filters are more attractive than their MACE counterparts because they require only the inversion of a single diagonal matrix.

5.4.2.3 Matching Module   For each class, a single MACE (UMACE) filter is synthesized. Once the MACE (UMACE) filter $H(u,v)$ has been determined, the input test image $f(x,y)$ is cross-correlated with it in the following manner:

$$c(x, y) = IFFT\{FFT(f(x, y)) * H^*(u,v)\} \tag{5.3}$$

where the test image is first transformed to a frequency domain and then reshaped in the form of a vector. The result of the previous process is convolved with the conjugate of the MACE (UMACE) filter. This operation is equivalent with cross-correlation with the MACE (UMACE) filter. The output is transformed again in the spatial domain.

5.4.2.4 Similarity Measurement

(A). *Max Peak Size.* The maximum peak value is taken as the maximum correlation peak value over a correlation plane. The height of this peak can be used as a good similarity measure for image matching (Figure 5.5a).

(B). *Peak-to-Side Lobe Ratio.* Typically, the PSR is used as a performance measure for the sharpness of the correlation peak. PSRs are typically large for true class and small for false category. Thus, the PSR is used to evaluate the degree of similarity of the correlation planes. The significance of the PSR is that it measures the sharpness of the correlation function. PSR can be calculated as

$$PSR = \frac{peak - mean}{\sigma} \tag{5.4}$$

Peak is the maximum located peak value in the correlation plane, *mean* is the average of the side lobe region surrounding the peak (bigger region: 40×40 pixels for a 128×128 pixel image, with a mask region: 5×5 excluded zone around the peak) and σ is the standard deviation of the side lobe region values (Figure 5.5b).

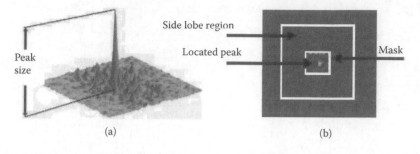

Side lobe region

Located peak

Peak size

Mask

(a)   (b)

Figure 5.5 Similarity matching: (a) Max peak size and (b) PSR.

5.4.2.5 Normalization and Decision Process Before finding the decision, a Min–Max normalization scheme was employed to transform the score values computed into similarity measurements in the same range. The Min–Max normalization formulation is given by

$$D_n = \frac{D - \min(D)}{\max(D) - \min(D)} \tag{5.5}$$

where D represents the matching scores for all database templates and D_n represents the normalized vector. Therefore, these scores are compared and the highest score provides the identity of the test image for the different modalities.

The final step of a person identification system is the decision of either accepting or rejecting the subject based on the security threshold, T_0. Suppose that the best score is D_0, where

$$D_0 = \max\{D_n\} \tag{5.6}$$

This score, D_0 is compared with the decision threshold T_0. When $D_0 \geq T_0$, the claimed identity is accepted; otherwise it is rejected.

5.4.3 Fusion Process

The goal of the fusion process is to investigate the system's performance when information from different hand biometrics (palmprint, fingerprint, or FKP) is fused. In fact, in such a case, the system works as a kind of multimodal system with a single biometric trait but with multiple units. Therefore, the information presented by different modalities (palmprint, fingerprint, or FKP) is fused to make the system efficient. Multimodal biometric systems use various levels of fusion: (i) fusion at the feature extraction level, in which the features extracted using two or more sensors are concatenated; (ii) fusion at the matching score level, in which the matching scores obtained from multiple matchers are combined; (iii) fusion at the image level, in which two or more images are combined into a single image; (iv) fusion at the decision level, in which the accept/reject decisions of multiple systems are consolidated [29]. In this work, we present the fusion at the matching score level and fusion at the decision level.

Fusion at the matching score level is preferred in the field of biometric recognition because it is easy to access and combines the matching scores [30]. In our system, we adopted the combination approach, in which the individual matching scores are combined to generate a single scalar score that is then used to make the final decision. During the system design, we experimented with five different fusion schemes: sum score, min score, max score, mul score, and sum-weighting score [31]. Suppose that the quantity F_{0i} represents the score of the ith matcher (i = 1, 2, 3) for different modalities (palmprint, fingerprint, or FKP) and F_D represents the fusion score. Therefore, F_D is given by

sum score (SUS):
$$F_D = \sum_{i=1}^{n} F_{0i}$$

min score (MIS):
$$F_D = min\{F_{0i}\}$$

max score (MAS):
$$F_D = max\{F_{0i}\}$$

mul score (MUS):
$$F_D = \prod_{i=1}^{n} F_{0i}$$

sum-weighting score (SWS)
$$F_D = \sum_{i=1}^{n} w_i \cdot F_{0i}$$

$$w_i = \frac{\dfrac{1}{\sum_{j=1}^{n}\left(\dfrac{1}{EER_j}\right)}}{EER_i} \tag{5.7}$$

where w_i denotes the weight associated with the matcher i, with $\sum_{i=1}^{m} w_i = 1$, and EER_1 is the equal error rate of matcher i, respectively.

5.5 Experimental Results and Discussion

In the identification mode, the biometric system attempts to determine the identity of an individual. A biometric is collected and compared with all the templates in a database. Identification is closed set if the person is assumed to exist in the database. In open set identification, the person is not guaranteed to exist in the database. The proposed method was tested through both testing modes.

5.5.1 Databases

To evaluate the performance of the proposed multimodal identification scheme, a database was constructed by merging three separate databases (of 148 users each) collected using different sensors and over different periods, all these databases (palmprint, fingerprint, or FKP) are available at the Hong Kong Polytechnic University (PolyU) [32–34]. The multimodal database consists of six palmprint images, six fingerprint images, and FKP images per person with a total of 148 persons. Two random samples of each palmprint, fingerprint, and FKP were selected to construct a training set. The rest of the samples were taken as the test set. It has been noted that our FKP database contains FKPs from four types of fingers, left index fingers (LIF), left middle fingers (LMF), right index fingers (RIF), and right middle fingers (RMF).

5.5.2 Evaluation Criteria

The measure of any biometric recognition system for a particular application can be described by two values [35]. The false acceptance rate (FAR) is the ratio of the number of instances of pairs of different palmprints found to match the total number of match attempts. The false rejection rate (FRR) is the ratio of the number of instances of pairs of the same modality found not to match to the total number of match attempts. FAR and FRR trade off against one another. That is, a system can usually be adjusted to vary these two results for a particular application; however, decreasing one increases the other and vice versa. The system threshold value is obtained based on the equal error rate (EER) criteria where FAR = FRR. This is based on the rationale that both rates must be as low as possible for the biometric system to work effectively.

Another performance measurement is obtained from FAR and FRR, which is called the genuine acceptance rate (GAR). It represents the identification rate of the system. To visually depict the performance of a biometric system, the receiver operating characteristic (ROC) curves are usually used. The ROC curve displays how FAR changes with respect to the GAR and vice versa [36]. Biometric systems generate matching scores that represent how similar (or dissimilar) the input is compared with the stored template.

5.5.3 Unimodal System Identification Test Results

The goal of this experiment was to evaluate the system performance when we used information from each modality (palmprint, fingerprint, or FKP). For this, there were a total of 200 training images and 400 test images for each modality, respectively. Therefore, there were a total of 400 genuine comparisons and 39,600 impostor comparisons were generated. MACE and UMACE filters were applied to evaluate the identification performance. The PSR and the peak were used for matching.

5.5.3.1 Open Set System Identification Palmprint

The ROC shown in Figure 5.6a depicts the performance of the open set palmprint identification system at all filters and performance measures. Our identification system can achieve a best EER of 0.9094% for To = 0.4623 and the maximum GAR = 99.0906% in the case of MACE filter and PSR matching. For example, the described identification system can recognize palmprints quite accurately with an EER of 1.3483% and To = 0.4918 with MACE filter and peak matching. When the threshold, To, is 0.6183, the EER is equal to 2.3917% with UMACE filter and peak matching. Finally, the UMACE filter and PSR matching give an EER equivalent to 1.500% at To = 0.6016. The ROC curve of

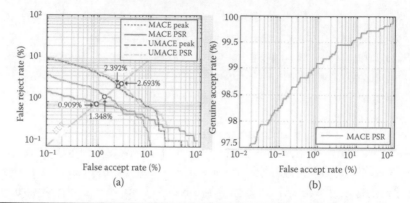

Figure 5.6   Unimodal open set system identification test results: (a) the ROC curves for palm-print modality and (b) the ROC curves for palmprint with MACE filter and PSR matching.

GAR against FAR in the case of MACE filter and PSR matching for various thresholds is shown in Figure 5.6b. The performance of the system identification under different values of To, which control the FAR and the FRR, is shown in Table 5.1.

5.5.3.2 Closed Set System Identification Palmprint   For the evaluation of the system performance, in the case of closed set identification, Table 5.2 shows the performance of palmprint identification by using MACE, UMACE filters, and PSR PEAK for matching. The performance of the identification system is significantly improved by using the MACE filter and PSR matching. For example, if UMACE filter with PSR matching is used for identification, we

Table 5.1   Open Set Palmprint Identification Test

	PEAK			PSR	
To	FAR	FRR	To	FAR	FRR
MACE					
0.3000	7.3301	0.4054	0.2000	7.2231	0.5405
0.4918	1.3483	1.3483	**0.4623**	**0.9094**	**0.9094**
1.0000	0.0392	6.1712	1.0000	0.0165	2.4775
UMACE					
0.4000	8.1899	0.8108	0.4000	8.9937	0.7658
0.6183	2.3917	2.3917	0.6042	2.6930	2.6930
0.9000	0.2292	8.0180	0.9000	0.2261	8.6036

Table 5.2 Closed Set Palmprint Identification Test Results

	MACE				UMACE			
	PEAK		PSR		PEAK		PSR	
	ROR	RPR	ROR	RPR	ROR	RPR	ROR	RPR
50	93.8461	50	94.4615	50	89.6923	42	89.3846	47
100	92.8462	98	96.4615	100	88.7692	87	88.4610	94
148	92.8794	143	**97.1413**	**148**	87.8378	132	87.1102	141

have ROR = 87.1102% with a lowest rank (rank of perfect rate) of 141, the rank-one recognition (ROR) is increased to 89.6923% with RPR equal to 42 if a UMACE filter with PEAK matching is used. A MACE filter with PSR matching improves the result (ROR = 97.1413% with RPR equal to 148).

5.5.3.3 Open Set System Identification Fingerprint In this experiment, we plot the fingerprint system performance against the different filters and different similarity measurements (see Figure 5.7a). The performance of the identification system is significantly improved by using the UMACE filter and PEAK matching. For example, if MACE filter with PEAK matching is used for identification, we have EER = 3.765% at the threshold To = 0.5135. In the case of using MACE filter with PSR matching, EER was 2.842% at the threshold To = 0.5173, and if UMACE filter with PSR matching is used, the EER was 1.641% at the threshold To = 0.6045. UMACE filter

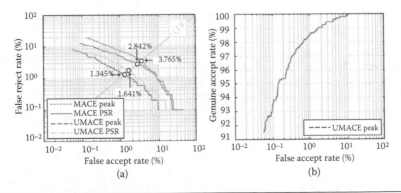

Figure 5.7 Unimodal open set system identification test results: (a) the ROC curves for fingerprint modality and (b) the ROC curves for fingerprint with UMACE filter and PEAK matching.

with peak matching improves the result (1.345% at the threshold To = 0.5998) for a database size equal to 148 users, and the ROC curve obtained by the UMACE filter and PEAK matching is plotted in Figure 5.7b. The performance of the system identification under different values of To, which control the FAR and the FRR, is shown in Table 5.3.

5.5.3.4 Closed Set System Identification Fingerprint   In the case of a closed set identification, a series of experiments were carried out to select the best filter and similarity measurement. This was done using all filters and performance measures that give the best identification rate. Table 5.4 presents experimental results obtained using the best results of rank-one recognition for the UMACE filter and PEAK matching producing 94.8571% with the lowest rank (rank of perfect rate) of 10.

5.5.3.5 Open Set System Identification FKP   In this experiment, MACE and UMACE filters are applied to evaluate the identification performance. The PSR and the peak matching are determined and the identification performance of the four fingers is illustrated in Figure 5.8a to d. From these figures, we can observe the benefits of using the RMF modality with a MACE filter and PSR matching in term of EER (see Figure 5.8d). It is noted that the MACE filter and PSR matching provide the best performance for all finger modalities. Therefore, if the RMF modality is used, we have EER = 1.2617% at the threshold To = 0.5332 if MACE filter and PEAK matching are used. In the case of using the UMACE filter and PEAK matching, EER was 2.3437%

Table 5.3   Open Set Fingerprint Identification Test Results

	PEAK			PSR		
To	FAR	FRR	To	FAR	FRR
MACE					
0.4500	5.9040	1.8340	0.4000	6.7260	1.5440
0.5135	3.7650	3.7650	0.5173	2.8420	2.8420
0.6500	1.4180	6.4670	0.7500	0.5230	6.4670
UMACE					
0.4000	6.1530	0.2900	0.4000	7.0520	0.3860
0.5998	**1.3450**	**1.345**	0.6045	1.6410	1.6410
0.7500	0.4030	2.7990	0.7500	0.5110	4.0540

Table 5.4 Closed Set Fingerprint Identification Test Results

	MACE				UMACE			
	PEAK		PSR		PEAK		PSR	
	ROR	RPR	ROR	RPR	ROR	RPR	ROR	RPR
50	85.7143	13	91.1429	25	**94.8571**	**10**	94.2857	18
100	80.0000	77	86.5714	90	91.1429	65	91.8571	77
148	80.2122	133	86.8726	128	91.5058	99	92.0849	117

at the threshold To = 0.6744. This EER was 5.2525% at To = 0.6271 for the UMACE filter and PSR matching. RMF modality improves the result (0.3367% at the threshold To = 0.5616) in the case of using MACE filter and PSR matching for a database size equal to 148 users. Therefore, the system can achieve higher accuracy at RMF modality compared with the other fingers. The ROC curve of GAR against FAR of RMF modality in the case of MACE filter and PSR matching for various thresholds is shown in Figure 5.8e. Finally, the system was tested with different thresholds and the results are shown in Table 5.5.

5.5.3.6 Closed Set System Identification FKP In the case of a closed set identification, a series of experiments were carried out to select the best filter and similarity measurement. This was done using all the filters and performance measures that provided the best identification rates. Table 5.6 presents the experimental results obtained. The best results of rank-one recognition for the MACE filter and PSR matching produce 92.0849% with the lowest rank (rank of perfect rate) of 77.

5.5.4 Multiple-Instances System Identification Test Results

The goal of this experiment was to investigate the system's performance when we fused information from two or more fingers of a person. In fact, in such a case, the system works as a kind of multimodal system with a single biometric trait but with multiple units. The fusion is carried out by using two levels of fusion: matching score levels and decision levels.

5.5.4.1 Fusion at the Matching Scores Level The information presented by two or all finger FKPs is fused at the matching score level to make the system efficient. For that, a series of experiments were carried

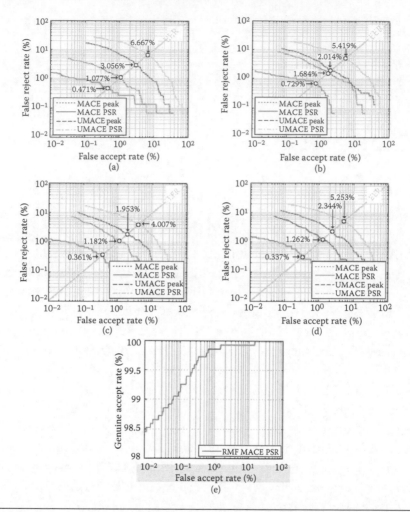

Figure 5.8 Unimodal open set identification test results (FKP): (a) the ROC curves for LIF modality; (b) the ROC curves for LMF modality; (c) the ROC curves for RIF modality; (d) the ROC curves for RMF modality; and (e) the ROC curves of RMF modality with MACE filter and PSR matching.

out to select the best fusion rule that minimized the EER using the best unimodal result [LIF (MACE PSR), LMF (MACE PSR), RIF (MACE PSR), RMF (MACE PSR)]. During the system design phase, we experimented on five different fusion schemes: sum score (SUM), sum-weighting score (SUM WHT), min score (MIN), max score (MAX), and mul score (MUL).

5.5.4.1.1 Open Set FKPs System Identification In the case of open set systems, Table 5.7 presents the test results for all combinations

Table 5.5   Open Set FKP Identification Test Results

	PEAK			PSR	
To	FAR	FRR	To	FAR	FRR
MACE					
0.3000	9.4313	0.2020	0.3000	3.3999	0.0673
0.5332	1.2617	1.2617	**0.5616**	**0.3367**	**0.3367**
1.0000	0.0472	7.7441	1.0000	0.0094	1.5488
UMACE					
0.5000	9.3636	0.6734	0.6000	6.4922	4.5791
0.6744	2.3437	2.3437	0.6271	5.2525	5.2525
0.8000	0.6841	5.4545	0.7000	2.8854	6.9360

possible [(1) LIF-RIF, (2) LMF-RMF, (3) LIF-LMF, (4) RIF-RMF, and (5) LIF-LMF/RIF-RMF]. The identification system described can achieve an EER equal to 0.0000% when the fusion of LIF-LMF/RIF-RMF with SUM, WHT, and Mul rule is used. However, it can be concluded that the fusion of the modalities yields much better identification results compared with one modality.

5.5.4.1.2 Closed Set FKPs System Identification   In the case of closed set systems, we can see the same results as in the open set system, that in which the fusion of all FKPs (LIF-LMF/RIF-RMF) with SUM, WHT, and Mul rule is used. Thus, the best result of rank-one recognition is given as 100% with the lowest rank (rank of perfect rate) of 1 (Table 5.8).

Table 5.6   Closed Set FKP (RMF) Identification Test Results

	PEAK		PSR	
	ROR	RPR	ROR	RPR
MACE				
LIF	94.8918	77	98.5281	97
LMF	91.1111	91	98.1145	93
RIF	92.4579	62	98.6532	70
RMF	91.9884	70	**98.9884**	**77**
UMACE				
LIF	82.6840	128	70.7359	147
LMF	88.6195	142	79.7306	135
RIF	89.4276	97	82.0875	139
RMF	88.0309	124	80.1158	123

Table 5.7 Open Set FKP Score Fusion

	LIF-LMF		LIF-RIF		RIF-RMF		RMF-LMF		ALLS	
	To	EER	To	EER	To	EER	To	EER	To	EER
SUM	0.8792	0.0041	0.9481	0.0033	0.6760	0.0224	0.6296	0.0594	**0.6994**	**0.0000**
WHT	0.7388	0.0178	0.8852	0.0041	0.6731	0.0249	0.6690	0.0673	**0.7438**	**0.0000**
MAX	0.9990	0.0213	0.9990	0.0164	0.7346	0.1252	0.8322	0.0673	0.9990	0.0410
MAX	0.6125	0.0673	0.5137	0.0673	0.5340	0.0673	0.6122	0.0720	0.5190	0.0665
MUL	0.6752	0.0049	0.7862	0.0049	0.0074	0.0074	0.4188	0.0394	**0.5040**	**0.0000**

Table 5.8 Closed Set FKP Score Fusion

	LIF-LMF		LIF-RIF		RIF-RMF		RMF-LMF		ALLS	
	ROR	RPR	ROR	RPR	ROR	RPR	ROR	RPR	ROR	RPR
SUM	99.9327	3	99.7980	3	99.7980	10	99.7306	8	**100.000**	**1**
WHT	99.5960	10	99.8653	5	99.7980	10	99.3939	10	**100.000**	**1**
MAX	98.1818	2	98.3838	2	98.7879	26	98.5859	19	97.3064	3
MAX	99.5960	30	99.6633	74	99.6633	30	99.4613	73	99.7980	17
MUL	99.9327	3	99.7980	6	99.7980	8	99.6633	8	**100.000**	**1**

5.5.4.2 Fusion at the Decision Level   The individual decisions from the three or all finger FKP representations were also combined (majority voting) to examine the performance improvement. From Table 5.9, 100% of the GAR can be achieved for all combinations.

5.5.5 Multimodal System Identification Test Result

The goal of this experiment was to investigate the system's performance when we fused information from palmprint, fingerprint, and FKP modalities. Therefore, information presented by different biometrics was fused to make the system efficient using two levels of fusion: matching score level and decision level.

5.5.5.1 Fusion at the Matching Scores Level   Fusion at the matching score level is preferred in the field of biometrics because there is sufficient information content and it is easy to access and combine the matching scores [12]. In our system, we adopted the combination approach in which the individual matching scores were combined to generate a single scalar score, which is then used to make the final decision.

5.5.5.1.1 Open/Closed Set Palmprint + Fingerprint Identification   In this experiment, the performance results were obtained by fusing the scores from two modalities (palmprints and fingerprints) with MACE filter (PSR matching) and UMACE filter (PEAK matching), respectively.

In the case of an open set system, the best results, in terms of EER, are shown in Table 5.10 (EER = 0.0350% at To = 0.7301), in which a SUM rule is used. From Table 5.11, we can see that the SUM rule is also preferred in closed set systems, in which the rank-one recognition is given as 99.7104% with the lowest rank (rank of perfect rate) of 16.

Table 5.9 Open Set FKP Decision Fusion

LIF-LMF-RIF			LIF-LMF-RMF			RIF-RMF-LIF			RIF-RMF-LMF			ALLS		
FAR	FRR	GAR	FAR	FRR	GAR	FAR	FRR	GAR	FAR	FRR	GAR	FAR	FRR	GAR
0.00	100	100	0.00	0.00	100	0.00	0.00	100	0.00	0.00	100	0.00	0.00	100

Table 5.10   Open Set Palm + Fingerprint Identification

SUM		WHT		MAX		MIN		MUL	
To	EER	To	EER	To	EER	To	EER	To	EER
0.7301	**0.0350**	0.6172	0.1675	0.9555	0.0965	0.4899	0.2896	0.3115	0.1762

Table 5.11   Closed Set Palm + Fingerprint Identification

SUM		WHT		MAX		MIN		MUL	
ROR	RPR	ROR	RPR	ROR	RPR	ROR	RPR	ROR	RPR
99.7104	**16**	99.4208	42	93.6293	4	99.6139	124	99.7104	72

5.5.5.1.2 Open/Closed Set Palmprint + FKP Identification   The information presented by the two modalities [palmprint and FKP(RMF)] with MACE (PSR matching) and MACE (PSR matching), respectively, at the matching score level demonstrate the performance of this system under different fusion rules. The results of this experiment are shown in Tables 5.9 and 5.10.

From Tables 5.12 and 5.13, we can observe that SUM rule–based fusion has the best performance between the two modes. Thus, the best results in the case of open test systems in terms of EER is given as 0.0960% with To of 0.6028, and in the case of closed sets, the rank-one recognition is given as 99.9035% with the lowest rank (rank of perfect rate) of 33.

5.5.5.1.3 Open/Closed Set Fingerprint + FKP Identification   The fusion in this experiment, under different fusion rules, is based on the information presented by the scores in the two modalities [fingerprint and FKP (RMF)] with UMACE filter (PEAK matching) and MACE

Table 5.12   Open Set Palm + FKP (RIF) Identification

SUM		WHT		MAX		MIN		MUL	
To	EER	To	EER	To	EER	To	EER	To	EER
0.6028	**0.0960**	0.6631	0.0998	0.8703	0.0965	0.4900	0.1931	0.3259	0.0965

Table 5.13   Closed Set Palm + FKP (RIF) Identification

SUM		WHT		MAX		MIN		MUL	
ROR	RPR	ROR	RPR	ROR	RPR	ROR	RPR	ROR	RPR
99.9035	**33**	99.5170	8	98.8417	10	99.5170	115	99.8069	68

filter (PSR matching), respectively. Tables 5.14 and 5.15 present the results of this experiment.

The best results between the two modes was obtained when using the SUM and MUL rules of fusion. Thus, in an open set, the system can work with an EER of 0.000% at To = 0.9693; in a closed set, a rank-one recognition (ROR) of 100.00% can be achieved, with the lowest rank (rank of perfect rate) of 1.

5.5.5.1.4 Open/Closed Set Palmprint + Fingerprint + FKP Identification   In this experiment, the matching scores were carried out by fusion of the scores from all modalities [palmprint, fingerprint, and FKP(RMF)] with MACE filter (PSR matching), UMACE filter (PEAK matching), and MACE filter (PSR matching), respectively, under different fusion rules.

From Tables 5.16 and 5.17, we can observe that the SUM rule–based fusion has the best performance of the two modes. Thus, the best results in the case of open test systems, in terms of EER, is given as 0.001%

Table 5.14   Open Set Fingerprint + FKP (RIF) Identification

SUM		WHT		MAX		MIN		MUL	
To	EER	To	EER	To	EER	To	EER	To	EER
0.9693	**0.0000**	0.7035	0.0965	0.9990	0.0617	0.8103	0.0091	**0.9578**	**0.0000**

Table 5.15   Closed Set Fingerprint + FKP (RIF) Identification

SUM		WHT		MAX		MIN		MUL	
ROR	RPR	ROR	RPR	ROR	RPR	ROR	RPR	ROR	RPR
100.000	1	99.1313	7	94.6911	2	99.8069	5	**100.000**	1

Table 5.16   Open Set All Identification (Score)

SUM		WHT		MAX		MIN		MUL	
To	EER	To	EER	To	EER	To	EER	To	EER
0.8790	**0.001**	0.7120	0.0307	0.9990	0.0840	0.5475	0.0965	0.3754	0.0131

Table 5.17   Closed Set All Identification (Score)

SUM		WHT		MAX		MIN		MUL	
ROR	RPR	ROR	RPR	ROR	RPR	ROR	RPR	ROR	RPR
99.9035	2	99.8069	3	93.7259	2	99.8069	108	99.9035	14

with a To of 0.8790; and in the case of closed sets, the rank-one recognition is given as 99.9035% with the lowest rank (rank of perfect rate) of 2.

5.5.5.2 Fusion at the Decision Level   Individual decisions from the three modalities [palmprint, fingerprint, and FKP (RMF)] were also combined (majority voting) to examine performance improvement. A GAR of 100% can be achieved with a FAR of 0.00%.

5.6 Comparing Results

The experimental results presented in Section 5.5 show that a significant improvement in performance can be achieved from the combination of multibiometric modalities (palmprint, fingerprint, or FKP) compared with the results from unibiometric modalities in previous work (referenced in Section 5.1).

In the case of unimodal systems, Table 5.18 shows a comparison between previous works [37–41] and our work, which uses a different approach to extract features. We can see that our proposed method gives the best results compared with previous works.

In the case of multimodal systems, Table 5.19 shows a comparison between previous works [37,39,40] and our work, which uses a

Table 5.18 Comparing Results, Recognition Performance (Unimodal)

REF.	METHOD	IDENTIFICATION	VERIFICATION
PALMPRINT (GAR)			
[40]	Binary DB (100)	X	95.91
[38]	Gray code DB (136)	X	98.02
Ours	(U)MACE DB (148)	99.09	X
FINGERPRINT (GAR)			
[41]	LDA DB (100)	X	97.97
[37]	SLPCCAM DB (136)	89.06	X
Ours	(U)MACE DB (148)	98.66	X
FKP (EER)			
[39]	Daubechies DB (165)	X	1.95
[38]	LGIC DB (165)	X	0.402
Ours	(U)MACE DB (148)	0.336	X

Table 5.19   Comparing Results, Recognition Performance (Multimodal)

	REFERENCE			
FUSION	OURS	[41]	[43]	[44]
Palmprint + Fingerprint	0.035	X	X	0.0045
Palmprint + FKP	0.096	X	99.84	X
FKP + Fingerprint	**0.000**	X	X	X
Palmprint + Fingerprint + FKP	0.001	X	X	X
Fingerprint + Finger vein	X	98.75	X	X

different approach to extract features. The results presented are for fusion at the score level. We can see that the proposed method gives the best results compared with the previous work. The proposed method can achieve an EER equal to 0.00% when a fusion of FKP and fingerprint modalities is used.

5.7 Conclusion

In this chapter, a multimodal biometric identification system based on the fusion of three biometric traits, palmprint, fingerprint, and FKP, has been proposed. The fusion of these three biometric traits is carried out at the matching score level and decision level. A system using MACE and UMACE filters has been proposed. Using several fusion rules, fusion was performed at the matching score and image levels. Peak and PSR values were used for recognizing a palmprint, FKP, or fingerprint test image. The proposed system was evaluated using the palmprint, FKP, and fingerprint images of PolyU's database. To compare the proposed multimodal system with the unimodal systems, a series of experiments were performed using open set identification and closed set identification, and it was found that the proposed multimodal system gives a considerable performance gain over the unimodal systems in the two cases.

References

1. A.A. Ross, K. Nandakumar, and A.K. Jain. *Handbook of Multibiometrics.* Springer Science+Business Media, LLC, New York, 2006.
2. A. Kumar, and D. Zhang. Improving biometric authentication performance from the user quality. *IEEE Transactions on Instrumentation and Measurement* 59(3), 730–735, 2010.

3. J. Ortega-Garcia, J. Bigun, D. Reynolds, and J. Gonzalez-Rodriguez. Authentication gets personal with biometrics. *IEEE Signal Processing Magazine* 21, 50–62, 2004.

4. A.K. Jain, A. Ross, and S. Prabhakar. An introduction to biometric recognition. *IEEE Transactions on Circuits and Systems for Video Technology* 14(1), 4–20, 2004.

5. B. Ulery, A. Hicklin, C. Watson, W. Fellner, and P. Hallinan. *Studies of Biometric Fusion—Executive Summary, NISTIR7346*, National Institute of Standards and Technology, September 2006.

6. F. Yang, and B. Ma. A new mixed-mode biometrics information fusion based-on fingerprint, hand-geometry, and palm-print. In *International Conference on Image and Graphics 2007*, 689–693, 2007.

7. J. Fierrez-Aguilar, L. Nanni, J. Ortega-Garcia, R. Cappelli, and D. Maltoni. Combining multiple matchers for fingerprint verification: A case study in FVC2004. In *Proceedings 13th International Conference on Image Analysis and Processing (ICIAP2005)*, Cagliari, September 2005.

8. L. Nanni, and A. Lumini. Ensemble of multiple palmprint representation. *Expert Systems with Applications* 36(3), 4485–4490, 2009.

9. A. Lumini, and L. Nanni. When fingerprints are combined with iris—a case study: FVC 2004 and CASIA. *International Journal of Network Security* 4(1), 27–34, 2007.

10. E. Marasco, and C. Sansone. Improving the accuracy of a score fusion approach based on likelihood ratio in multimodal biometric systems. In P. Foggia, C. Sansone, and M. Vento, editors, *Image Analysis and Processing—ICIAP 2009, 15th International Conference Vietri sul Mare, Italy, September 8–11, 2009, Proceedings*. Volume 5716 of *Lecture Notes in Computer Science*, Springer, 509–518, 2009.

11. S. Kar, S. Hiremath, D.G. Joshi, V.K. Chadda, and A. Bajpai. A multi-algorithmic face recognition system. In *International Conference on Advanced Computing and Communications, 2006. ADCOM 2006*, Surathkal, 321–326, 2007.

12. Q. Zhao, D. Zhang, L. Zhang, and N. Luo. Adaptive fingerprint pore modeling and extraction. *Pattern Recognition* 43, 2833–2844, 2010.

13. R. Zhao, K. Li, M. Liu, and X. Sun. A novel approach of personal identification based on single knuckleprint image. In *Asia-Pacific Conference on Information Processing, APCIP*, 2009.

14. D. Zhang, W.K. Kong, J. You, and M. Wong. On-line palmprint identification. *IEEE Transactions on Pattern Analysis and Machine Intelligence* 25(9), 1041–1050, 2003.

15. W. Jia, B. Ling, K.-W. Chau, and L. Heutte. Palmprint identification using restricted fusion. *Applied Mathematics and Computation* 205, 927–934, 2008.

16. G. Lu, D. Zhang, and K. Wang. Palmprint recognition using eigenpalms features. *Pattern Recognition Letters* 24(9–10), 1463–1467, 2003.

17. D. Maltoni, D. Maio, A.K. Jain, and S. Prabhakar. *Handbook of Fingerprint Recognition*. Springer, New York, 2003.

18. N.K. Ratha, K. Karu, S. Chen, and A.K. Jain. A real-time matching system for large fingerprint databases. *IEEE Transactions on Pattern Analysis and Machine Intelligence* 18(8), 799–813, 1996.

19. A.K. Jain, S. Prabhakar, L. Hong, and S. Pankanti. Filter bank-based fingerprint matching. *IEEE Transactions on Image Processing* 9(5), 846–859, 2000.

20. A.J. Willis, and L. Myers. A cost-effective fingerprint recognition system for use with low-quality prints damaged fingertips. *Pattern Recognition* 34(2), 255–270, 2001.

21. A. Ross, A.K. Jain, and J. Reisman. A hybrid fingerprint matcher. *Pattern Recognition* 36(7), 1661–1673, 2003.

22. A. Kumar, and C. Ravikanth. Personal authentication using finger knuckle surface. *IEEE Transactions on Information Forensics and Security* 4(1), 98–109, 2009.

23. A. Kumar, V. Kanhangad, and D. Zhang. A new framework for adaptive multimodal biometrics management. *IEEE Transactions on Information Forensics and Security* 5(1), 92–102, 2010.

24. M. He, S.-J. Horng, P. Fan, R.-S. Run, R.-J. Chen, J.-L. Lai, M.K. Khan, and K.O. Sentosa. Performance evaluation of score level fusion in multimodal biometric systems. *Pattern Recognition* 43(5), 1789–1800, 2010.

25. M. Hanmandlu, J. Grover, A. Gureja, and H.M. Gupta. Score level fusion of multimodal biometrics using triangular norms. *Pattern Recognition Letters* 32, 1843–1850, 2011.

26. L. Zhang, L. Zhang, and D. Zhang. Finger-knuckle-print: A new biometric identifier. In *Proceedings of the ICIP09*, 2009.

27. D.A. Ramli, S.A. Samad, and A. Hussain. A UMACE filter approach to lipreading in biometric authentication system. *Journal of Applied Sciences* 8, 280–287, 2008.

28. A. Hussain, R. Ghafar, S.A. Samad, and N.M. Tahir. Anomaly detection in electroencephalogram signals using unconstrained minimum average correlation energy filter. *Journal of Computer Science* 5(7), 501–506, 2009.

29. R. Ghafar, A. Hussain, S.A. Samad, and N.M. Tahir. UMACE filter for detection of abnormal changes in EEG: A report of 6 cases. *World Applied Sciences Journal* 5(3), 295–301, 2008.

30. M. Faundez-Zanuy. Data fusion in biometrics. *IEEE Aerospace and Electronic Systems Magazine* 20(1), 34–38, 2005.

31. A. Ross, A. Jain, and J.-Z. Qian. Information fusion in biometrics. In *Audio and Video-Based Biometric Person Authentication,* 354–359, 2001.

32. R. Singh, M. Vatsa, and A. Noore. Hierarchical fusion of multispectral face images for improved recognition performance. In *Science Direct, Information Fusion* 9(2), 200–210, 2008.

33. The Hong Kong Polytechnic University, PolyU Palmprint Database. Available on: http://www.Comp.polyu.edu.hk/biometrics.

34. PolyU Fingerprint Database. Available on: http://www.comp.polyu.edu.hk/~biometrics/HRF/HRF.htm.

35. PolyU. Finger KnucklePrint Database. Available on http://www.comp.polyu.edu.hk/biometrics/FKP.htm.

36. T. Connie, A. Teoh, M. Goh, and D. Ngo. Palmprint recognition with PCA and ICA. In *Palmerston North, 2003 Conference of Image and Vision Computing New Zealand*, 227–232, 2003.
37. J. Yang, and X. Zhang. Feature-level fusion of fingerprint and finger-vein for personal identification, 2011 Elsevier B.V. *Pattern Recognition Letters* 33, 623–628, 2012.
38. L. Zhang, L. Zhang, D. Zhang, and H. Zhu. Ensemble of local and global information for finger–knuckle-print recognition. *Pattern Recognition Letters* 44, 1990–1998, 2011.
39. M. Goh Kah Ong, C. Tee, and A.T. Beng Jin. An innovative contactless palm print and knuckle print recognition system. *Pattern Recognition Letters* 31(12), 1708–1719, 2010.
40. A. Kumar, D.C.M. Wong, H.C. Shen, and A.K. Jain. Personal authentication using hand images. *Pattern Recognition Letters* 27, 1478–1486, 2006.
41. T. Savic, and N. Pavešic. Personal recognition based on an image of the palmar surface of the hand. *Pattern Recognition* 40, 3152–3163, 2007.

6

On Deciding the Dynamic Periocular Boundary for Human Recognition

SAMBIT BAKSHI, PANKAJ KUMAR SA, AND BANSHIDHAR MAJHI

Contents

Abstract

There has been a significant amount of research in recognizing humans through images of the iris captured under near-infrared illumination and constrained scenarios, whereas recognition under visual spectrum and unconstrained scenarios is relatively recent and challenging. Hence, several attempts have been made by researchers to identify humans not only through the iris but also through recognizing patterns existent in the periocular (periphery of the ocular) region. In such biometric systems, images of the periocular region are considered as biometric templates to be used for recognition. Effort has been made in this article to specify a rectangular boundary around the eye region (periocular region) in a facial image that is potentially optimal for human recognition. A comparatively larger template of the periocular image can be slightly more potent for recognition but slows down the biometric system by making feature extraction computationally intensive and increasing the database's size. A smaller template, however, cannot yield desirable accurate recognition, although it performs faster because of the low computation needed for feature extraction. These two contradictory objectives (i.e., to minimize the size of the periocular template to be considered for recognition and to maximize recognition through the template) are intended to be optimized through the proposed research. This article proposes four different approaches for dynamic optimal localization of the periocular region. Feature extractors are found to work efficiently on the periocular region when employed to evaluate the proposed localization. The optimal localization methods are tested on the publicly available unconstrained UBIRIS.v2 and FERET databases and satisfactory results have been achieved. The results assure that optimization of the aforementioned two objectives can be achieved to mark an optimized size of the periocular region.

6.1 Introduction

A biometric system comprises a physical or behavioral trait of a person that can recognize that person uniquely. The face is one of the primitive means of human recognition. Computer-aided identification of a person through facial biometrics has increased in importance through the last decade and researchers have attempted to find unique facial nodal points. However, changes in facial data with expression and age make recognition using the face challenging. A stringent necessity to identify a person on partial facial data has been felt in such scenarios. There are forensic applications in which antemortem information is based on parts of the face. These motives led researchers to derive auxiliary biometric traits from facial images, that is, the iris, ear, lip, and periocular region. Iris recognition yields very low accuracy for images taken in the visible spectrum. In particular, the periocular region has been exploited to examine the existence of uniqueness because there are many nodal points in the periocular region. Classification and recognition through the periocular region show significant accuracy, given the fact that periocular biometrics uses only approximately 25% of a complete face data.

Periocular (peripheral area of the ocular) region refers to the immediate vicinity of the eye, including the eyebrow and lower eyefold as depicted in Figure 6.1. Face recognition has been the main attention of biometric researchers due to its ease of unconstrained acquisition and because of its uniqueness. The face has been proven to have approximately 18 feature points [1], which can be included in the formation of a unique template for authentication. The major challenge in face detection that researchers have to deal with is the change in the human face that comes with age, expression, etc. With the advent of low-cost hardware to fuse multiple biometrics in real time, the emphasis shifted to extracting a subset of the face that could partially resolve the aforementioned issues (Table 6.1). Hence, investigations of the ear, lip, and periocular region have started gaining priority. Furthermore, capturing eye or face images automatically acquires the periocular image. This gives the flexibility of recognizing an individual using periocular data along with iris data without extra storage or acquisition cost. Moreover, periocular features can be used when an iris image does not contain subtle details, which mostly occurs due to poor image quality. Periocular biometrics also comes into play

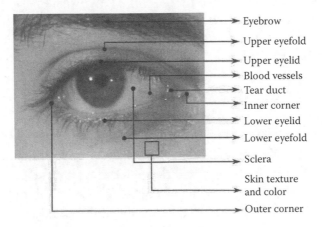

Figure 6.1 Important features from a periocular image.

Table 6.1   Comparison of Biometric Traits Present in the Human Face

TRAIT	ADVANTAGES	POSSIBLE CHALLENGES
Iris	High dimensional feature can be extracted Difficult to spoof Permanence of iris Secured within eye folds Can be captured in noninvasive way	Yields accuracy in NIR images than VS images Cost of NIR acquisition device is high Low recognition accuracy in unconstrained scenarios Low recognition accuracy for low resolution Occlusion due to use of lens Eye may close at the time of capture Does not work for patients with keratoconus and keratitis
Face	Easy to acquire Yields accuracy in VS images Most available in criminal investigations	Not socially acceptable for some religions Full face image makes database large Variation with expression and age
Periocular Region	Can be captured with face/iris without extra acquisition cost	Fewer features in case of infants
Lip	Existence of both global and local features	Less acceptable socially Shape changes with human expression Possible partial occlusion by moustache Pattern may not be visible due to lipstick
Ear	Easy segmentation due to presence of contrast in the vicinity	Difficult to acquire Can be partially occluded by hair

as a candidate for fusion with face image for better recognition accuracy. Figure 6.2 illustrates a working model of a biometric system that employs the eye region (periocular region) as a trait for recognition.

This article attempts to fit an optimal boundary to the periocular region that is sufficient and necessary for recognition. Unlike other biometric traits, edge information is not a required criterion to exactly localize the periocular region. Rather, the periocular region can be localized as where the periphery of the eye contains no further information. Researchers have considered a static rectangular boundary around the eye to recognize humans and have termed this localized rectangle as the periocular region. However, this approach is naïve as the same static boundary does not work for every face image (e.g., when the face image is captured through different distances from the camera, or when there is a tilt of the face or camera during acquisition). Thus, there is a need to derive a dynamic boundary to describe the periocular region. While deciding the periocular boundary, the objective of achieving the highest recognition accuracy should also be

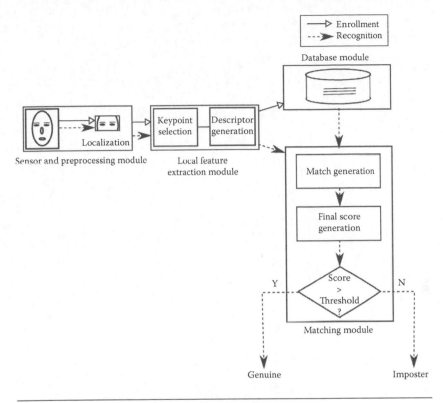

Figure 6.2 Working model of periocular biometric system.

maintained. The article specifies a few metrics through which the peri-ocular region can be localized in a scale and rotation invariant manner.

6.2 Literature Review

Table 6.2 summarizes the comparative study of accuracy obtained by several benchmark iris localization techniques that deal with near-infrared (NIR) eye images as input. We can conclude from the results that high localization accuracy has been achieved for NIR iris images. Several global and local matching techniques have been applied for matching NIR iris images, and researchers have obtained high accuracy. However, when it comes to recognizing a person only through his or her iris image captured under the visible spectrum, the results have been observed to be unsatisfactory. Therefore, researchers have been motivated to take into account not only the iris but also its peripheral regions when recognizing from images in the visible spectrum.

Table 6.2 Performance Comparison of Some Benchmark NIR Iris Localization Approaches

YEAR	AUTHORS	APPROACH	TESTING DATABASE	ACCURACY RESULTS
2002	Camus et al. [2]	Multiresolution coarse-to-fine strategy	Constrained iris images (640 without glasses, 30 with glasses)	Overall 98% (99.5% for subjects without glasses and 66.6% for subjects wearing glasses)
2004	Sung et al. [3]	Bisection method, canny edge map detector, and histogram equalization	3176 images acquired through a CCD camera	100% inner boundary and 94.5% for collarette boundary
2004	Bonney et al. [4]	Least significant bit plane and standard deviations	108 images from CASIA v1 and 104 images from UNSA	Pupil detection 99.1% and limbic detection 66.5%
2005	Liu et al. [5]	Modification to Masek's segmentation algorithm	317 gallery and 4249 probe images acquired using Iridian LG 2200 iris imaging system	97.08% Rank-1 recognition
2006	Proenca et al. [6]	Moment functions dependent on fuzzy clustering	1214 good quality images, 663 noisy images acquired from 241 subjects in two distinct sessions	98.02% on good data set and 97.88% on noisy data set
2008	Pundlik et al. [7]	Markov random field and graph cut–based energy minimization	WVU nonideal database	Pixel label error rate 5.9%
2009	He et al. [8]	Adaboost-cascade iris detector for iris center prediction	NIST Iris Challenge Evaluation (ICE) v 1.0, CASIA-Iris-V3-lamp, UBIRISv1.0	0.53% EER for ICEv1.0 and 0.75% EER for CASIA Iris-V3-lamp
2010	Jin et al. [9]	K-means cluster	CASIAv3 and UBIRIS.v2.0	1.9% false positive and 21.3% false negative (on a fresh data set not used to tune the system)
2010	Tan et al. [10]	Gray distribution features and gray projection	CASIAv1	99.14% accuracy with processing time of 0.484 second/image
2011	Bakshi et al. [11]	Image morphology and connected component analysis	CASIAv3	95.76% accuracy with processing time of 0.396 second/image

The task of recognition is more challenging than classification and hence draws more attention. The most commonly used feature extraction techniques, in the context of periocular recognition, are scale-invariant feature transform and local binary patterns. Tables 6.3 and 6.4 outline the methods used and performance obtained toward periocular classification and recognition in visual spectrum (VS) images, respectively. However, the portion of the eye on which it is applied is not computationally justified in the literature. Any arbitrary rectangular portion

(a) Will the accuracy obtained from this arbitrary boundary increase if a larger region is considered?
(b) How much of the periocular region being considered is actually contributing to recognition?
(c) Is there any portion within this arbitrarily considered periocular region that can be removed and accuracy can still be comparably achieved?

The derivation of optimal dynamic periocular region gives a simultaneous solution to the aforementioned questions.

6.3 Why Localization of the Periocular Region Is Required

Unlike other biometric traits, the periocular region has no boundary defined by any edge information. Hence, the periocular region cannot be detected through differential changes in pixel value in different directions. Rather, the location of the boundary is the region that is smooth in terms of pixel intensity, that is, a region with no

Table 6.3 Survey on Classification through Periocular Biometric

AUTHORS	CLASSIFICATION TYPE	ALGORITHM	CLASSIFIER	TESTING DATABASE	ACCURACY (%)
Abiantum et al. [13]	Left vs. right eye	Adaboost, Haar, Gabor features	LDA, SVM	ICE	89.95%
Bhat et al. [14]	Left vs. right eye	ASM	SVM	ICE, LG	Left eye, 91% Right eye, 89%
Merkow et al. [15]	Gender	LBP	LDA, SVM, PCA	Downloaded from the Web	84.9%
Lyle et al. [16]	Gender and ethnicity	LBP	SVM	FRGC	Gender, 93% Ethnicity, 91%

Table 6.4 Survey on Recognition through Periocular Biometric

YEAR	AUTHORS	ALGORITHM	FEATURES	TESTING DATABASE		PERFORMANCE RESULTS
2010	Hollingsworth et al. [18]	Human analysis	Eye region	NIR images of 120 subjects		Accuracy of 92%
2010	Woodard et al. [19]	LBP fused with iris matching	Skin	MBGC NIR images from 88 subjects	Left eye Rank-1 RR:	Iris, 13.8%; periocular, 92.5%; both, 96.5%
					Right eye Rank-1 RR:	Iris, 10.1%; periocular, 88.7%; both, 92.4%
2010	Miller et al. [20]	LBP	Color information, Skin texture	FRGC Neutral expression, different session	Rank-1 RR:	Periocular, 94.10%; face, 94.38%
				FRGC Alternate expression, same session	Rank-1 RR:	Periocular, 99.50%; face, 99.75%
				FRGC Alternate expression, different session	Rank-1 RR:	Periocular, 94.90%; face, 90.37%
2010	Miller et al. [21]	LBP, City Block Distance	Skin	FRGC VS images from 410 subjects	Rank-1 RR:	Left eye, 84.39%; right eye, 83.90%; both eyes, 89.76%
				FERET VS images from 54 subjects	Rank-1 RR:	Left eye, 72.22%; right eye, 70.37%; both eyes, 74.07%
2010	Adams et al. [22]	LBP, GE	Skin	FRGC VS images from 410 subjects	Rank-1 RR:	Left eye, 86.85%; right eye, 86.26%; both eyes, 92.16%
				FERET VS images from 54 subjects	Rank-1 RR:	Left eye, 80.25%; right eye, 80.80%; both eyes, 85.06%
2010	Woodard et al. [23]	LBP, Color Histograms	Skin	FRGC Neutral expression, different session	Rank-1 RR:	Left eye, 87.1%; right eye, 88.3%; both eyes, 91.0%
				FRGC Alternate expression, same session	Rank-1 RR:	Left eye, 96.8%; right eye, 96.8%; both eyes, 98.3%
				FRGC Alternate expression, different session	Rank-1 RR:	Left eye, 87.1%; right eye, 87.1%; both eyes, 91.2%

information. Park et al. [12] have localized the periocular region statically by taking a rectangle having a dimension of $6R_{iris} \times 4R_{iris}$ centering the iris. However, this localization method fails when the eye is tilted or when the gaze is not frontal. Moreover, the method presumes the location of the iris' center to be accurately detectable. However, the iris center cannot be detected for some eye images due to the low-resolution nature of the image.

The objective of the article is to attain a dynamic boundary around the eye that will define the periocular region. The region hence derived should have the following properties: (a) it should be able to recognize humans uniquely, (b) it should be achievable for low-quality visible spectrum (VS) images, (c) should contain the main identifiable features of the eye region identifiable by a human being, and (d) no subset of the derived periocular region should be as equally potent as the derived region for recognition.

6.4 Proposed Periocular Localization Methods

To achieve the above stated properties, four different dynamic models are proposed through which the periocular region can be segmented out. These models are based on (a) human anthropometry, (b) demand of the accuracy of biometric system, (c) human expert judgment, and (d) subdivision approach.

6.4.1 Through Human Anthropometry

In a given face image, the face can be extracted by neural training to the system or by fast color-segmentation methods. The color-segmentation methods detect the skin region in the image and finds the connected components in such a region. Depending on the connected components having skin color, the system labels the largest component as the face. Algorithm 6.1 proposes a binary component analysis–based skin detection. The thresholds are experimentally fitted to obtain the highest accuracy in segmenting the skin region in face images comprising skin colors with different skin tones. The algorithm takes RGB face image as input. It first converts the face image to YC_bC_r color space and normalizes the pixel values. In the next step, the average luminance value is calculated by summing up the Y component values of each pixel and dividing by the total number of pixels in the image. A brightness-compensated image is generated depending on the value of average luminance as specified in the algorithm. In the obtained brightness-compensated image, a compound condition is applied and, finally, a thresholding is performed to obtain the skin map. Through a connected component analysis of the skin map in YC_bC_r color space, the open eye region can be obtained as explained in Algorithm 6.2. The reason for segmenting the open eye region is to obtain the non-skin region within the detected face, which can be labeled as the eye and thus achieve the approximate location of the eye's center.

Once the eye region is detected, the iris' center can be obtained using conventional pupil detection and integro-differential approaches for finding the iris' boundary; a static boundary can also be fitted. As described previously, Park et al. [12] bounded the periocular region with a $6R_{iris} \times 4R_{iris}$ rectangle centering the iris. However, no justification is given regarding the empirically taken height and width of this periocular boundary. This process of finding the periocular boundary has prerequisite knowledge of the coordinates of the iris center and radius of the iris.

Anthropometric analysis [17] of the human face and eye region gives information about the ratio of the eyes and iris, as well as the ratio of width of the face and eyes. A typical block diagram in Figure 6.3 depicts the ratios of different parts of the human face with respect to the height or width of the face. From this analysis, it is found that

$$\text{width}_{eye} = 0.42 \times \frac{\text{height}_{face}}{2} \tag{6.1}$$

$$\text{height}_{eye} = 0.13 \times \frac{\text{width}_{face}}{2} \tag{6.2}$$

This information can be used to decide the boundary of the periocular region. In Equation 6.1, the width of the eye is expressed as a function of the width of the human face. Hence, to gauge the width of the periocular boundary, there is no need to have knowledge of the iris' radius. However, knowledge of the coordinates of the iris' center is necessary. From this information, a bounding box can be

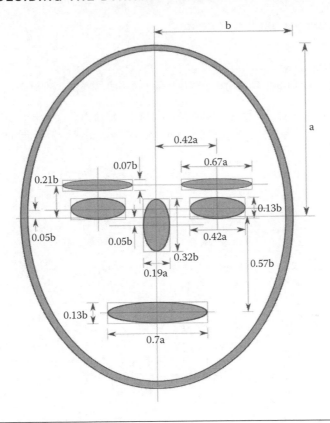

Figure 6.3 Different ratios of portions of the face from human anthropometry.

fit composing all visible portions of the periocular region, for example, the eyebrows, eyelashes, tear ducts, eye fold, eye corner, etc. This approach is crude and dependent on human supervision or intelligent detection of these nodal points in the human eye. This method achieves periocular localization without knowledge of the iris' radius. Hence, it is suitable for the localization of the periocular region for unconstrained images in which the iris' radius is not detectable by machines due to the low quality of the image, partial closure of the eye, or luminance of the visible spectrum eye image.

However, to make the system work in a more unconstrained environment, the periocular boundary can be achieved through sclera detection, for scenarios in which the iris cannot be properly located due to unconstrained acquisition of the eye, or when the image captured is a low-quality color face image captured from a distance.

Algorithm 6.1 Skin_Detection

Require: I: RGB face image of size $m \times n$
Ensure: S: Binary face image indicating skin map

1. Convert RGB image I to YC_bC_r color space
2. Normalize $_IY_{i,j}$ to $[0,255]$ where $_IY_{i,j}$ denotes Y value for the pixel (i, j)
3. Compute the average luminance value of image I as

$$_IY_{\text{avg}} = \left(\sum_{i=1}^{m} \sum_{j=1}^{n} {}_IY_{i,j} \right) \Big/ mn$$

4. Brightness compensated image $_IC'$ is obtained as

$$_IC' = \left\{ {}_IR'_{i,j}, {}_IG'_{i,j}, {}_IB'_{i,j} \right\}$$

5. Skin map S is detected from $_IC'$ as

$$S_{i,j} = \begin{cases} 0 \\ 1 \end{cases} \text{if} \left(\frac{R_{i,j}+1}{G_{i,j}+1} > 1.08 \text{ and } \frac{R_{i,j}+1}{B_{i,j}+1} > 1.08 \text{ and } G_{i,j} > 30 \text{ and } G_{i,j} < 140 \atop \text{otherwise} \right)$$

     where $S_{i,j} = 0$ indicates skin region and $S_{i,j} = 1$ indicates nonskin region.
6. **return** S

Algorithm 6.2 Open_Eye_Detection

Require: I: RGB face image of size $m \times n$, S: Binary face image indicating skin map
Ensure: EM: Binary face image indicating open eye regions

1. Convert RGB image I to YC_bC_r color space
2. Normalize $_IY_{i,j}$ to $[0,255]$ where $_IY_{i,j}$ denotes Y value for the pixel (i, j)
3. FC = Set of connected components in S
4. EM = FC
5. For each connected component EM_p in S, repeat steps 5 to 8

6. $EB_p = 0$

7. For each pixel (i, j) in EM_p, the value of EB_p is updated as

$$EB_p = \begin{cases} EB_p + 0 & \text{if} \quad 65 < {}_IY_{i,j} < 80 \\ EB_p + 1 & \text{otherwise} \end{cases}$$

8. If EB_p = number of pixels in EM_p, then do $EM = EM - EM_p$ (removal of pth connected component in set EM)

9. **return** EM

6.4.1.1 Detection of Sclera Region and Noise Removal The sclera is localized and noise is removed from localized sclera map through the following steps:

1. The input RGB iris image *im* is converted to grayscale image im_gray.

2. The input RGB iris image im is converted to HSI color model, where the S component of each pixel can be determined by

$$S = 1 - \frac{3}{R+G+B}[\min(R,G,B)]$$

where R, G, and B denotes the red, green, and blue color components of a particular pixel. Let the image hence formed containing S components of each pixel be saturation_im.

3. If $S < \tau$ (where τ is a predefined threshold), then that pixel is marked as the sclera region, else as a nonsclera region. Chen et al. [24] have experimented with $\tau = 0.21$ to get a binary map of sclera region through binarization of saturation_im as follows:

$$\text{sclera\_noisy} = \text{saturation\_im} < \tau$$

Only a noisy binary map of sclera "sclera noisy" can be found through this process, in which white pixels denote noisy sclera region, and black pixels denote nonsclera region.

4. im_bin is formed as follows:

$$\begin{aligned} \text{im\_bin}(i,j) &= \text{average intensity of } 17 \times 17 \text{ window around the pixel } (i,j) \text{ in im\_gray}(i,j), \\ &= 0, \end{aligned}$$

for each nonzero pixel (i,j) in sclera_noisy

for each zero pixel (i,j) in sclera_noisy

5. sclera_adaptive is formed as

$$\begin{aligned} \text{sclera\_adaptive}(i,j) &= 0, \\ &= 1, \end{aligned}$$

if sclera_noisy$(i,j) = 1$
or
im_gray$(i,j) <$ im_bin(i,j)
else

6. All binary connected components present in sclera_adaptive are removed except for the largest and second largest components.
7. If the size of the second largest connected component in sclera_adaptive is less than 25% of that of the largest one, it is interpreted that the largest component is the single sclera detected and the second largest connected component is therefore removed. Else, both the components are retained as binary maps of the sclera.

After processing these above specified steps, the binary image would only contain one or two components describing the sclera region after removing noise.

6.4.1.2 Content Retrieval of Sclera Region After a denoised binary map of the sclera region within an eye image is obtained, it is necessary to retrieve information about the sclera, whether two parts of the sclera on two sides of the iris are separately visible, or if only one of them is detected, or if both parts of the sclera are detected as a single component.

There can be three exhaustive cases in the binary image found as sclera: (a) the two sides of the sclera is connected and found as a single connected component, (b) two sclera regions are found as two different connected components, and (c) only one side of the sclera is detected due to the position of the eye in the image.

If two connected components are found, then it is classified as case b (as shown in Figure 6.4a–c) and two components are treated

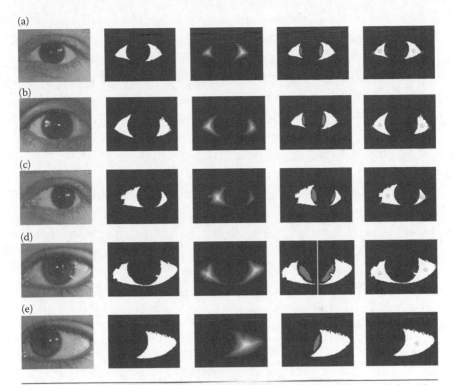

Figure 6.4 Results of proposed gaze estimation through sclera detection: (a–c) detection of nodal points on both sides of the sclera as two separate components; (d) detection of nodal points on the sclera as a single component; (e) detection of nodal points on only one side of the sclera.

as two portions of the sclera. Else, if a single connected component is obtained, it is checked for the length and width ratio of the best-fitted oriented bounding rectangle. If the ratio is greater than 1.25, then it belongs to case a, else in case c (as shown in Figure 6.4e). For case a, the region is subdivided into two components (by detecting the minimal cut that divides the joined sclera into two parts, as shown in Figure 6.4d) and further processing is performed.

Each sclera is subjected to following processing through which three nodal points are detected from each sclera region, that is, (a) center of the sclera, (b) center of the concave region of the sclera, and (c) eye corner. Therefore, in general cases in which two parts of the sclera are detected, six nodal points will be detected. The method of nodal point extraction is illustrated below:

1. *Finding the center of the sclera:* The sclera component is subjected to a distance transform in which the value of each white pixel (indicating the pixels belonging to the sclera) is replaced by its minimum distance from any black pixel. The pixel that is farthest from all black pixels will have the highest value after this transformation. That pixel is chosen as the center of the sclera.

2. *Finding the center of the concave region of the sclera:* The midpoints of every straight line joining any two border pixels of the detected sclera component are found as shown in Figure 6.5. The midpoints lying on the component itself (shown by the red point between P_1 and P_2 in Figure 6.5) are neglected. The midpoints lying outside the component (shown by the yellow point between P_3 and P_4 in Figure 6.5) are taken into account. Due to discrete computation of straight lines, the midpoints of many such straight lines drawn overlap. A separate matrix having the same size as the sclera itself is introduced, which initially has a zero value for each pixel. For

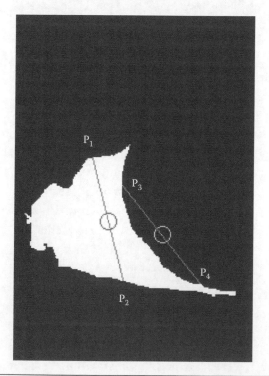

Figure 6.5   Method of formation of concave region of a binarized sclera component.

every valid midpoint, the value of the corresponding pixel in this new matrix is incremented. Once this process is done, more than one connected component of nonzero values will be obtained in the matrix signifying concave regions. The largest connected component is retained whereas others are removed. The pixel with the maximum value in the largest component is marked as the center of the concave region.

3. *Finding the eye corner:* The distances of all pixels lying on the boundary of the sclera region from the sclera's center are also calculated to find the center of the sclera as described above. The boundary pixel which is furthest from the center of the sclera is marked as the eye corner.

The result of extracting these nodal points from eye images helps in finding the tilt of the eye along with the position of the iris. Figure 6.4 depicts five sample images from the UBIRIS.v2 data set and the outputs obtained from their processing through the aforementioned nodal point extraction technique. This information can be useful in the localization of the periocular region.

6.4.2 *Through Demand of Accuracy of Biometric System*

Beginning with the center of the eye (pupil's center), a bounding rectangular box is taken enclosing only the iris. Figure 6.6 shows how the eye image changes when it is cropped with the pupil's center and the bounding size is gradually increased. The corresponding accuracy of every cropped image is tested. In subsequent steps, the coverage of this bounding box is increased with a width of 2% of the diameter of the iris and a change in accuracy is observed. After certain number of iterations of this procedure, the bounding box will come to a portion of the periocular region where there is no more change in intensity; hence, the region

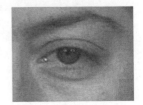

Figure 6.6   Cropped images from an iris image at the pupil's center.

is low in entropic. Hence, no more local features can be extracted from this region even if the bounding box is increased. In such a scenario, the saturation accuracy is achieved, and on the basis of saturation accuracy, the corresponding minimum bounding box is considered as the desired periocular region. Because the demand for different biometric systems may vary, the bounding box corresponding to certain predefined accuracies can also be segmented according to the periocular region. Similar results have also been observed for the FERET database.

The exact method of obtaining the dynamic boundary is as follows:

1. For i = 0 to 100, follow steps 2 to 4
2. For each image in the database, find the approximate iris location in the eye image
3. For each image in the database, centering at the iris' center, crop a bounding box whose width w = 100 + 2 × i % of diameter of iris, height h = 80% of w
4. Find the accuracy of the system with this image size
5. Observe the change in accuracy with w

Figure 6.7 illustrates a plot of accuracy against w, which shows that the accuracy of the biometric system is saturated after a particular size of the bounding box. Increasing the box size further does not increase the accuracy. To carry out this experiment, a local binary pattern

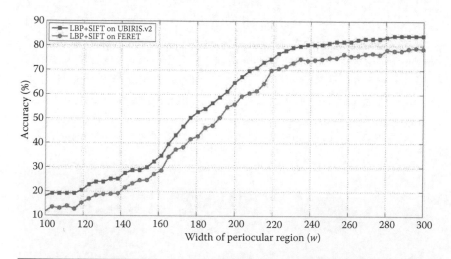

Figure 6.7   Change of recognition accuracy (LBP + SIFT considered as the feature set) with a change in the width of the cropped periocular area tested on UBIRIS.v2 and FERET data sets.

(LBP) [25] along with a scale-invariant feature transform (SIFT) [26] are employed as feature extractors from the eye images. First, LBP is applied and the resulting image is subjected to extraction of local features through SIFT. In the process, a maximum accuracy of 85.64% is achieved while testing with 50 randomly chosen eye images of 12 subjects from the UBIRIS.v2 data set [27]. When the same experiment was executed for 50 randomly chosen eye images of 12 subjects from the FERET data set [28], a maximum accuracy of 78.29% was achieved. These saturation accuracy values were obtained when a rectangular boundary with a width that is 300% of the diameter of the iris or a wider rectangular eye area is taken into consideration. Therefore, to minimize template size without compromising accuracy, the smallest wide rectangle with saturation accuracy can be used as the localization boundary to periocular region.

6.4.3 Through the Subdivision Approach and Automation of Human Expertise

During the enrollment phase of a biometric system, a human expert needs to manually verify whether the captured image includes the expected region of interest. Through the automated labeling of different sections of the eye, the portion that is necessary for identification can be stated (from human expert knowledge already discussed) and an automated failure to acquire detection system can be made. Hence, there is no need for a human expert to verify the existence of important portions of the human eye in an acquired eye image.

The challenge in incorporating this localization strategy in the periocular region is the automatic detection of portions of the human eye such as the eyelids, eye corners, tear ducts, lower eyefolds, etc. An attempt to perform subdivision detection in the eye region can be achieved through color detection and analysis and by applying different transformations.

6.5 Conclusions

The literature survey and the proposed works progressed thus far signify why recognition through VS periocular image has gained so much importance and how the present approaches work. To implement a biometric system that works for the whole nation, enrollment of every citizen is necessary. Optimization of each template size, even for a small amount, will result in an effective reduction of the whole database's size. This chapter prescribes four metrics for the optimization of VS's periocular image and experimentally establishes its relevance in terms of satisfying expected recognition accuracy. These methods can be used to localize the periocular region dynamically so that an optimized region can be selected that is best suitable for recognition in terms of two contradictory objectives: (a) minimal template size and (b) maximal recognition accuracy.

References

1. A.S.M. Sohail, and P. Bhattacharya. Detection of facial feature points using anthropometric face model. *Multimedia Systems and Applications Series* 31, 189–200, 2008. doi: 10.1007/978-0-387-72500-017.
2. T.A. Camus, and R. Wildes. Reliable and fast eye finding in close-up images. In *16th International Conference on Pattern Recognition* 1, 389–394, 2002.
3. H. Sung, J. Lim, J. Park, and Y. Lee. Iris recognition using collarette boundary localization. In *17th International Conference on Pattern Recognition* 4, 857–860, 2004.
4. B. Bonney, R. Ives, D. Etter, and D. Yingzi. Iris pattern extraction using bit planes and standard deviations. In *Conference Record of the Thirty-Eighth Asilomar Conference on Signals, Systems and Computers*, 2004.
5. X. Liu, K.W. Bowyer, and P.J. Flynn. Experiments with an improved iris segmentation algorithm. In *Fourth IEEE Workshop on Automatic Identification Advanced Technologies* 118–123, 2005.
6. H. Proenca, and L.A. Alexandre. Iris segmentation methodology for non-cooperative recognition. In *IEE Proceedings on Vision, Image and Signal Processing* 153(2):199–205, 2006.
7. S.J. Pundlik, D.L. Woodard, and S.T. Birchfield. Non-ideal iris segmentation using graph cuts. In *IEEE Computer Society Conference on Computer Vision and Pattern Recognition Workshops*, 1–6, 2008.
8. Z. He, T. Tan, Z. Sun, and X. Qiu. Toward accurate and fast iris segmentation for iris biometrics. *IEEE Transactions on Pattern Analysis and Machine Intelligence* 31(9):1670–1684, 2009.
9. L. Jin, F. Xiao, and W. Haopeng. Iris image segmentation based on k-means cluster. In *IEEE International Conference on Intelligent Computing and Intelligent Systems (ICIS)* 3, 194–198, 2010.
10. F. Tan, Z. Li, and X. Zhu. Iris localization algorithm based on gray distribution features. In *IEEE International Conference on Progress in Informatics and Computing (PIC)* 2, 719–722, 2010.

11. S. Bakshi, H. Mehrotra, and B. Majhi. Real-time iris segmentation based on image morphology. In *International Conference on Communication, Computing and Security (ICCCS '11)*, 335–338, 2011.

12. U. Park, R.R. Jillela, A. Ross, and A.K. Jain. Periocular biometrics in the visible spectrum. *IEEE Transactions on Information Forensics and Security* 6(1):96–106, 2011.

13. R. Abiantum, and M. Savvides. Tear-duct detector for identifying left versus right iris images. *IEEE Applied Imaginary Pattern Recognition*, 1–4, 2008.

14. S. Bhat, and M. Savvides. Evaluating active shape models for eye-shape classification. In *IEEE International Conference on Acoustics, Speech, and Signal Processing*, 5228–5231, 2008.

15. J. Merkow, B. Jou, and M. Savvides. An exploration of gender identification using only the periocular region. In *4th IEEE International Conference on Biometrics: Theory, Applications, and Systems (BTAS)*, 2010.

16. J.R. Lyle, P.E. Miller, S.J. Pundlik, and D.L. Woodard. Soft biometric classification using periocular region features. In *4th IEEE International Conference on Biometrics: Theory, Applications, and Systems (BTAS)*, 2010.

17. Ramanathan, and H. Wechsler. Robust human authentication using appearance and holistic anthropometric features. *Pattern Recognition Letters* 31(15), 2010.

18. K. Hollingsworth, K.W. Bowyer, and P.J. Flynn. Identifying useful features for recognition in near-infrared periocular images. In *4th IEEE International Conference on Biometrics: Theory, Applications and Systems (BTAS)*, 2010.

19. D.L. Woodard, S.J. Pundlik, and P.E. Miller. On the fusion of periocular and iris biometrics in non-ideal imagery. In *20th International Conference on Pattern Recognition (ICPR)*, 201–204, 2010.

20. P.E. Miller, J.R. Lyle, S.J. Pundlik, and D.L. Woodard. Performance evaluation of local appearance based periocular recognition. In *4th IEEE International Conference on Biometrics: Theory, Applications and Systems (BTAS)*, 2010.

21. P.E. Miller, A.W. Rawls, and S.J. Pundlik. Personal identification using periocular skin texture. In *ACM Symposium on Applied Computing (SAC '10)*, 2010.

22. J. Adams, D.L. Woodard, G. Dozier, P.E. Miller, K. Bryant, and G. Glenn. Genetic-based type II feature extraction for periocular biometric recognition: Less is more. In *20th International Conference on Pattern Recognition (ICPR)*, 205–208, 2010.

23. D.L. Woodard, S.J. Pundlik, P.E. Miller, and J.R. Lyle. Appearance-based periocular features in the context of face and non-ideal iris recognition. *Journal of Signal, Image and Video Processing* 5(4):443–455, 2011.

24. Y. Chen, M. Adjouadi, C. Han, J. Wang, A. Barreto, N. Rishe, and J. Andrian. A highly accurate and computationally efficient approach for unconstrained iris segmentation. *Image and Vision Computing* 28(2):261–269, 2010.

25. T. Ojala, M. Pietikinen, and D. Harwood. A comparative study of texture measures with classification based on featured distributions. *IEEE Transactions on Information Forensics and Security* 29(1):51–59, 1996.
26. D.G. Lowe. Distinctive image features from scale-invariant keypoints. *International Journal of Computer Vision* 60(2), 2004.
27. H. Proenca, S. Filipe, R. Santos, J. Oliveira, and L.A. Alexandre. The UBIRIS.v2: A database of visible wavelength iris images captured on-the-move and at-a-distance. *IEEE Transactions on Pattern Analysis and Machine Intelligence* 32(8), 2010.
28. J.P. Phillips, H. Moon, S.A. Rizvi, and P.J. Rauss. The FERET evaluation methodology for face-recognition algorithms. *IEEE Transactions on Pattern Analysis and Machine Intelligence* 22(10):1090–1104, 2000.

7

RETENTION OF ELECTROCARDIOGRAM FEATURES INSIGNIFICANTLY DEVALORIZED AS AN EFFECT OF WATERMARKING FOR A MULTIMODAL BIOMETRIC AUTHENTICATION SYSTEM

NILANJAN DEY, BIJURIKA NANDI,
POULAMI DAS, ACHINTYA DAS,
AND SHELI SINHA CHAUDHURI

Contents

Abstract

In recent times, identification authentication has been facing a number of challenges in verifying a person's identity. Accurate verification is necessary, or else the person might suffer from identity crisis. Also, unauthorized access might result in misuse of personal information. To eliminate such discrepancies, many authentication processes have come into being. Of all the authentication techniques in use, the biometric authentication process that deals with human anatomical features provides the most reasonable solution. The work in this chapter proposes combining of electrocardiogram (ECG) and finger-print features to design a robust biomedical authentication system. According to the proposed methodology, after recording and extracting the ECG and fingerprint features, they are stored in templates in remote databases. On login attempt, the person's fingerprint and ECG features are recorded to produce a watermarked ECG signal. The watermarked signal is transmitted over a communication channel and matched with the data stored in the database, at a remote feature matcher. Comparing the two, a match is found if the result obtained lies within a previously set threshold. To develop the watermarked ECG signal, the size of a gray fingerprint image, taken as the watermark, is calculated. The ECG signal recorded is converted to 2D signal as per the size of the fingerprint image. After decomposing the 2D signal by SWT into 4 subbands, DCT is applied to the subband $Cd1$. SVD is applied on the resultant image. SWT is also applied to the fingerprint image and decomposed into 4 sub bands, to each of which DCT is applied. Subsequently SVD is applied to the resultant image. Singular value of the 2D signal is modified using the singular value of $Cd1$ band of the watermark image. Finally IDCT and ISWT are applied to embed the watermark into 1D signal, which is subsequently reshaped into 1D signal. The method serves to be a strong authentication system.

7.1 Introduction

In today's world, identification authentication has emerged as a very important aspect of our daily lives. It faces a number of challenges in accurately verifying a person's identity to allow that person to gain access over any sort of application or transaction. Any discrepancy, either on the part of the authentication system used or due to any unauthorized access, can lead to the identity crisis of any individual. A biometric authentication system, in this respect, provides quite a reasonable solution because it uses human anatomical or behavioral features for the verification process. The multimodal biometric authentication system, which uses a combination of modalities, has advantages over its unimodal counterpart, especially in areas of False Acceptance Rate (FAR) and False Rejection Rate (FRR). In this chapter, according to the proposed methodology, electrocardiograms (ECG) and fingerprints are combined to achieve a robust multimodal biometric system. Here, the ECG signal of a person is watermarked by the grayscale image of his fingerprint. The watermarked ECG signal of the individual, after being transmitted through a communication channel, is matched with his original ECG and fingerprint features, which are stored at a remote database. If the result obtained has a value within a previously defined threshold, then a match is found. This approach helps to compare the original fingerprint with the recovered one based on the structural similarity index metric (SSIM) and the correlation value. In addition, the methodology also does a comparative study between the original ECG signal and its watermarked version on the basis of the peak signal to noise ratio (PSNR) value. The watermarked ECG signal has an acceptable level of imperceptibility and distortion. A comparative study is done for the intervals between two consecutive "RR," "QQ," "SS," "TT," "PR," "QT," and "QTc" peaks as well as for the QRS complex duration. In addition to this, a comparative study between the discrete wavelet transformation, discrete cosine transformation, and singular value decomposition (DWT-DCT-SVD) and stationary wavelet transformation, discrete cosine transformation, and singular value decomposition

(SWT-DCT-SVD)–based watermarking techniques is also done to prove the efficacy and robustness of the proposed method. In the first part of this chapter, the method successfully shows that even after watermarking, the ECG signal does not get much devalorized and hence the initial ECG signal is successfully retained. In the latter part of the chapter, the robustness of the newly proposed technique was proved by showing the method's immunity toward additive white Gaussian noise.

7.2 Unimodal and Multimodal Biometric Systems

The biometric system gauges and analyzes the physiological characteristics of the human body such as the face, fingerprints, eyes, retinas, irises, voice patterns, or behavioral characteristics for enrollment, verification, or detection. Presently, a considerable amount of work has been done in ECG-based biometric authentication systems. A multimodal biometric authentication system helps to overcome the limitations of the unimodal biometric system by reducing one or more of the false accept, false reject, and failure to enroll rates.

Computer networks across the globe are interconnected by the Internet. The Internet serves billions of users around the world. In modern times, the Internet is the most useful technology that has made communications and business transactions a lot easier. E-commerce, e-governance, social networking, online gaming, and many other online modes of communications or transactions have gained huge popularity among the ever-increasing number of Internet users [1]. This calls for a secured system that will authenticate online transactions and protect them from unauthorized use. With the huge volume of information being exchanged all day long through the Internet, interception of this information by attackers has also gained prominence. Hence, Internet security today faces the most important challenge of authenticating a user. Several methods have been incorporated to check unauthorized access to data and information during online transaction processes. The most commonly used process is the ID password system. This password-based system is highly popular among users owing to its simplicity. Moreover, the vast population of Internet users is adapted to this environment of security, and so, even if this system is vulnerable to attacks, it is the one mostly in use. This system also demands that the user should remember the password to proceed with any sort of transaction or communication [2]. One-time password tokens or certificates are other means of authentication processes. However, they are not as frequently used due to the complexity of the methods. A more robust authentication process is biometric authentication. The term *biometrics* is derived from the Greek words *bios* (life) and *metrikos* (to measure) [3]. Biometric authentication refers to the identification of humans by their various characteristics or traits, which are unique, such as fingerprints, facial features, DNA, characteristics of voice, etc. This authentication process is becoming widely popular in today's world. Biometric authentication provides a superior means of securing data from the hands of imposters. This system does not require the user to remember any sort of password. In addition, biometric systems also keep track of when and where a particular user accesses the system [4]. The biometric system stores a large amount of biometric data. By comparing the data entered after enrollment (first time storing of data of an individual in the system), to the data stored in the database of the system, a match is either made or rejected. The biometric authentication procedure involves two basic steps: enrollment and verification. In the first step, that is, the enrollment process, an individual's biometric data are captured, transformed into a template, and stored. During the verification process, a new template is formed after a live scan of the person's biometric features. This new template is compared with the templates already stored in the database [5]. Either a match is found or it is rejected. This identification mode involves one-to-many comparisons against the biometric database to establish the person's identity [6]. The person is identified only when the outcome of the comparison between the new template of biometric data and the templates already stored in the system falls within a previously set threshold. During this identification process, the biometric system is subjected to two types of errors: false acceptance and false rejection. The performance of any biometric system is hence measured by the two parameters, FAR and FRR. FAR is the measure of all likelihood by which a biometric system falsely accepts access by an unauthorized user. Similarly, the FRR is the percentage of identification instances when an authorized user is denied access [7]. Both parameters are measured in percentages; for example, if FAR is 0.1%, it denotes that out of 2000 imposters, two are successful in breaching the system. Similarly, if FRR is 0.05%, then it denotes that 1 out of 2000 authorized users is denied access to the system. In the biometric authentication process, FAR is often called type II error, and FRR as type I error [8]. When these two errors are the same, they give rise to the equal error rate or ERR. Mathematically, ERR is given by (FAR + FRR)/2. A perfect biometric system should have zero ERR [9]. Biometric systems can be broadly divided into two classes: unimodal biometric systems and multimodal biometric systems. The unimodal biometric system uses a single representation and a single matcher for recognition decision [10]. Therefore, unimodal systems use any one of the many features such as fingerprint recognition, hand geometry, face recognition, iris recognition, etc., as biometric features. In the facial recognition process, the overall facial structure such as distance between the eyes, nose, mouth, and jaw edges are measured. Using these features, a template is formed and stored in the database, with which all subsequent captures are compared to find a match. In the hand geometry process, distinct features of the hand such as the length, width, thickness, surface area of the finger along with the palm size are taken into account and extracted, and thereafter stored in templates, which are later used for verification process. Rings, furrows, and freckles present in the colored tissues surrounding the pupil are considered for iris recognition process. Here, these features are extracted and the templates are stored in the database. Fingerprint recognition involves feature extraction of the fingers, such as ridges, furrows, and minutiae. Like all the other systems, here the features are also stored in templates and used later for each and every verification process [11]. Of all other conventional biometric features, the use of fingerprints is relatively more widespread. An impression left by the friction ridges (the raised portion of the epidermis on the fingers, toes, palm of the hand, or sole of the foot, consisting of one or more connected ridge units of friction ridge skin) of a human finger is termed as a fingerprint. The process of comparing two instances of friction ridge skin impressions from human fingers or toes, or palm of the hand or sole of the foot, to determine whether these impressions belong to the same individual, is referred to as fingerprint identification or dactyloscopy. No two fingerprints or palmprints are exactly the same in every detail. In fact, two impressions recorded immediately after one another from the same hand may vary to some extent. Fingerprint identification is thus also known as individualization because it helps to identify a particular individual. The history of fingerprints dates back to hundreds of years [12]. However, its uniqueness and characteristics were first pointed out in 1892 by Sir Francis Galton, a British anthropologist and cousin to Charles Darwin, in his first book on fingerprints [13]. The unique characteristics of fingerprints, as identified by Galton, officially came to be known as minutiae. However, they are often referred to as "Galton's details." The patterns of furrows, ridges, and minutiae (local ridge characteristics occurring at either a ridge bifurcation or a ridge ending point) on the fingers make the fingerprints of any individual unique. Minutiae are the major features of fingerprints and are used extensively in biometric authentication processes. These minutiae can be of varied types such as ridge endings (abrupt end of a ridge), ridge bifurcations (a single ridge dividing into two ridges), short ridges or independent ridges (a ridge that ends after travelling a short distance), islands (a single small ridge inside a short ridge or a ridge ending not connected to all other ridges), ridge enclosures (a single ridge that bifurcates and joins again right after to continue as a single ridge), spurs (a bifurcation with a short ridge branching off a longer ridge), crossover or bridge (a short ridge running between two parallel ridges), delta (Y-shaped ridge meeting), and core (U-turn in the ridge pattern). Fingerprints are generally grouped into five classes, namely, whorls, right loops, left loops, arches, and tented arches, depending on the furrow, ridge, and minutiae patterns [14]. Fingerprint recognition is a technique of biometric authentication. It uses pattern recognition techniques based on high-resolution fingerprint images of the individual. Fingerprint recognition includes the following steps: image acquisition, preprocessing, feature extraction, and matching. The noise present in fingerprint images leads to spurious minutiae points. To overcome this problem, feature extraction of fingerprints is done, which helps to locate the minutiae points effectively. Among a number of biometric authentication processes, fingerprint authentication method is the most popular one due to its unique features and easy extraction procedures. A fingerprint feature extraction methodology locates, measures, and encodes ridge edgings and bifurcations in the fingerprint. There are many ways for minutiae extraction. A lot of care needs to be taken in extracting minutiae from grayscale fingerprint image because even the slightest of errors may degrade the extraction process to a large extent. In the traditional approach, the first step includes enhancement of the ridge–valley structures. This enhancement procedure is necessary to eliminate the noise present in the fingerprint image. The simplest way to enhance the image is to use a low-pass filter in which the high-frequency noise is eliminated. Another approach divides the image into 32 × 32 pixel blocks, on each of which fast Fourier transform (FFT) is performed. The result is non-linearly processed to enhance the image. One of the best approaches, however, is passing the image through the Gabor filter. A Gabor filter is a band-pass filter that enhances some spatial frequencies and attenuates the others. The real valued Gabor filter is defined by the pointwise multiplication of a cosine with a Gaussian window. Here, a filter that enhances those structures that agree with the local ridge orientation is applied to each pixel. After enhancement, the image is turned into a black and white image from the grayscale one. This is called a binarized image. The next step involves thinning, in which the width of each ridge is reduced to a single pixel. Finally, the actual minutiae detection in the skeleton image is done, with the help of a lookup table. Then, postprocessing takes place, which eliminates false minutiae points. Other than this traditional approach, few other methodologies have been developed for fingerprint feature extraction (Figure 7.1). One was genetic programming and the other one was reinforcement learning. Both were unsuccessful due to lack of robustness in their techniques. Therefore, the more widely used fingerprint extraction method, to date, is the traditional approach [15].

Although the unimodal biometric system provides a promising solution in the field of authentication processes, this system also has some serious drawbacks. The verification process of the biometric system fails at times because individual facial features, voice, etc., change with age or illness. Serious security issues in cases of data privacy and identity theft may also crop up if these biometric data fall into the wrong hands. Biometric data collected for one application can be shared or used to gain access to other applications of a particular user because the biometric features of a user are entitled to remain the same for any application. Unimodal biometric systems are susceptible to noise, which ultimately leads to improper matching. In cases of

Figure 7.1 Extracted fingerprint features.

identical features, which generally occur in identical twins, the unimodal system is not robust enough to match perfectly. In addition, the unimodal biometric system is also vulnerable to spoofing, wherein data can be imitated or forged [16]. Therefore, to deal with all these problems, and to provide better authentication processes, multimodal biometric systems were developed. Multimodal biometric systems use more than one correlated biometric feature, such as multiple impressions of a finger, multiple images of a face, or any other combination. Due to the various combinations of biometric features that the multimodal biometric system uses, this system is more robust than the unimodal system. Multimodal systems are less vulnerable to spoofing, are resistant to noise, and can almost accurately find matches in case of intraclass similarities such as facial features. Multimodal biometric systems reduce both FAR and FRR, making the system even more efficient. In unimodal and multimodal systems, fingerprints, hand geometry, iris recognition, and facial recognition are widely used. However, these biometric features often pose problems during the authentication processes. If the fingertips get dirty or if the user has skin problems, the fingerprints will not match with the stored template. In case of identical twins, it is difficult to accurately recognize facial features. Moreover, poor image quality and changes in facial features due to age or illness might not yield proper results. The hand recognition system does not work for children, people with arthritis, and those with missing fingers. Iris recognition is highly intrusive, rendering discomfort to users during enrollment. To top it all, the face is sensitive to artificial disguise, fingerprints can be regenerated using latex, and the iris can be contorted by using contact lenses with copied iris features printed on them. Therefore, research has been carried out to find any other unique biometric feature that would help in developing a secured authentication process. Recent investigations have cited the possibility of using electrocardiography as a new biometric modality for human identity recognition. There are physiological and geometrical differences of the hearts of different individuals that make ECG signals unique. ECG signals have different wave shapes, amplitudes, intervals, and segments due to the difference in the physical conditions of the heart [17]. Presently, considerable amount of work has been done in ECG-based biometric authentication systems.

The detection of the voltage within the heart against time is known as an electrocardiography or ECG. The word electrocardiograph is coined from three Greek words: *electro*, because it is related to electrical activity; *kardio*, for heart; and *graph*, a Greek root word meaning "to write." The direction and magnitude of the electrical activity of the heart, caused by the depolarization and repolarization of the atria and ventricles, are graphically recorded by ECG. ECG is used to measure the rate and regularity of heartbeats, as well as the size and position of the chambers, the presence of any damage to the heart, and the effects of drugs or devices used to regulate the heart. ECG varies from person to person, depending on the shape, size, and position of heart, and the weight, height, and chest configuration, etc., of the person involved. The heart's electrical activity shows distinctive characteristics regarding the working conditions of the heart and the various ailments associated with it. The body's natural electric current causes the heart muscles to contract and pump blood through the heart's chambers and throughout the body. To measure the electrical impulses that lead to heart contractions, electrodes are attached to selected parts of the patient's torso, directly on the skin. Small pads are placed between the skin and the electrodes to improve electrical conductivity and to function as buffers to reduce any discomfort that patient may face. These electrode leads must be placed at very specific points in the body, which are more directly connected to specific kinds of cardiac electrical signals. The electrodes are extremely sensitive. To measure heart muscle activity, they should be capable of detecting the minutest of minute changes in potential energy on the body's skin. The ECG device detects and amplifies the tiny electrical changes on the skin that are caused when the heart muscle depolarizes during each heartbeat. These changes are communicated through electrical signals measuring only about 1 mV or less. A typical ECG graph of the cardiac cycle consists of a P wave, a QRS complex, a T wave, and a U wave. The baseline voltage of the ECG is known as the isoelectric line. Typically, the isoelectric line is measured as the portion of the tracing following the T wave and preceding the next P wave. The first wave of the ECG is the P wave. It denotes the spread of electrical impulse through the atrial musculature (activation or depolarization). The P wave normally lasts less than 0.11 s. In left atrial enlargement, an abnormally long P wave results as it takes more time for the electrical wave to reach the entire atrium. The height of the P wave is normally less than 0.25 mV, gently rounded, not pointed or notched. Hypertrophy of the right atrium, which causes larger amounts of electricity to flow over the atrium, makes the P wave abnormally tall. On the other hand, hyperkalemia reduces the P wave's height. The QRS complex represents the activation of the ventricle. The QRS complex is normally less than 0.10 s in length. Prolonged QRS complex indicates some blockage of the electrical action in the conducting system due to a number of factors like ischemia, necrosis of the conducting tissue, electrolyte abnormality, or hypothermia. Electrical systole of the ventricles starts with the beginning of the QRS complex. The first downward deflection of the QRS complex, known as the Q wave, represents the activation of the ventricular septum. Significant Q waves, longer than 0.04 s or larger than 1/4 of the R wave, indicate either myocardial infarction or obstructive septal hypertrophy (IHSS). The first upward deflection of the QRS complex is called the R wave. Most of the ventricle is activated during the R wave. The R wave may be lengthened if the ventricle is enlarged, and may be unusually high if the ventricular muscle tissue is hypertrophied. The S wave is any downward deflection following the R wave. Like the R wave, an abnormally large S wave may indicate hypertrophy of the ventricle. If a second upward deflection is seen, it is called an R-prime wave. R-prime waves are considered abnormal, and are assumed to be associated with a problem in the ventricular conduction system. The T wave represents the wave of repolarization. The normal shape of the T wave is slightly rounded and slightly asymmetrical, lasting no longer than 0.16 s. Tall T waves may be seen in hyperkalemia or very early myocardial infarction. The occurrence of flat T waves denotes certain abnormalities related to the heart. Inverted T waves may be seen in both ischemia and infarction, late in pericarditis, ventricular hypertrophy, bundle branch block, and cerebral disease. The U wave is assumed to be caused by the repolarization of the interventricular septum. They normally have low amplitude, and at times are completely absent. Large U waves may be seen in electrolyte abnormality (such as hypokalemia), or with drug effects. Apart from these main parts of the ECG signal, the signal can also be divided into a number of segments and intervals. The study of the characteristics and durations of these segments and intervals are also vital to detecting any abnormality of the heart (Figure 7.2).

Following the P wave is the PR segment. This segment connects the P wave and the QRS complex. During the PR segment, the electrical wave moves slowly through the atrioventricular (AV) node. The time duration of the PR segment ranges from 0.05 to 0.12 s. The time from the beginning of the P wave until the beginning of the QRS complex is the PR interval. The PR interval reflects conduction

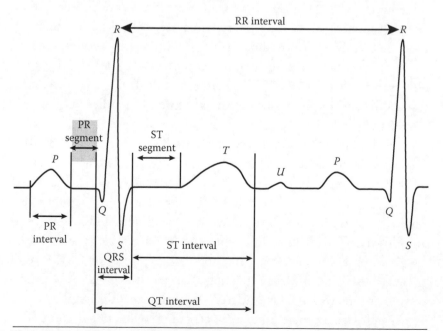

Figure 7.2   P-QRS-T complex detected ECG signal.

through the AV nodes. This interval is normally between 0.12 and 0.2 s. Degenerative disease of the node, or digoxin, hyperkalemia, hypercalcemia, or hypothermia causes the conduction of the electrical wave through the AV node to be slow, resulting in a larger PR interval. First-degree AV blocks are represented by prolonged PR intervals. The PR interval may be abnormally short with rapid conduction. A mildly short PR interval may be observed with hypokalemia or hypocalcemia. An artificially short PR interval occurs with an early start of the QRS complex, similar to what happens in extra conducting bundle—Wolff–Parkinson–White syndrome [18–20]. The time intervals between consecutive heartbeats are generally measured in the ECG from the beginning of a QRS complex to the beginning of the next QRS complex. Therefore, these intervals might be called QQ intervals, PP intervals, or TT intervals, but they are conventionally named RR intervals. Although the beginning of the QRS complex should customarily be taken as the reference point, this point can, however, be difficult to locate in noisy or low amplitude ECGs, leading to erroneous results. The RR interval, apart from being the most prominent peak of the ECG, also depicts ventricular contraction. If the PP interval is used, junctional syndromes of ECG will be hard to figure out. All other intervals do not serve as prominent and good reference points. Hence, the R wave peak is the most preferred reference point because this measurement can be made with smaller errors. The RR interval is the time interval between the R wave peaks of two consecutive QRS complexes. The RR interval has its primary importance in calculating the heart rate. The duration of RR interval is generally of 0.6 to 1 s that, respectively, corresponds to a heart rate of 60 to 100 beats per minute (bpm). The heart rate can be given by HR = 60,000/RR interval in milliseconds. Therefore, a person with an RR interval of 700 ms has a HR of approximately 85 bpm. However, the calculated heart rate can be quite different from the measured pulse even in a normal person due to the heart rate variations associated with respiration (the sinus arrhythmia). Resting heart rates below 60 bpm are referred to as bradycardia, whereas those above 100 bpm are called tachycardia [21,22]. The ST segment lies between the QRS complex and the T wave. The point at which it begins is called the J (junction) point. The ventricle contracts during this segment, but no electricity flows. The

ST segment therefore coincides with the baseline. The duration of the *ST* segment is between 0.08 and 0.12 s. The ST segment is shortened by increasing the heart rate. Abnormality of electrolytes may also affect the ST segment length. Upward or downward shifts in the ST segment are very important. A deviation of the ST segment from the baseline can indicate infarction or ischemia, pericarditis, electrolyte abnormality, or ventricular strain [18–20]. The QT interval is measured from the beginning of the QRS complex until the end of the T wave. The duration of the QT interval is around 0.32 s to 0.43 s. Normally, the QT interval should be less than half the preceding RR interval. Very fast heart rates shorten the QT length. The QT interval may be prolonged with electrolyte abnormality (hypokalemia, hypocalcemia, hypomagnesemia) or myocardial ischemia [23]. The QT interval at a heart rate of 60 bpm is estimated by the corrected QT interval (QTc). This helps to compare QT values over time at different heart rates and thereby aids in the better detection of patients at increased risk of arrhythmias. A number of formulae have been developed to calculate QTc. They are as follows:

Bazett's formula: $QTc = QT/\sqrt{RR}$
Fredericia's formula: $QTc = QT/RR^{1/3}$,
Framingham's formula: $QTc = QT + 0.154(1 - RR)$,
Hodges' formula: $QTc = QT + 1.75 \text{ (heart rate} - 60)$

Normal duration of QTc lies between 0.35 and 0.46 s in women and 0.44 s in men. Prolonged QTc can be due to hypokalemia, hypomagnesemia, hypocalcemia, hypothermia, myocardial ischemia, postcardiac arrest, congenital QT syndrome, etc. Short duration of QTc can be due to hypercalcemia, congenital short QT syndrome, or digoxin effect. ECG thus helps us in detecting a number of diseases related to the heart [24].

7.3 Proposed Multimodal Biometric Authentication System

In this chapter, a multimodal biometric authentication system based on the features of ECG signals and fingerprints has been proposed. Here, the ECG signal of an individual is watermarked by that person's fingerprint image to generate a secure and robust authentication system.

Watermarking is the process of embedding data into a one-dimensional (1-D) or two-dimensional (2-D) signal for security purposes. A blind watermarking scheme does not require the original signal or any other data. An embedding algorithm is used to insert a watermark into the original image. Watermarking patterns in 2-D signal processing can either be in spatial domain or in transformed domain. Insertion of a least significant bit (LSB) to the embedding information in a 2-D signal is a very easy and is a typical approach in spatial domains. However, this approach has a serious limitation of being vulnerable to even the minutest of 2-D signal manipulations. Conversion of the image, which is a 2-D signal, from one format to another format and back, could potentially damage the information hidden in LSBs. Watermarked images can easily be detected by statistical analysis like histogram analysis. In this technique, N number of LSBs from each pixel of a container image are replaced with the data from a watermark. The watermark is destroyed as the value of N increases. In frequency domain analysis, data can be kept hidden by using DCT. However, the limitation of this approach is in blocking artifacts. DCT pixels are grouped into 8 × 8 blocks, and the pixel blocks are transformed into 64 DCT coefficients for each block. Any modification of a single DCT coefficient will affect all 64 image pixels in that block. In modern times, one of the techniques used for watermarking is the DWT approach [25]. The results obtained at each step of the DWT are half the size of the original signal. Contrary to this, stationary wavelet transform or SWT does not subsample the signal. Rather, the corresponding low-pass and high-pass filters are padded with zeros to upsample the signal at each level of decomposition. The primary advantage of SWT over DWT is that the spatial information of the original image at each step is restored, which aids in achieving the translation invariance that remains impossible to be carried out with conventional approaches. In this approach, the imperceptibility and distortion of the watermarked 2-D signal is acceptable. SVD uses nonfixed orthogonal bases in place of fixed orthogonal bases that other transforms use. SVD thus renders a good deal of accuracy, robustness, and imperceptibility in resolving rightful ownership of the watermarked image. The proposed watermarking method deals with a SWT-DCT-SVD–based gray fingerprint image watermarking in the P, QRS, and T components detected

ECG signal. Analysis and experimental results show that the new watermarking method is robust and also provides good security [26].

Recently, a considerable amount of work has been done based on DWT-DCT-SVD, in the domain of watermarking. This chapter proposes a watermarking technique based on SWT-DCT-SVD to overcome the above discussed limitation of a DWT-DCT-SVD–based approach. Later in this chapter, the calculated PSNR, correlation value, and SSIM by SWT-DCT-SV–based approach will clearly prove that the resultant value is quite satisfactory compared with the previous approach, that is, DWT-DCT-SVD. Although the extracted ECG features from watermarked signals in both cases remain almost unchanged (Figure 7.3).

The work described in this chapter proposes the following methodology. In the very beginning, the finger scan device scans an individual's fingerprints, and the ECG machine records his ECG signal. These two biometric features are recorded and extracted (Figure 7.4). The extracted features of both the fingerprint and the ECG signal are then stored in templates in some remote database. Then, when a person wants to log-in to the system from any region, his or her fingerprints are scanned and that person's ECG signal is recorded. These fingerprints and ECG signal together generate the watermarked ECG signal. The watermarked signal is transmitted through some communication channel. At a remote feature-matcher, features are extracted from both the watermarked ECG signal and the fingerprints extracted from the watermarked ECG signal received by the communication channel. The remote feature-matcher then compares these extracted biometric features with those stored in the remote database with the help of a feature-matcher. This proposed watermarking technique is an irreversible watermarking technique. Thus, it may so happen that the extracted features from the watermarked signal do not perfectly map with the stored features of the actual signal. Therefore, a certain threshold is defined for matching purposes. Upon comparison, if the result obtained lies within the previously set threshold, then a match is found or else the biometric features remain unmatched.

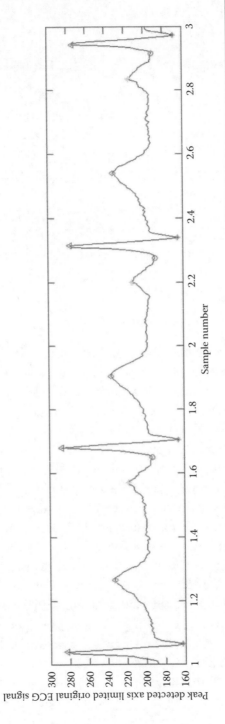

Figure 7.3 Extracted ECG features.

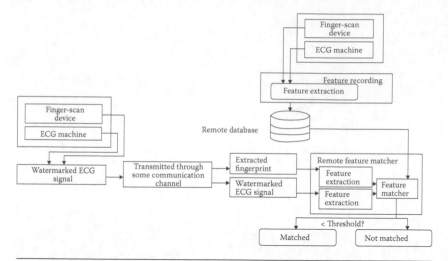

Figure 7.4   Architecture of proposed multimodal biometric authentication system.

7.4 Methodology

7.4.1 Discrete Wavelet Transformation

The wavelet transform describes a multiresolution decomposition process with respect to a signal expansion into a set of wavelet-based functions. DWT is characterized by an excellent space frequency localization property. To build up the multiresolution time–frequency plane, DWT uses filter banks. A filter bank is composed of filters that separate a signal into a number of frequency bands. The application of DWT in 1-D signal corresponds to a 1-D filter in each dimension. The Daubechies wavelet, taken as the input, is referred to as the mother wavelet and is divided into eight nonoverlapping multiresolution subbands by the filters, namely, db1, db2, db3 up to db8, where db is the abbreviation for Daubechies. Further processing is done on the subband to attain the next coarser level of wavelet coefficients, until some final scale "N" is reached. Of the eight levels formed from the signal disintegration, the db6 subband signal best exhibits the original signal because, according to the wavelet theory, the approximation signal at level n is the result of aggregation of the approximation at level $n-1$ added to the detail at level $n-1$.

For 2-D signals, the wavelet transform describes a multiresolution decomposition process in terms of an image expansion into a set of wavelet-based functions. Quite similar to the case of 1-D signals,

DWT application on 2-D images also corresponds to 2-D filter image processing in each dimension. Here, the loaded image is segmented into four nonoverlapping multiresolution subbands by the filters, namely, LL_1 (approximation coefficients), LH_1 (vertical details), HL_1 (horizontal details), and HH_1 (diagonal details). The subband (LL_1) is again processed to obtain the next coarser scale of wavelet coefficients, until a final level "N" is reached. When "N" is reached, $3N + 1$ subbands composed of the multiresolution subbands are obtained. These are, namely, LL_X and LH_X, HL_X, and HH_X where "X" ranges from 1 until "N." In general, the maximum portion of the image energy is stored in the LL_X subbands.

The simplest possible wavelet is the Haar wavelet. Being discontinuous, the Haar wavelet is not differentiable. This characteristic proves to be advantageous for the analysis of signals with sudden transitions. The Haar wavelet is the easiest orthogonal wavelet transform. The Haar basis is given by

$$\psi_{\text{Haar}}(t) = \begin{cases} 1 & \text{for } 0 < t < 0.5 \\ -1 & \text{for } 0.5 < t < -1 \\ 0 & \text{otherwise} \end{cases} \tag{7.1}$$

Its scaling function, $\phi(t)$, can be described as

$$\phi(t) = \begin{cases} 1 & 0 \le t < 1, \\ 0 & \text{otherwise} \end{cases} \tag{7.2}$$

To remove the process of decimation at every transformation level, DWT (Figure 7.5) is further modified to develop SWT (Figure 7.6), which is translation-invariant in nature. Translation-invariance is achieved by discarding the use of downsamplers and upsamplers in the DWT. Rather, upsampling of the filter coefficients by a factor of $2^{(j-1)}$ in the jth level is done in the algorithm. SWT is an inherently redundant scheme as the output of each level contains the same number of samples as the input. So, for decomposition of the N level, there is a redundancy of N in the wavelet coefficients. This algorithm proposed by Holdschneider is also known as "algorithme à trous." The algorithm involves the insertion of zeros in the filters [27].

(a)

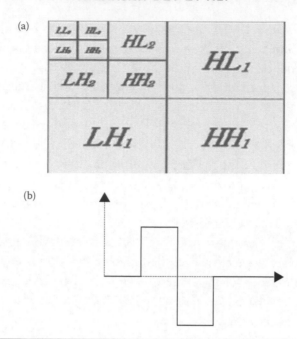

(b)

Figure 7.5   Three-phase decomposition using DWT (a), and the Haar wavelet (b).

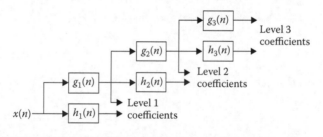

Figure 7.6   Three-phase decomposition using SWT.

7.4.2 Discrete Cosine Transformation

A DCT is basically a methodology for the conversion of a signal into fundamental frequency components. The cosine functions oscillating between different frequencies, mainly used for image compression, are summed up to represent a sequence of finitely numerous data points. The application was pioneered by Chen and Pratt in 1984.

The DCT is almost similar to the discrete Fourier transform (DFT) with some variations.

- The DCT shows better efficiency concentrating energy into lower order coefficients over DFT in case of image data.
- The DCT is purely real whereas the DFT is complex (magnitude and phase).
- Operating on a block of pixels, the DCT generates coefficients that are similar to the frequency domain coefficients produced by a DFT operation. Being closely related to a 2N point DFT, N point DCT has the same frequency resolution. The N frequencies of a 2N point DFT correspond to N points on the upper half of the unit circle in the complex frequency plane.
- Assuming a periodic input, the magnitude of the DFT coefficients is spatially invariant (phase of the input does not matter), which is not so in the case of DCT. For processing 1-D signals such as speech waveforms, 1-D DCT is used. For analysis of 2-D signals such as images, a 2-D version of the DCT is required. The 2-D DCT is separable in the two dimensions because it can be determined by applying 1-D transforms independently to the rows and columns [27].

For an $N \times N$ digital image $f(x, y)$, its 2-D DCT and its inverse transformation is defined by the following equations:

$$C(u,v) = \alpha(u)\alpha(v) \sum_{x=0}^{N-1} \sum_{y=0}^{N-1} f(x,y) \cos\left[\frac{\pi(2x+1)u}{2N}\right] \cos\left[\frac{\pi(2y+1)v}{2N}\right]$$

(7.3)

$$f(x,y) = \sum_{x=0}^{N-1} \sum_{y=0}^{N-1} \alpha(u)\alpha(v)c(u,v) \cos\left[\frac{\pi(2x+1)u}{2N}\right] \cos\left[\frac{\pi(2y+1)v}{2N}\right]$$

(7.4)

where $C(u, v)$ is the result of discrete transform, and is also known as the DCT coefficient; $u, v = 0, 1, 2,... N-1$ and $x, y = 0, 1, 2,... N-1$; and $\alpha(u)$ is defined as

$$\alpha(u) = \sqrt{(1/N)}\ u = 0;\ \text{and}\ \alpha(u) = \sqrt{(2/N)}\ u = 1, 2...N-1 \quad (7.5)$$

7.4.3 Singular Value Decomposition

To perform a number of operations, and most importantly, to find a solution for the least square problems, SVD has been developed. Nowadays, SVD has a wide range of image processing applications such as image hiding, image compression, noise reduction, image watermarking, etc. The property, that addition of small interference in an image does not cause great changes in the singular values of the image, has subsequently increased the use of SVD in different image processing schemes [27].

Suppose M is the matrix that represents the input image. M is an $N \times N$ matrix whose rank r is less than or equal to N, that is, $r \leq N$. SVD is applied on the input image matrix M to decompose it in UPV^T. U is an $N \times N$ orthogonal matrix that can be represented as

$$\begin{bmatrix} u_{1,1} & \cdots & u_{1,N} \\ \vdots & \ddots & \vdots \\ u_{N,1} & \cdots & u_{N,N} \end{bmatrix},$$

V is also an $N \times N$ orthogonal matrix that can be represented as

$$\begin{bmatrix} v_{1,1} & \cdots & v_{1,N} \\ \vdots & \ddots & \vdots \\ v_{N,1} & \cdots & v_{N,N} \end{bmatrix}^T,$$

P is a diagonal matrix with diagonal entries

$$P = \begin{bmatrix} \sigma_1 & 0 & \cdots & 0 \\ 0 & \sigma_2 & \cdots & 0 \\ \vdots & \vdots & \ddots & 0 \\ 0 & 0 & \cdots & \sigma_N \end{bmatrix}$$

where $\sigma_1 \geq \sigma_2 \geq \sigma_3 \geq \ldots \ldots \geq \sigma_r \geq \sigma_{r+1} \geq \ldots \ldots \geq \sigma_N = 0$

Therefore, the SVD of the square matrix M can be represented as

$$M = UPV' = \begin{bmatrix} u_{1,1} & \cdots & u_{1,N} \\ \vdots & \ddots & \vdots \\ u_{N,1} & \cdots & u_{N,N} \end{bmatrix} \times \begin{bmatrix} \sigma_1 & 0 & \cdots & 0 \\ 0 & \sigma_2 & \cdots & 0 \\ \vdots & \vdots & \ddots & 0 \\ 0 & 0 & \cdots & \sigma_N \end{bmatrix}$$

$$\times \begin{bmatrix} v_{1,1} & \cdots & v_{1,N} \\ \vdots & \ddots & \vdots \\ v_{N,1} & \cdots & v_{N,N} \end{bmatrix} = \sum_{i=0}^{r} P_i U_i V_i^T \tag{7.6}$$

7.5 Proposed System

7.5.1 Fingerprint Image Embedding in ECG Signal

Step 1. A gray fingerprint image is taken as a watermark.

Step 2. The size of the watermark image is calculated.

Step 3. The ECG signal is converted into a 2-D signal with the same size as the grayscale fingerprint image.

Step 4. By applying SWT, the 2-D signal is decomposed into four subbands (Ca_1, Cv_1, Ch_1, and Cd_1).

Step 5. DCT is applied on the Cd_1 subband.

Step 6. SVD is applied on the resultant signal.

Step 7. By applying SWT, the fingerprint image is decomposed into four subbands (Ca_1, Cv_1, Ch_1, and Cd_1).

Step 8. DCT is applied on every subband of the decomposed watermark image.

Step 9. SVD is applied on every resultant image after applying DCT on the four subbands of the decomposed watermark.

Step 10. Singular value of the 2-D signal is modified using singular value of the Cd_1 subband of the watermark image after applying SWT and DCT.

Step 11. Inverse DCT (IDCT) is applied on the resultant signal followed by inverse SWT (ISWT) to embed the watermark within the 2-D signal.

Step 12. The watermarked ECG signal is reshaped into a 1-D signal (Figure 7.7).

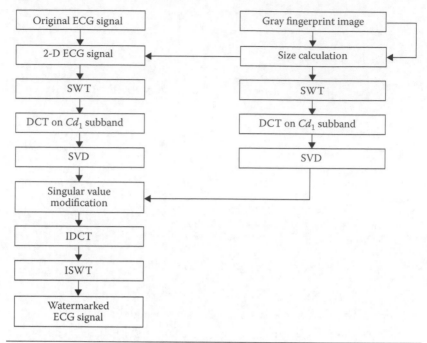

Figure 7.7   Watermark (fingerprint) embedding.

7.5.2 Fingerprint Image Extraction from Watermarked ECG Signal

Step 1. The watermarked ECG signal is reshaped into a 2-D signal again.

Step 2. By applying SWT, the watermarked ECG signal is decomposed into four subbands (Ca_1, Cv_1, Ch_1, and Cd_1).

Step 3. DCT is applied on the Cd_1 subband of the signal.

Step 4. SVD is applied on the resultant signal.

Step 5. Singular value of the watermarked signal is modified to extract the watermark from it.

Step 6. IDCT is applied followed by ISWT on the resultant signal to extract the fingerprint image from the watermarked signal (Figure 7.8).

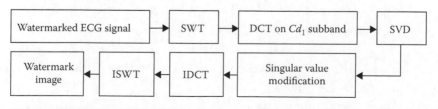

Figure 7.8   Watermark (fingerprint) extraction.

7.5.3 *Comparative Study between Original ECG Signal*
Features and Watermarked ECG Signal Features

Step 1. Modified Pan–Tompkins algorithm [25,28] is applied on the original ECG signal for the detection of P, QRS, and T components.

Step 2. ECG features, that is, RR, PP, QQ, SS, PR, QT, and QTc are measured from the peak detected ECG signal.

Step 3. Modified Pan–Tompkins algorithm is applied on the watermarked ECG signal for the detection of P, QRS, and T components.

Step 4. ECG features, that is, RR, PP, QQ, SS, PR, QT, and QTc are measured from the peak detected ECG signal.

Step 5. Extracted ECG features of the original ECG signal are stored in a remote database.

Step 6. Extracted ECG features of the watermarked ECG signal are fetched into a remote feature-matcher.

7.5.4 *Joint Feature Matching*

Step 1. Extracted features are stored on a remote database using any fingerprint feature extraction algorithm from the original fingerprint image.

Step 2. Extracted features are stored on a remote feature-matcher using the same fingerprint feature extraction algorithm from the recovered fingerprint image.

Step 3. Joint features are obtained from the extracted watermarked image (finger print) and watermarked ECG signal are matched in the feature-matcher for multimodal biometric authentication systems (Figure 7.9).

7.6 Results and Discussions

MATLAB® 7.0.1 software is extensively used for the study of the ECG watermarking embedding and extraction processes [32–34]. The resulting images are shown in Figures 7.10 through 7.12.

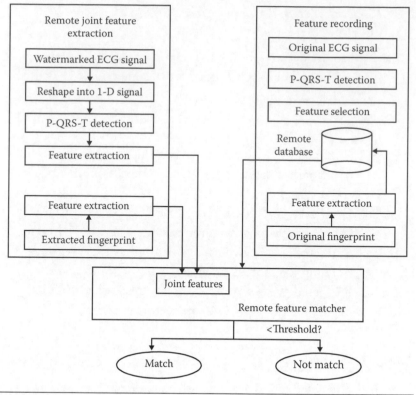

Figure 7.9 Joint feature matching.

7.6.1 Peak Signal to Noise Ratio

PSNR measures the quality of a watermarked signal. This performance metric is used to determine perceptual transparency of the watermarked signal with respect to the original signal. The PSNR is basically the ratio between the maximum possible value (power) of a signal and the power of noise that affects the original signal quality [29].

$$PSNR = \frac{XY \max\limits_{x,y} P_{x,y}^2}{\sum\limits_{x,y} \left(P_{x,y} - \bar{P}_{x,y}\right)^2}
\qquad (7.7)$$

where M and N are the number of rows and columns in the input signal, $P_{x,y}$ is the original signal, and $\bar{P}_{x,y}$ is the watermarked signal. PSNR between the original signal and the watermarked signal for this SWT-DCT-SVD–based method is 40.1034.

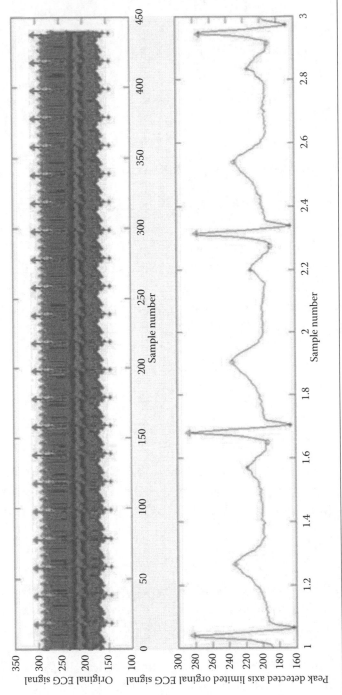

Figure 7.10 Peak detected original ECG signal and peak detected axis limited original ECG signal.

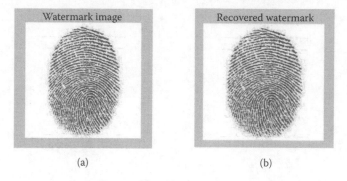

Figure 7.11   Watermark image (a) and recovered image (b).

7.6.2 Correlation Coefficient

After a secret image embedding process, the similarity of original signal x and watermarked signal x' is measured by the standard correlation coefficient (c). This coefficient measures the strength and the direction of linear relationship between two variables. The correlation coefficient is also referred to as the Pearson product moment correlation [30]. C is expressed as follows:

$$C = \frac{\displaystyle\sum_m \sum_n (x_{mn} - x')(y_{mn} - y')}{\sqrt{\left(\displaystyle\sum_m \sum_n (x_{mn} - x')^2\right)\left(\displaystyle\sum_m \sum_n (y_{mn} - y')^2\right)}} \tag{7.8}$$

where y and y' are transforms of x and x'. The correlation value between the original watermark fingerprint and the recovered watermark fingerprint image for this SWT-DCT-SVD–based method is 0.9884.

7.6.3 Structural Similarity Index Metric

SSIM is based on the structural information of the image. It provides a good measure for different kinds of images, from natural scenes to medical images [31]. SSIM is a recently proposed approach for image quality assessment. The SSIM index is capable of measuring similarities between two images. This particular index has also been designed to improve traditional metrics such as PSNR and mean squared error, which have been proved to be inconsistent with human eye perception.

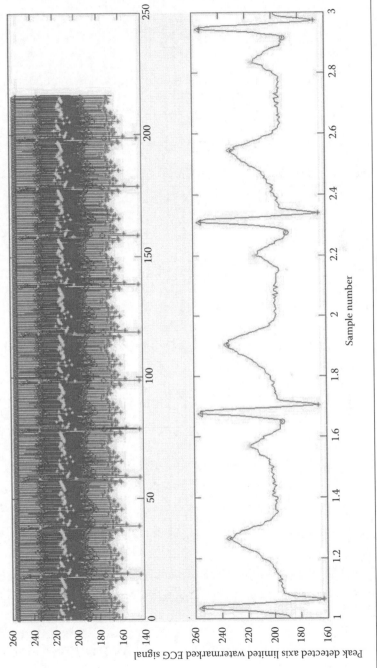

Figure 7.12 Peak detected watermarked ECG signal and peak detected axis limited watermarked ECG signal.

If two nonnegative images are placed together, mean intensity can be represented by the following equation:

$$\mu_x = 1/N \sum_{i=1}^{N} x_i \tag{7.9}$$

Standard deviation can be represented by the following equation:

$$\sigma_x = \left(\frac{1}{N-1} \sum_{i=1}^{N} (x_i - \mu_x)^2 \right)^{1/2} \tag{7.10}$$

Contrast comparison $c(x, y)$—difference of σ_x and σ_y

$$c(x, y) = \frac{2\sigma_x \sigma_y + C_2}{\sigma_x^2 + \sigma_y^2 + C_2} \tag{7.11}$$

Luminance comparison can be defined by the following equation:

$$l(x, y) = (2\mu_x \mu_y + C_1)/\mu_x^2 + \mu_y^2 + C_1 \tag{7.12}$$

where C_1 and C_2 are constants. Structure comparison is conducted $s(x, y)$ on these normalized signals ($x - \mu_x)/\sigma_x$ and ($y - \mu_y)/\sigma_y$

$$S(x, y) = f(l(x, y), c(x, y), s(x, y)) \tag{7.13}$$

$$\text{SSIM}(x, y) = [l(x, y)]^{\alpha} \cdot [C(x, y)]^{\beta} \cdot [S(x, y)]^{\gamma} \tag{7.14}$$

$$\text{SSIM}(x, y) = \left[(2\mu_x \mu_y + C_1)(2\sigma_{xy} + C_2) \right] / \left(\mu_x^2 + \mu_y^2 + C_1 \right) \left(\mu_x^2 + \mu_y^2 + C_2 \right) \tag{7.15}$$

α, β, and γ are parameters used to adjust the relative importance of the three components.

The SSIM between the original watermark fingerprint and the recovered watermark fingerprint image for this SWT-DCT-SVD–based method is 0.9830.

Tables 7.1 through 7.8 show that ECG features remained almost unaffected by watermarking for both cases of DWT-DCT-SVD based and SWT-DCT-SVD based approaches. However, Table 7.9 shows that the SWT-DCT-SVD–based approach remarkably improved the

Table 7.1   RR Intervals of Two Consecutive Peaks before and after Watermarking

SL. NO.	INTERVAL	TIME INTERVALS BEFORE WATERMARKING (s)	DWT-DCT-SVD–BASED APPROACH TIME INTERVALS AFTER WATERMARKING (s)	SWT-DCT-SVD–BASED APPROACH TIME INTERVALS AFTER WATERMARKING (s)
1	RR	0.6450	0.6450	0.6450
2		0.6400	0.6400	0.6400
3		0.6350	0.6350	0.6350
4		0.6300	0.6350	0.6350
5		0.6250	0.6250	0.6250
6		0.6250	0.6200	0.6200
Average		0.633333	0.633333	0.633333

Table 7.2   SS Intervals of Two Consecutive Peaks before and after Watermarking

SL. NO.	INTERVAL	TIME INTERVALS BEFORE WATERMARKING (s)	DWT-DCT-SVD–BASED APPROACH TIME INTERVALS AFTER WATERMARKING (s)	SWT-DCT-SVD–BASED APPROACH TIME INTERVALS AFTER WATERMARKING (s)
1	SS	0.6300	0.6450	0.6450
2		0.6400	0.6400	0.6400
3		0.6350	0.6350	0.6350
4		0.6350	0.6350	0.6350
5		0.6200	0.6200	0.6200
6		0.6250	0.6250	0.6250
Average		0.630833	0.633333	0.633333

Table 7.3   QQ Intervals of Two Consecutive Peaks before and after Watermarking

SL. NO.	INTERVAL	TIME INTERVALS BEFORE WATERMARKING (s)	DWT-DCT-SVD–BASED APPROACH TIME INTERVALS AFTER WATERMARKING (s)	SWT-DCT-SVD–BASED APPROACH TIME INTERVALS AFTER WATERMARKING (s)
1	QQ	0.6300	0.6300	0.6300
2		0.6550	0.6550	0.6550
3		0.6250	0.6250	0.6250
4		0.6400	0.6400	0.6400
5		0.6000	0.6000	0.6000
6		0.6500	0.6500	0.6450
Average		0.633333	0.633333	0.6325

Table 7.4   TT Intervals of Two Consecutive Peaks before and after Watermarking

SL. NO.	INTERVAL	TIME INTERVALS BEFORE WATERMARKING (s)	DWT-DCT-SVD–BASED APPROACH	SWT-DCT-SVD–BASED APPROACH
			TIME INTERVALS AFTER WATERMARKING (s)	TIME INTERVALS AFTER WATERMARKING (s)
1	TT	0.6450	0.6450	0.6500
2		0.6400	0.6400	0.6400
3		0.6350	0.6400	0.6400
4		0.6400	0.6300	0.6350
5		0.6200	0.6250	0.6100
6		0.6200	0.6100	0.6200
Average		0.633333	0.631666667	0.6325

Table 7.5   Consecutive PR Intervals before and after Watermarking

SL. NO.	INTERVAL	TIME INTERVALS BEFORE WATERMARKING (s)	DWT-DCT-SVD–BASED APPROACH	SWT-DCT-SVD–BASED APPROACH
			TIME INTERVALS AFTER WATERMARKING (s)	TIME INTERVALS AFTER WATERMARKING (s)
1	PR	0.1100	0.1050	0.1050
2		0.1150	0.1100	0.1100
3		0.1100	0.1050	0.1050
4		0.1150	0.1100	0.1100
5		0.1100	0.1100	0.1100
6		0.1100	0.1100	0.1100
Average		0.111667	0.108333	0.108333

Table 7.6   Consecutive QT Intervals before and after Watermarking

SL. NO.	INTERVAL	TIME INTERVALS BEFORE WATERMARKING (s)	DWT-DCT-SVD–BASED APPROACH	SWT-DCT-SVD–BASED APPROACH
			TIME INTERVALS AFTER WATERMARKING (s)	TIME INTERVALS AFTER WATERMARKING (s)
1	QT	0.2550	0.2550	0.2500
2		0.2700	0.2700	0.2700
3		0.2550	0.2550	0.2550
4		0.2650	0.2700	0.2700
5		0.2650	0.2600	0.2650
6		0.2850	0.2850	0.2750
Average		0.265833	0.265833	0.264167

Table 7.7 Consecutive QTc Intervals before and after Watermarking

			DWT-DCT-SVD–BASED APPROACH	SWT-DCT-SVD–BASED APPROACH
SL. NO.	INTERVAL	TIME INTERVALS BEFORE WATERMARKING (s)	TIME INTERVALS AFTER WATERMARKING (s)	TIME INTERVALS AFTER WATERMARKING (s)
1	QTc	0.3175	0.3175	0.3175
2		0.3375	0.3375	0.3375
3		0.3200	0.3388	0.3200
4		0.3339	0.3388	0.3326
5		0.3352	0.3415	0.3352
6		0.3605	0.3429	0.3620
Average		0.3341	0.336167	0.334133

Table 7.8 Consecutive QRS Complex Durations before and after Watermarking

			DWT-DCT-SVD–BASED APPROACH	SWT-DCT-SVD–BASED APPROACH
SL. NO.	DURATION	TIME INTERVALS BEFORE WATERMARKING (s)	TIME INTERVALS AFTER WATERMARKING (s)	TIME INTERVALS AFTER WATERMARKING (s)
1	QRS	0.0550	0.0550	0.0550
2		0.0700	0.0700	0.0700
3		0.0550	0.0550	0.0550
4		0.0650	0.0650	0.0650
5		0.0600	0.0600	0.0600
6		0.0800	0.0800	0.0800
Average		0.064167	0.064167	0.064167

Table 7.9 PSNR, Correlation, and SSIM Index

	DWT-DCT-SVD–BASED APPROACH	SWT-DCT-SVD–BASED APPROACH
PSNR between Original ECG and Watermarked ECG	39.9900	40.1034
Correlation between Original and Fingerprint Extracted Fingerprint	0.9815	0.9884
SSIM Index between Original and Fingerprint Extracted Fingerprint	0.9341	0.9830

value of PSNR, correlation, and SSIM, which claims the efficacy of the proposed method.

As discussed, the basic measure of error of a verification system is FRR and FAR. Due to the high correlation and SSIM values of the recovered fingerprint image, it is possible to retrieve most of the feature points of the fingerprint at the remote end. The above results

RR intervals

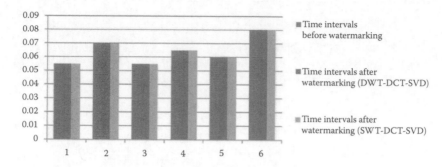

Figure 7.13 RR intervals.

QRS complex

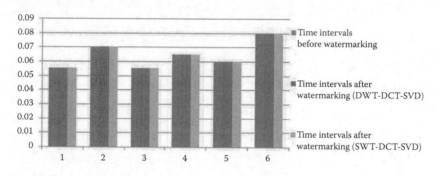

Figure 7.14 QRS complex.

QTc intervals

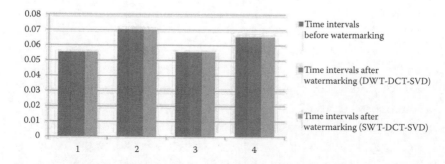

Figure 7.15 QTc intervals.

also show that even after watermarking, the devalorized ECG features have been successfully retained. Therefore, it can be concluded that FRR and FAR can be significantly improved by this proposed multimodal system in comparison to any unimodal system, although here, the FRR and FAR solely depend on the selection of fingerprint extraction algorithms (Figures 7.13–7.15).

7.6.4 Robustness Test of the Proposed Algorithm

Different types of digital signal processing attacks can remove or degrade the watermarks. The parameter that measures the immunity of the watermark against such changes by digital signal processing attacks is called robustness. In the proposed method described in this chapter, the results obtained as a measure for the robustness of the technique, for one of the most common digital signal processing attacks (Gaussian white noise), have been presented.

7.6.4.1 *Effect of White Gaussian Noise*   The following equation represents a simple model of the ECG signal

$$f(t) = s(t) + n(t) \tag{7.16}$$

where $f(t)$ is the vector signal. $s(t)$ and $n(t)$ denote ECG signals and white Gaussian noise $N(0, \sigma2)$, respectively.

Table 7.10   Change of Extracted Features as an Effect of White Gaussian Noise

SIXTH INTERVAL	WATERMARKED SIGNAL (SWT-DCT-SVD–BASED APPROACH)	NOISY WATERMARKED SIGNAL (SWT-DCT-SVD–BASED APPROACH) (dB = 40)	NOISY WATERMARKED SIGNAL (SWT-DCT-SVD–BASED APPROACH) (dB = 50)
RR	0.6200	0.6200	0.6200
SS	0.6250	0.6250	0.6250
QQ	0.6450	0.6500	0.6450
TT	0.6200	0.6050	0.6100
PR	0.1100	0.1100	0.1150
QT	0.2750	0.2900	0.2850
QTc	0.3620	0.3620	0.3620
Sixth QRS Duration	0.0800	0.0800	0.0800

Table 7.11   Change of PSNR, Correlation, and SSIM Index as an Effect of White Gaussian Noise

	SWT–DCT–SVD–BASED APPROACH	EFFECT OF WHITE GAUSSIAN NOISE IN SWT-DCT-SVD–BASED APPROACH (dB = 40)	EFFECT OF WHITE GAUSSIAN NOISE IN SWT-DCT-SVD–BASED APPROACH (dB = 50)
PSNR between Original ECG and Watermarked ECG	40.1034	40.1096	40.1096
Correlation between Original and Fingerprint Extracted Fingerprint	0.9884	0.9886	0.9886
SSIM Index between Original and Fingerprint Extracted Fingerprint	0.9830	0.9828	0.9841

Because the watermarked signal size entirely depends on the fingerprint image dimension, apart from the compression attack, the above results show that the proposed watermarking technique is robust enough against the most common signal processing attack, Gaussian noise (Tables 7.10 and 7.11). Hence, the efficacy of the proposed method also claims robustness against common signal attacks such as noise.

7.7 Conclusion

The proposed method is a multimodal biometric authentication system. Being a multimodal system, it enjoys various advantages over the unimodal biometric system. This method is less susceptible to noise, less vulnerable to spoofing, and resistant to intraclass similarity. Moreover, this multimodal system also provides significantly better FAR and FRR over other systems. Immunity to common signal attacks makes the method robust as well. Another advantage of this technique is that, in most of the blind watermarking methods, binary images are hidden. However, the grayscale image has been successfully hidden as a watermark in this methodology. Although this proposed method has a bunch of advantages, there are a few weaknesses that need attention for the betterment of this technique. The FAR and FRR of the system depend on the selection of a fingerprint feature algorithm because FAR and FRR values vary with different types of algorithms. In addition, because the fingerprint image is capable of watermarking only that portion of the signal that is equal to the size of the image, the remaining part of the signal gets wasted; this ultimately decreases the PSNR value. Overall, the method serves as a secure and strong authentication system. It also provides scope for further research in areas of watermarking with various types of images. Further investigation can lead to the use of colored fingerprint images for the purpose of watermarking.

References

1. R. Belguechi, V. Alimi, E. Cherrier, P. Lacharme, and C. Rosenberger. An Overview on Privacy Preserving Biometrics. Université de Caen Basse-Normandie, Caen, France. In *Recent Application in Biometrics*. July 2011. Dr. Jucheng Yang (Ed.), ISBN:978-953-307-488-7, InTech, Available from: http://www.intechopen.com/books/recent-application-inbiometrics/an-overview-on-privacy-preserving-biometrics.
2. F. Beritelli and A. Spadaccini. Human Identity Verification Based on Heart Sounds: Recent Advances and Future Directions. Dipartimento di Ingegneria Elettrica, Elettronica ed Informatica (DIEEI), University of Catania, Italy. 2011.
3. Available at http://onlinemca.com/seminars/biometrix.php.
4. Available at http://www.superpages.com/supertips/advantages-of-bio metrics.html.
5. Frost and Sullivan. *A Best Practices Guide to Fingerprint Biometrics Ensuring a Successful Biometrics Implementation.* http://www.frost.com/prod/servlet/cpo/240303611.
6. Available at http://www.mistralsolutions.com/hs-downloads/tech-briefs/nov10-article-1.html.
7. Available at http://www.webopedia.com/TERM/F/false_acceptance.html.
8. Available at http://searchsecurity.techtarget.com/definition/false-acceptance.
9. P. Lacharme and A. Plateaux. *PIN-Based Cancelable Biometrics.* GREYC Research Lab, Ensicaen-UCBN-CNRS, 6 Boulevard Maréchal Juin, 14000 Caen, France.
10. Available at http://www.scribd.com/doc/70263759/03-Bio-Metrics-Exercise-3-2005.
11. S. Latifi and N. Solayappan. *A Survey of Unimodal Biometric Methods, Security and Management.* Department of Electrical Engineering, University of Nevada at Las Vegas, NV. 57–63, 2006.
12. Available at http://en.wikipedia.org/wiki/Fingerprint.
13. Available at http://www.crimescene-forensics.com/History_of_Fingerprints.html.
14. D. Maltoni, D. Maio, A.K. Jain, and S. Prabhakar. *Handbook of Fingerprint Recognition,* 1st Edition. Springer, 2003, ISBN 0-387-95431-7.
15. A.M. Bazen. *Fingerprint Identification—Feature Extraction, Matching, and Database Search.* Final version: August 19, 2002. Available at http://doc.utwente.nl/64943/1/Bazen02_thesis_Fingerprint_Matching_-_Feature_Extraction,_Matching,_and_Database_Search.pdf.

16. Ashish Mishra. Multimodal biometrics it is: Need for future Systems. *International Journal of Computer Applications* 3(4), 28–33, June 2010. Published By Foundation of Computer Science.

17. Y. Wang, F. Agrafioti, D. Hatzinakos, and K.N. Plataniotis. Analysis of human electrocardiogram for biometric recognition. *EURASIP Journal on Advances in Signal Processing* 2008. Hindawi Publishing Corporation. Article ID 148658. doi:10.1155/2008/148658.

18. Available at http://en.wikipedia.org/wiki/Electrocardiography.

19. Available at http://www.mauvila.com/ECG/ecg_artifact.htm.

20. M.E. Cain, J.L. Anderson, M.F. Arnsdorf, J.W. Mason, M.M. Scheinman, and A.L. Waldo. Signal-averaged electrocardiography, *J. Am. Coll. Cardiol.* 27, 238–249, 1996. American College of Cardiology Expert consensus Document.

21. Available at http://www.cs.wright.edu/~phe/EGR199/Lab_1/.

22. Available at http://en.wikipedia.org/wiki/RR_interval.

23. Available at http://physionet.incor.usp.br/tutorials/hrv/.

24. N. Dey, S. Mukhopadhyay, A. Das, and S. Sinha Chaudhuri. Analysis of P-QRS-T components modified by blind watermarking technique within the electrocardiogram signal for authentication in wireless telecardiology using DWT. *International Journal of Image, Graphics and Signal Processing* 4(7), 33–46, 2012.

25. Available at http://en.wikipedia.org/wiki/Stationary_wavelet_transform.

26. N. Dey, A. Bardhan Roy, P. Das, A. Das, and S. Sinha Chaudhuri. DWT-DCT-SVD based intravascular ultrasound video watermarking. *World Congress on Information and Communication Technologies (WICT 2011)*, Trivandrum, November 10–12, 2012.

27. J. Pan and W.J. Tompkins. Real time QRS detection algorithm. *IEEE Transactions on Biomedical Engineering BME* 32(3), 230–236, March 1985.

28. Available at http://www.ni.com/white-paper/13306/en.

29. Available at http://mathbits.com/MathBits/TISection/Statistics2/correlation.htm.

30. H.K. Maity and S.P. Maity. Intelligent modified difference expansion for reversible watermarking. *The International Journal of Multimedia & Its Applications* 4(4), 83–95 August 2012.

31. Available at http://en.wikipedia.org/wiki/Structural_similarity.

32. R.M. Rangayyan, http://www.enel.ucalgary.ca/People/Ranga/enel563/SIGNAL_DATA_FILES/.

33. R.M. Rangayyan. *Biomedical Signal Analysis: A Case-Study Approach*. IEEE Press and Wiley, New York. 516 pp. 2002. ISBN 0-471-20811-6.

34. R.M. Rangayyan, Editor. *Biomedical Signal Processing*. Special Issue of the Journal Medical and Life Sciences Engineering, published by the Biomedical Engineering Society of India, vol. 13, 1994.

8

Facial Feature Point Extraction for Object Identification Using Discrete Contourlet Transform and Principal Component Analysis

N. G. Chitaliya and A. I. Trivedi

Contents

Abstract

In this chapter, facial feature point extraction from a face data set is particularly of interest mainly for mobile robotics applications as well as for visual surveillance systems. A feature-based classification approach using fast discrete contourlet transform and Principal Component Analysis (PCA) is used in this method. The preprocessing and filtering steps are applied to each image of the face data set. These are the main steps of the proposed algorithms because they are used to sharpen the images that are able to extract efficient feature vectors from the edges in later stages. The discrete contourlet transform is applied to the preprocessed image. Each face is decomposed using the contourlet transform. Low-frequency and high-frequency contourlet coefficients are obtained at different scales and various angles. The frequency coefficients are used as feature vectors for later processes. PCA is used to reduce the dimensionality of the feature vector. Finally, the eigen feature vector is used for the classifier. The test database is projected on a Contourlet-PCA subspace to retrieve the reduced coefficients. These coefficients are used to match the feature vector coefficients of the training data set using a Euclidian distance classifier. The experiments were carried out using Face94 and IIT_Kanpur databases. Recognition rates using the contourlet transform with and without preprocessing were compared with two distance measure classifiers (Euclidean distance classifier and neural network). A Euclidean distance classifier with preprocessing provides an improvement of almost 4% to 10% in the recognition rate compared with other methods.

8.1 Introduction of Object Recognition Systems

Humans recognize an object with little effort. However, for a machine, an image is a projection of a three-dimensional (3-D) structure into two-dimensions (2-D). The differing appearance of the same object with variations in different viewpoints, viewing distance, scaling, translation, rotation, varying illumination, cluttered background, intracategory appearance variations, etc., make this task difficult. This task is still a challenge in machine vision.

A complete object recognition system consists of the following modules [4], as shown in Figure 8.1:

A. Data acquisition
B. Preprocessing
C. Feature extraction and feature selection
D. Training
E. Performance evaluation

A. Data Acquisition. One of the most important requirements for designing a successful object recognition system is to have adequate and representative training and testing data sets. A sufficient number of training data sets is required to learn a decision boundary as a functional mapping between the feature vectors and the correct class labels. There is no rule that specifies how much data is sufficient. The designer must select the types of sensors or measurement schemes that provide the data such that it should be able to outline the classifier effectively [4].

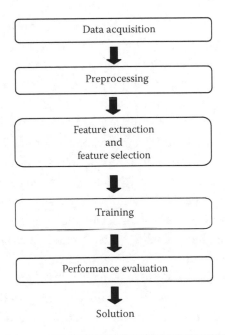

Figure 8.1 Modules of object recognition system.

B. *Preprocessing.* The goal is to condition the acquired data such that noises from various sources are removed as much as possible. Various filtering techniques are used if the user has prior knowledge regarding the spectrum of the noise. Conditioning may include the normalization of the data with respect to the mean and variance of the amplitude of the data normally, which is called the feature value. Preprocessing used for deblurring, image enhancement, or edge detection depends on the application domain [4,6].

C. *Feature Extraction and Feature Selection.* The goal of this step is to find a preferably small number of features that are particularly distinguishing or informative for the classification process and that are invariant to irrelevant transformations of the data. Better discriminating information may reside in the spectral or frequency domains. Feature extraction is usually obtained from a mathematical transformation of the data. In the spatial domain, feature descriptors are extracted using colors and geometric primitives such as lines, circles, or textures. In the frequency domain, feature extractions are performed by applying Discrete Cosine Transform, Discrete Fourier Transform (DFT), Fast Fourier Transform (FFT), Discrete Wavelet Transform (DWT), etc. Some of the methods find intensity discontinuity points, which are invariant to rotation, translation, and scale [1,4].

D. *Training.* After acquiring, preprocessing, and extracting the most informative features of the training data set, the classifier and training algorithms are selected. Classification can be considered as a function approximation problem that can use a variety of mathematical tools such as optimization algorithms. Most common object recognition algorithms use statistical approaches or neural network approaches. Statistical pattern recognition uses Bayes' classifier, naïve Bayes' classifier, *k*-nearest neighbor classifier, etc. Neural network approaches use multilayer perceptron, radial basis function, support vector machines, and self-organizing maps [1,3,4], among others.

E. *Performance Evaluation.* To get a good estimate of the generalization ability of a classifier, different methods like split-sample[6], cross-validation[7], Boot strapping[2] are used. Performance evaluation can be done by splitting the entire data set into two parts—a training data set and a testing data set. The training data set is used for actual training and the testing data set is used for testing the true field performance of the algorithm. Because an adequate and representative training data set is highly important for successful training, there are no fixed rules about the size of the training and testing data sets [2,3].

8.2 Designing the Classifier

The task of designing the classifier involves different modules such as feature extraction and feature matching. To validate the effectiveness of the classifier, different performance metrics were measured. This section covers the literature review on the related work done thus far in this area.

8.2.1 Different Approaches Used for Feature Extraction

A pattern recognition system that adjusts its parameters to find the correct decision boundaries, through a learning algorithm using a training set such that a cost function (mean square error between numerically encoded values of actual and predicted labels) is minimized, can be referred to as a classifier or model [6].

The object classification task uses two types of learning methods: supervised and unsupervised learning. Supervised learning is the term used to describe the training of a classifier with target data available for the training set. The aim of the object classifier is to find the correct mapping between the input data and the target data. Unsupervised learning does not use target data. The goal of learning is to find clusters in data or modeling distributions as opposed to finding the mapping.

Feature extraction (a set of variables that carry discriminating and characterizing information about an object) and feature selection algorithms are mainly important for object classification. There are basically three approaches used for feature extraction [2,4,6]:

A. Geometry-based approaches
B. Feature point–based approaches
C. Appearance-based approaches

A. Geometry-Based Approaches. Geometrical model–based feature extraction can be done by extracting geometric primitives such as lines, curves, or circles. They cannot handle variations in the lighting and viewpoints with certain occlusions. An excellent review of geometry-based object recognition can be found in the book by Mundy [10]. This chapter reviews the key advances of the geometric era and the underlying causes of the movement away from formal geometry and prior models toward the use of statistical learning methods based on appearance features. Although geometry-based approaches are invariants to viewpoints and illumination, dependency and complexity on statistical functions have made limited use of the method.

B. Feature Point–Based Approaches. The main idea behind the feature point–based object recognition algorithm lies in finding interest points, often occurring at intensity discontinuities that are invariant to change due to scale, illumination, and affine transformation. Feature point–based approaches find the different points that are invariant to the affine, rotation, translation, or scaling. Various feature-based algorithms are reviewed such as the Harris Corner Detector (HCD) [11], Scale-Invariant Feature Transform (SIFT) [12], Speeded-Up Robust Feature (SURF) transform [13], and Random Sample Consensus (RANSAC) [14].

HCD uses a combined corner and edge detector method based on the local correlation function to identify the regions of the image containing textures and isolated features. It shows good consistency and performance over a natural image. SIFT is invariant to image scaling, translation, and rotation and is partially invariant to illumination changes and affine or 3-D projection.

SIFT consists of four major stages: scale–space extrema detection, key point localization, orientation assignment, and key point descriptor. The first stage identifies key locations in the scale–space by looking for locations that are maxima–minima of a difference-of-Gaussian function [12]. Each point is used to generate a feature vector that describes the local image region sampled relative to its scale–space coordinate frame. Image keys are created from the feature vector, which allows for local geometric deformations by representing blurred image gradients in multiple orientation planes and at multiple scales. The keys were used as input for a nearest-neighbor indexing method that identified candidate object matches. Final verification of each match is achieved by finding a low-residual least-squares solution for the unknown model parameters.

SURF is a robust image detector and descriptor that was first presented by Herbert Bay [13]. SIFT and SURF algorithms employ slightly different ways of detecting features. SIFT builds an image pyramid, filtering each layer with Gaussians of increasing sigma values and taking the difference. SURF is based on sums of approximated 2-D Haar wavelet responses and makes an efficient use of integral images. It calculates the determinant of a Hessian blob detector, from which it uses an integer approximation. These computations are extremely fast with an integral image.

RANSAC, proposed by Fischler and Bolles [14], is an iterative method to estimate the parameters of a mathematical model from a set of observed data that contains outliers. It is a nondeterministic algorithm that produces a reasonable result only with a certain probability. The probabilities increase as more iterations are allowed. In RANSAC, there is a procedure that can estimate the parameters of a model that optimally explains or fits in the small data.

SURF is less time-consuming than SIFT whereas RANSAC is invariant to affine transform. SIFT-based methods are expected to perform better for objects with rich texture information because a sufficient number of key points can be extracted but require sophisticated indexing and matching algorithms for effective object recognition. An advantage of RANSAC is the ability to perform a robust estimation of the model parameters, that is, it can estimate the parameters with a high degree of accuracy even when a significant number of outliers are present in the data set. A disadvantage of RANSAC is that there is no upper bound on the time it takes to compute these parameters and a good initialization is needed.

C. *Appearance-Based Approaches*. Better discriminating information may reside in the spatial domain or frequency domain. Most recent appearance-based techniques involve feature descriptors and pattern recognition algorithms in the frequency domain.

Most widely used approaches perform linear transformations such as Principal Component Analysis (PCA) and Linear Discriminant Analysis (LDA). PCA, also known as Karhunen–Loeve transformation, is most commonly used as a dimensionality reduction technique in pattern recognition. It was originally developed by Pearson in 1901 [15] and generalized by Loeve in 1963. PCA does not take class information into consideration. The classes are best separated in the transformed space and is better handled by LDA, which considers intercluster as well as intracluster distances in its classification. PCA is used for two main purposes. First, it reduces the dimensions of data to a computationally feasible size. Second, it extracts the most representative features out of the input data so that although the size is reduced, the main features remain and are still be able to represent the original data [15,16].

The concept of the eigen picture was defined to indicate the eigen functions of the covariance matrix of a set of face images. Turk and Pentland [17] have developed an automated system using eigenfaces with the similar concept of classifying images into four different categories, which helps in recognizing the true/false positive of faces and in building a new set of image models. For nighttime detection and classification of vehicles, Thi et al. [18] used support vector machines with eigenvalues. Sahambi and Khorasani [19], used a neural network appearance–based 3-D object recognition using independent component analysis. The eigenfaces approach has been adopted in recognizing generic objects across different viewpoints and modeling illumination variations [20].

Frequency domain analysis is more attractive because it can provide more detailed information about the signal and its component frequencies. Over the past 10 years, wavelet theory has become an emerging and fast-evolving mathematical and signal processing tool for its many distinct merits. Different from the FFT, the wavelet transform can be used for multiscale analysis of the signal through dilation and translation, thus it can extract the time–frequency features of the signals effectively.

Wavelet transforms have been previously used for time series classification [21]. Originally, DFT was proposed for mapping the time domain function to the frequency domain. The wavelet transform [22] is expressed as the decomposition of a signal, $f(x) \in L^2(R)$, a family of functions that are translations and dilations of a mother wavelet function $\psi(x)$. The 2-D filter coefficients can be expressed as

$$h_{LL}(m,n) = h(m)h(n), \quad h_{LH}(k,l) = h(k)g(l)$$
$$h_{HL}(m,n) = g(m)h(n), \quad h_{HH}(k,l) = g(k)g(l) \tag{8.1}$$

where the first and second subscripts denote the low-pass and high-pass filtering, respectively, along the row and column directions of the image. Wavelet transform can be implemented (convolution and downsample) along the rows and columns separately. 2-D DWT is performed using low-pass and high-pass filters. After the decomposition of the four subbands, LL, LH, HL, and HH are obtained, which represent the average (A), horizontal (H), vertical (V), and diagonal (D) information respectively. The iteration of the filtering process produces the multilevel decomposition of an image. Wavelet transforms provide effective multiscale analysis but are not effective at representing the image with smooth contours in different directions. For acquiring more directional information, Multiscale Geometric Analysis (MGA) tools were proposed such as curvelet [28], ridgelet [24], bandlet [28], contourlet [23], etc.

Contourlet transform [23] is a multiscale and directional image representation that first uses a wavelet-like structure for edge detection, and then a local directional transform for contour segment detection. A double filter bank structure is used for obtaining sparse expansions for typical images having smooth contours. In the double filter bank structure, a Laplacian Pyramid (LP) is used to capture the point discontinuities, followed by a Directional Filter Bank (DFB), which is used to link these point discontinuities into linear structures. The contourlets have elongated supports at various scales, directions, and aspect ratios. This allows contourlets to efficiently approximate a smooth contour at multiple resolutions. In 2005, Zhou et al. [24] pioneered the use of nonsubsampled contourlets as the latest MGA tool. Yan et al. [25] proposed a face recognition approach based on contourlet transform, whereas Yang et al. [26] proposed a multisensor image fusion method based on nonsubsampled contourlet transforms. Extensive experimental results show that the scheme proposed by Yan, which is based on the contourlet transform, performs better than the method based on stationary wavelet transforms [23]. Srinivasan Rao et al. [27] used feature vectors using contourlet transform for content-based image retrieval system.

Donoho and Duncan [28] introduced a new multiscale transform named curvelet transform, which was designed to represent edges and other singularities along curves much more efficiently than traditional transforms, that is, using fewer coefficients for a given accuracy of reconstruction. The implementation of the curvelet transform involves the following steps: (1) subband decomposition, (2) smooth partitioning, (3) renormalization, and (4) ridgelet analysis. There were two separate Fast Discrete Curvelet Transform (FDCT) algorithms introduced by Starck et al. [29]. The first algorithm is called the Unequally Spaced FFT (FDCT via USFFT), in which the curvelet coefficients are found by irregularly sampling the Fourier coefficients of an image. The second algorithm is the wrapping transform, which uses a series of translation and a wraparound techniques. The wrapping FDCT is more intuitive and uses less computation time. Use of the curvelet transform for image denoising is explained by Starck et al. [29]. A comparative study based on wavelet-, ridgelet-, and curvelet-based texture classification is well explained by Dettori and Semler [30].

Contourlet transform can represent information better than wavelet transform for images having more directional information with smooth contours [23] due to its properties such as directionality and anisotropy. This method has been selected to extract features for performing object classification tasks and for comparisons.

8.2.2 Feature Matching

To establish the similarity or closeness of two feature vectors in some feature spaces, a wide range of distance matrices are used for feature matching. A distance matrix calculates the distance between two point sets in a matrix space [31].

8.2.2.1 Minkowski Norms   The most commonly used distance matrices are the Minkowski norms. It is defined based on the L_p norm. The norms are popular for their simplicity, speed of calculation, and

quality of results. Similarity distance d between two feature vectors is calculated using the following equation:

$$d_P(x, y) = \left(\left[\sum_{i=1}^{N} \left[|x_i - y_i|^P \right] \right]^{\frac{1}{P}} \right) \tag{8.2}$$

where $x = (x_1, x_2, ..., x_N)$ and $y = (y_1, y_2, ..., y_N)$ are the query and targeted feature vectors, respectively. N is the number of elements in the vectors.

When $P = 1$, $d_1(x, y)$ is the city block distance also known as Manhattan distance (L_1)

$$L_1 = d_1(x, y) = \sum_{i=1}^{N} |x_i - y_i| \tag{8.3}$$

When $P = 2$, $d_2(x, y)$ is the Euclidean distance (L_2) and is calculated as

$$L_2 = d_2(x, y) = \left(\left[\sum_{i=1}^{N} \left[|x_i - y_i|^2 \right] \right]^{\frac{1}{2}} \right) \tag{8.4}$$

8.2.2.2 Histogram Intersection The histogram intersection is another simple distance matrix that is often used. It was proposed by Swain and Ballard [8]. Their objective was to find known objects within images using color histograms. It is able to handle partial matches when the size of the object with a feature vector x is less than the size of the image with the feature vector. The histogram distance d is given as

$$d_{\text{hist}}(x, y) = 1 - \frac{\sum_{i=1}^{N} (\min(x_i, y_i))}{\min(|x|, |y|)} \tag{8.5}$$

Colors that are not present in the query image do not contribute to the intersection distance. This reduces the contribution of background colors. The sum is normalized by the histogram with the fewest samples.

8.2.2.3 Bhattacharyya Distance A statistical measure, known as Bhattacharyya distance measure, is often used for comparing two probability density functions, which are most commonly used to measure color similarity between two regions [9]. It is very closely related to the Bhattacharyya coefficient, which is used to measure the relative closeness of the two samples taken into consideration. Bhattacharyya distance can be calculated as

$$d_{\text{Bha}}(x, y) = \sum_{i=1}^{N} \sqrt{x_i} \sqrt{y_i} \qquad (8.6)$$

where x_i and y_i are the probability density functions.

Chi-squared, Kullback–Leibler, earth mover's distance, x^2 statistics and quadratic distances, Mahalnobis distance, chessboard distance, and cosine distance are well-known distance measures used for different applications. The choice of distance metric to be used greatly depends on the application. For general usage, the Minkowski norms will often be a good choice. For applications in which speed is preferred over accuracy, the L_1 norm or histogram intersection can be used. For applications in which the different components cannot be assumed to be independent, a metric such as the Mahalanobis distance may be preferable. In this method, Euclidean distance measure has been used for feature matching in the training and testing data sets.

8.3   Object Identification Using Contourlet Transform and PCA

Designing an object classifier using contourlet transform and PCA mainly involves two tasks: (A) training the classifier and (B) object identification of the query image.

(A) Training the Classifier
   The following steps are performed during classifier training:
   a. Resize all the images of data set
   b. Preprocessing to get the sharp images from the given data set and perform the feature extraction of enhanced images
   c. Generate eigenmatrix for dimensionality reduction for fast retrieval

(B) *Object Identification of the Query Image*

The object identification task involves the following steps:

a. Resize the unidentified image to the same size as the training data set

b. Perform preprocessing to get the sharp images and perform the feature extraction of enhanced images

c. Project the image into eigenspace using the eigenmatrix of the trained classifier

d. Compute the similarity measure using the Euclidean distance classifier or the neural network classifier for best match feature vector from the eigenmatrix of the trained data set

e. Identify and label the objects using best match feature vector

8.3.1 Block Diagram of the Object Classifier

The objective of the proposed work is to extract feature vectors for image identification. Figure 8.2 illustrates the overall process of calculating contourlet transform and PCA applied to the training images and recognition of the testing data set. The proposed methods are

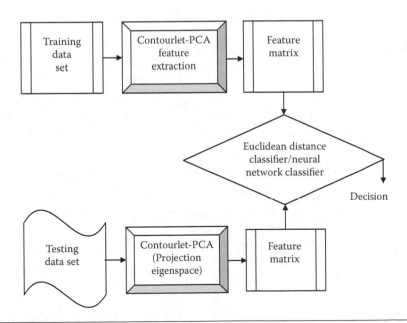

Figure 8.2   Block diagram of proposed object classifier system.

explained by Chitaliya and Trivedi [36,37] using Euclidean distance and neural networks. The first task of feature extraction and selection, and the second task of feature matching and object identification are executed as follows.

8.3.2 Data Set

For face identification, two different databases were used: Face94 and IIT_Kanpur data sets. The results for recognition using discrete curvelet transforms are compared with the discrete contourlet transform [23,28].

8.3.2.1 IIT_Kanpur Data Set
The IIT_Kanpur data set [34] consists of a total of 660 male and female images. The total database consists of 22 images of female faces and 38 images of male faces with 40 distinct subjects in upright, frontal position with tilting and rotation. Therefore, this is a more difficult database to work with. The size of each image is 640 × 480 pixels, with 256 gray levels per pixels. For each individual, three images were selected randomly for training and 10 images for testing. Figure 8.3a shows the original image of one female face having different positions and tilting. Figure 8.3b shows grayscale images of the IIT_Kanpur data set before filtering.

8.3.2.2 Face94 Data Set
The Face94 data set [35] consists of a total of 2,660 images. The data set consists of 20 female and 113 male face images with 20 distinct subjects containing variations in illumination and facial expression. For each individual, again three images were selected randomly for training and 10 images for testing out of 20 different types of face images. Figure 8.4a shows a female face image from the Face94 data set with different poses and Figure 8.4b shows some of the images from the Face94 data set used for training. Figure 8.5 shows the gray scale face images used for testing purpose from the Face94 data set.

8.3.3 Object Identification Modules

This subsection includes the theoretical background of the object identification task.

(a)

(b)

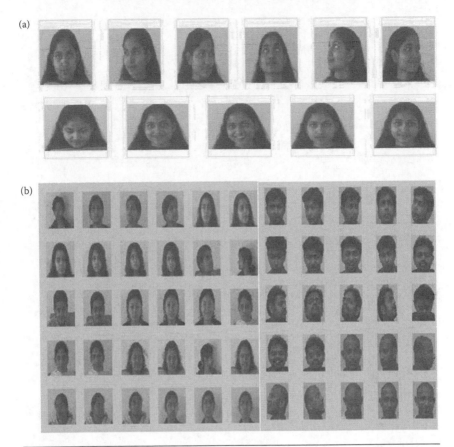

Figure 8.3 (a) Face images with different positions and tilting, and (b) grayscale images of the IIT_Kanpur data set.

8.3.3.1 Preprocessing

8.3.3.1.1 Unsharp Filter The unsharp filter is a simple sharpening operator that enhances edges and amplifies high-frequency components in an image via a procedure that subtracts an unsharped or smoothed version of an image from the original image [33]. Let S be the data set having P images for training and q images for testing. Color image $f_1(m, n)$ of size $m \times n$ is converted into a grayscale image. Unsharp masking produces an edge image $g(m, n)$ from an input image $f_1(m, n)$ by performing negative of Laplacian filter $f_{smooth}(m, n)$ as shown in Figure 8.6.

$$g(m, n) = f_1(m, n) \cdot f_{smooth}(m, n) \tag{8.7}$$

(a)

(b)

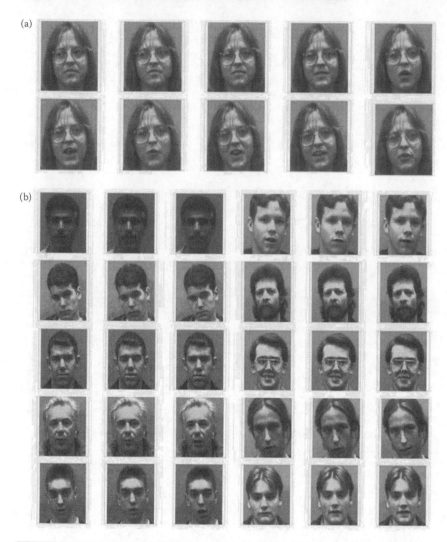

Figure 8.4 (a) Sample images from Face94 data set having different poses, and (b) some of the images from the Face94 data set used for training.

Convolution was performed with the unsharp mask U and the image $f_1(m, n)$ to get the edge image $g(m, n)$.

$$U = \frac{1}{(a+1)} \begin{bmatrix} -\alpha & \alpha-1 & -\alpha \\ \alpha-1 & \alpha+5 & \alpha-1 \\ -\alpha & \alpha-1 & -\alpha \end{bmatrix} \qquad (8.8)$$

The value of α controls the shape of the Laplacian function. The range of α is from 0 to 1.

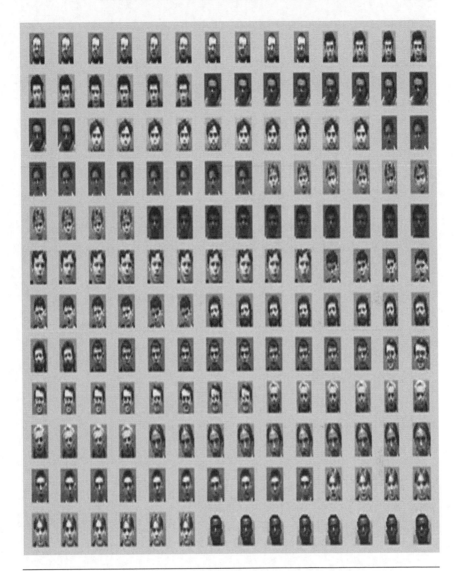

Figure 8.5   Some of the grayscale images from the Face94 data set used for testing.

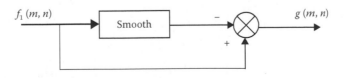

Figure 8.6   Spatial sharpening.

8.3.3.1.2 Thresholding Using Otsu's Method   Thresholding was applied on the image after applying the unsharp filter. Global thresholding was applied using Otsu's method [33]. Otsu's method is one of the better threshold selection methods with respect to uniformity and shape measures. The Otsu method is optimal for thresholding large objects from the background [32].

Otsu's algorithm performs the following steps:

1. Computes the normalized histogram of the input image. Denotes the components of the histogram by p_i where $i = 0, 1, 2, ..., L-1$, where L denotes distinct intensity levels in a digital image of size $m \times n$, and h_i denotes the total number of pixels with intensity i. The normalized histogram p_i is calculated as

$$p_i = \frac{h_i}{m \times n} \tag{8.9}$$

2. Calculates the cumulative sums, $P_1(k)$, for $k = 0, 1, 2, ... L-1$ using

$$P_1(k) = \sum_{i=1}^{k} p_i \tag{8.10}$$

3. Computes the cumulative means, $m(k)$, for $k = 0, 1, 2... L-1$ using

$$m(k) = \sum_{i=1}^{k} i p_i \tag{8.11}$$

4. Computes the global intensity mean m_G using

$$m_G = \sum_{i=0}^{L-1} i p_i \tag{8.12}$$

5. Calculates the class variance $\sigma_B^2(k)$ for $k = 0, 1, 2... L-1$ using

$$\sigma_B^2(k) = \frac{[m_G P_1(k) - m(k)]^2}{P_1(k)[1 - P_1(k)]} \tag{8.13}$$

6. Obtain Otsu's threshold, k^* as the value of k for which $\sigma_B^2(k)$ is maximum. If the maximum is not unique, obtain k^* by

averaging the values of k corresponding to the various maxima detected.

7. Obtain the separable measure, η^*, by evaluating Equation 8.20 at $k = k^*$.

$$\eta(k) = \frac{\sigma_B^2(k)}{\sigma_G^2} \qquad (8.14)$$

where σ_G^2 is the global variance and can be derived by

$$\sigma_G^2(k) = \sum_{i=0}^{L-1} (i - m_G)^2 \, p_i \qquad (8.15)$$

8.3.3.1.3 Removing Border Objects If the original image is considered as a mask, the marker image $f_{mask}(m, n)$ can be obtained [33] using Equation 8.16.

$$f_{mask}(m, n) = g(m, n) \text{ if } g(m, n) \text{ is on the border of the image} \qquad (8.16)$$
$$0 \quad \text{otherwise}$$

The clear border image can be constructed by

$$f(m, n) = g(m, n) - f_{mask}(m, n) \qquad (8.17)$$

The image, after preprocessing steps, is shown in Figure 8.7. Feature extraction is applied on the preprocessed images.

8.3.3.2 Feature Extraction Using Contourlet Transform and Curvelet Transform Feature extraction is an essential preprocessing step in pattern recognition and machine learning problems. Feature extraction maps a larger information data space into a smaller feature space. The fundamental idea of feature extraction is to perform all computations in a smaller, simpler space.

Feature extraction pattern involves three design steps:

- *Feature Construction*: This is the most challenging part of the pattern recognition system.
- *Feature Selection*: This decision determines the balance between the search time and the postprocessing time. For fast retrieval of the data set from the feature matrix, eigenvalues

(a)

(b)

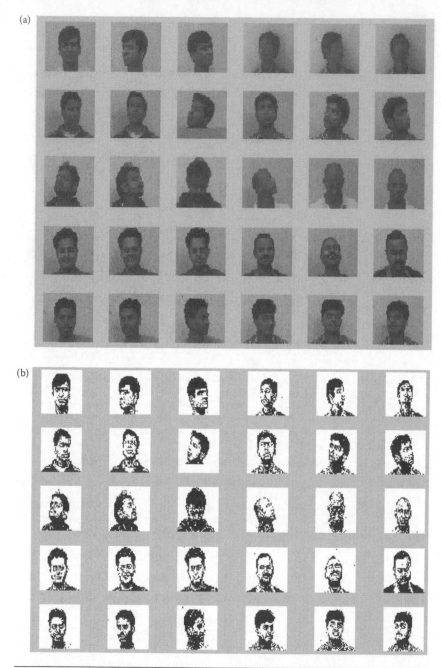

Figure 8.7   (a) Original image, and (b) image after applying preprocessing.

are constructed using the feature matrix in the proposed methodology.

- *Feature Matching*: This determines how fast the system can search the feature space. Euclidean distance classifier is used for feature matching. After comparison, Euclidean distance was found to be the more efficient method when comparing the recognition rates.

8.3.3.2.1 Feature Construction   After literature review, discrete contourlet transform and discrete curvelet transform were found to be efficient transforms for extracting feature points due to the directionality and anisotropy property compared with discrete wavelet transform.

- *Discrete Contourlet Transform:* Multiscale and time–frequency localization of an image is offered by the use of wavelet transforms. Wavelet transforms are not effective in representing the images with smooth contours in different directions. Contourlet transform eliminates this problem by providing two additional properties known as directionality and anisotropy [23,24]. Contourlet transform is divided into two main steps: (1) Laplacian Pyramid (LP) Decomposition and (2) Directional Filter Bank (DFB). LP decomposes the original image into a low-pass image and a band-pass image. Each band-pass image is further decomposed by DFB. The multiscale and multidirectional decomposition of the image will be obtained by repeating the same steps on the low-pass image [23]. Contourlet transform is a multiscale and multidirectional image representation that uses a wavelet-like structure for edge detection in the first stage, and then a local directional transform for contour segment detection.

  A double filter bank structure of the contourlet is shown in Figure 8.8. The contourlet transform obtains sparse expansions for images having smooth contours. In the double filter bank structure, LP [23] is used to capture the point discontinuities. DFBs, followed by LP, is used to link these point discontinuities into linear structures. The contourlets have elongated supports at various scales, directions, and aspect ratios. These allow the contourlet to efficiently approximate

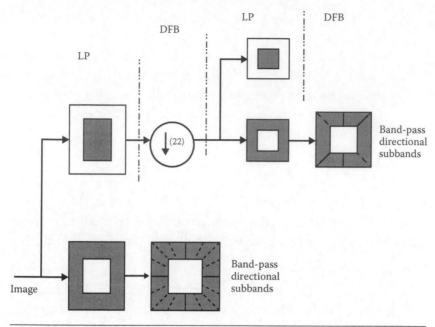

Figure 8.8   Double filter bank decomposition of discrete contourlet transform.

a smooth contour at multiple resolutions. In the frequency domain, the contourlet transform provides a multiscale and directional decomposition.

Band-pass images from the LP are applied to DFB so that directional information can be captured. The algorithm is applied on the coarse image. This combination of LP and DFB stages results in a double-iterated filter bank structure known as a contourlet filter bank. The contourlet filter bank decomposes the given image into directional subbands at multiple scales. The contourlet transform of two levels with a "pkva" filter is applied on the data set images $f(m, n)$. The resulting image gives the decomposed coefficients as C_1, C_{2-1}, C_{2-2},..., C_{n-1},..., C_{n-v}, where v is the number of directions, as shown in Figure 8.9. These coefficients are used to reorder the column vector I_i of the images. Image vector I_i is constructed by converting the coefficients to a column vector and then concatenation of all coefficient vectors. Let $I = (I_1, I_2, I_3,...I_p)$ be the feature image matrix constructed by a discrete contourlet coefficient, then eigenvalues and eigenvectors are calculated for I.

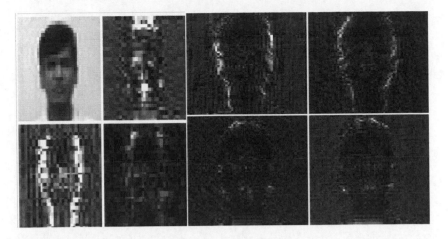

Figure 8.9 Decomposition of image using contourlet transform (two-level and pkva filter for pyramid and directional filter).

- *Discrete Curvelet Transform via Wrapping*: Candes and Donoho introduced a new multiscale transform called *curvelet transform*, which was designed to represent edges and other singularities along the curves much more efficiently than traditional transforms by using fewer coefficients for a given accuracy of reconstruction [28,29]. Implementation of curvelet transform involves subband decomposition, smooth partitioning, renormalization, and ridgelet analysis steps [29]. Candes et al. [38] introduced two separate Discrete Curvelet Transform algorithms. The first algorithm is the UnequiSpaced FFT transform (FDCT via USFFT), in which the curvelet coefficients are found by irregularly sampling the Fourier coefficients of an image. The second algorithm is the wrapping transform, which uses a series of translation and a wraparound techniques. FDCT based on the wrapping of Fourier samples has less computational complexity as it uses FFT instead of complex ridgelet transforms [29]. In FDCT via wrapping, a tight frame has been introduced as the curvelet support to reduce the data redundancy in the frequency domain [38]. Normally, ridgelets have a fixed length, which is equal to the image size, and a variable width, whereas curvelets have both variable width and length and represent more anisotropy. Therefore, the wrapping-based curvelet transform is simpler, less redundant, and faster in computation [30] than ridgelet-based curvelet transform.

Curvelet transform based on wrapping of Fourier samples takes a 2-D image as an input in the form of a Cartesian array $f(m, n)$ such that $0 \leq m < M, 0 \leq n < N$. It generates a number of curvelet coefficients indexed by scale j, an orientation l, and two spatial location parameters (k_1, k_2) as output. To form the curvelet texture descriptor, statistical operations are applied to these coefficients. Discrete curvelet coefficients can be defined as [29]:

$$C^D(j,l,k_1,k_2) = \sum_{\substack{0 \leq m \leq M \\ 0 \leq n \leq N}} f(m,n)\phi^D_{j,l,k_1,k_2}(m,n) \qquad (8.18)$$

Here, each $\phi^D_{j,l,k_1,k_2}(m,n)$ is a digital curvelet waveform. This curvelet approach implements the parabolic scaling law on the subbands in the frequency domain to capture the curved edges within an image more effectively. Curvelets exhibit an oscillating behavior in the direction perpendicular to their orientation in the frequency domain [29].

Wrapping-based curvelet transform is a multiscale transform with a pyramid structure consisting of many orientations at each scale. This pyramid structure consists of several subbands at different scales in the frequency domain. Subbands at high-frequency and low-frequency levels have different orientations and positions. The curvelet is nondirectional at the coarsest scale and becomes fine like a needle-shaped element at high scale. With an increase in the resolution level, the curvelet becomes finer and smaller in the spatial domain and shows more sensitivity to curved edges, which enables it to effectively capture the curves in an image.

To achieve higher level of efficiency, curvelet transform is usually implemented in the frequency domain. In the Fourier frequency domain, both the curvelet and the image are transformed and then multiplied. A combination of frequency responses of the curvelets at different scales and orientations gives the frequency tilting that covers the whole image in Fourier frequency domain as shown in Figure 8.10. The product of multiplication is called a wedge. The product is then inverse Fourier–transformed to obtain the curvelet coefficient.

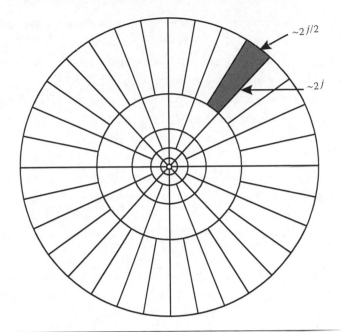

Figure 8.10   Curvelet in the Fourier frequency domain. (From D.L. Donoho, and M.R. Duncan, Digital Curvelet Transform: Strategy, Implementation and Experiments. Stanford University, California, Technical Report 1999.)

For collecting curvelet coefficients, inverse FFT is used. However, the trapezoidal wedge in the spectral domain is not suitable for use with the inverse Fourier transform. The wedge data cannot be accommodated directly into a rectangle the size of $2^j \times 2^{j/2}$. To overcome this problem, Candes et al. have formulated a wedge wrapping procedure in which a parallelogram with sides 2^j and $2^{j/2}$ is chosen as a support to the wedge data, as shown in Figure 8.11. The wrapping is

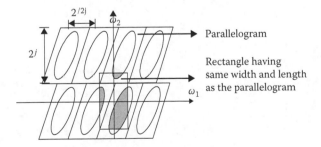

Figure 8.11   Wrapping wedge around the origin by periodic tilting of wedge data. The angle θ is in the range $\left(\dfrac{\pi}{4}, \dfrac{3\pi}{4} \right)$.

done by periodic tilting of the spectrum inside the wedge and then collecting the rectangular coefficient area in the center. The center rectangle of size $2^j \times 2^{j/2}$ collects all the information in that parallelogram. Discrete curvelet coefficients are obtained by applying 2-D inverse Fourier transform to this wrapped wedge data. Wrapping-based FDCT is much more efficient and provides better transform results than ridgelet-based curvelet transform.

Considering the total number of coefficients generated in the different levels of the curvelet transform and the execution speed for the generation of the coefficients, a lower coarse level is considered in the proposed method because it takes less execution time and provides only minor differences in the recognition rate compared with other levels.

The curvelet transform of one coarsest level and eight angles are applied on the data set images $f(m,n)$. In the proposed method, the images are decomposed into single scales using real-valued curvelets. The coefficients obtained using the curvelet transform are shown in Figure 8.12. These resultant curvelet coefficients are used to reorder the column vector I_i of the images. The FDCT via wrapping with preprocessing has been implemented in the proposed algorithm. Image vector X_i is constructed by converting coefficients to a column vector and then performing catenation of all coefficient vectors. Let $X = (X_1, X_2, X_3 \ldots X_P)$ be the feature image matrix constructed by discrete curvelet coefficient, then eigenvalue and eigenvectors are calculated for X.

Figure 8.12 Decomposition of image using curvelet transform.

8.3.3.2.2 *Feature Selection*   For selecting most efficient features, eigenvalues are calculated using PCA. PCA is used with two main purposes. First, it reduces the dimensions of the data to a computationally feasible size. Second, it extracts the most representative features out of the input data so that although the size is reduced, the main features remain, and are still able to represent the original data [17].

Eigenvectors and eigenvalues are calculated for the PCA. Eigenvectors are derived from the covariance matrix calculated from the feature matrix. Eigenvectors are invariant to the direction. The covariance matrix C of the input data is calculated from Equation 8.19

$$C = \frac{1}{P}\sum_{i=1}^{P}\phi_i\phi_i^T \tag{8.19}$$

where the difference ϕ_i between image vector I_i and mean are calculated as Equations 8.20 and 8.21.

$$\phi_i = I_i - \psi \tag{8.20}$$

$$\psi = \frac{1}{P}\sum_{i=1}^{P}I_i \tag{8.21}$$

All eigenvectors ν_i and eigenvalues λ_i of this covariance matrix are derived from Equation 8.22 as

$$\lambda_i = \frac{1}{P}\sum_{i=1}^{P}\left(v_i^T\phi_i^T\right)^2 \tag{8.22}$$

The set of eigenvectors will have corresponding eigenvalues associated with them, indicating the distribution of these eigenvectors in representing the whole data set. Typical references have shown that, only a small set of eigenvectors with top eigenvalues are enough to build up the whole image characteristic. PCA tends to find a P-dimensional subspace whose basis vectors correspond to the maximum variance direction in the original image space. New basis vectors define a subspace of images called eigenspace.

The value of eigenspace is represented using Equation 8.23

$$\varepsilon = \sum_{i=1}^{P} v_i \tag{8.23}$$

The weight ω_i of each input image vector I_i is calculated from the matrix multiplication of the different ϕ_i with the ε eigenspace matrix.

$$\omega_i = \phi_i \times \varepsilon \tag{8.24}$$

The image weight calculated from Equation 8.24 is the projection of an image on the object eigenspace, which indicates the relative "weight" of certainty that the image is that of a training data set or not.

The initial training set S consists of P different images. These images are transformed into a new set of vector T^w of all input training weights. Figure 8.13 shows the eigenimage after applying PCA to the contourlet transform with and without preprocessing. Figure 8.14 shows the eigenimage after applying PCA to the curvelet transform with and without preprocessing.

This transformation has showed how PCA has been used to reduce the original dimension of the data set $(P \times m \times n)$ to T^w [size $(P \times P)$]

Figure 8.13 Eigenfaces using contourlet-PCA after the preprocessing stage.

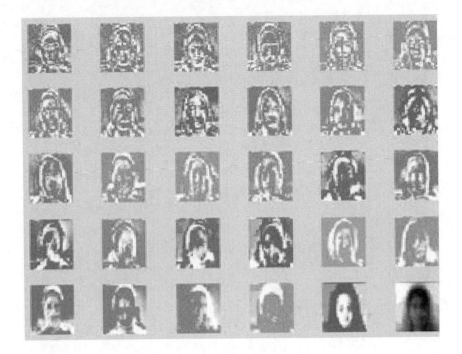

Figure 8.14 Eigenfaces using curvelet-PCA after the preprocessing stage.

where generally $P \ll m \times n$. Thus, the dimensions are greatly reduced and the most representative features of the whole data set still remain within P eigenfeatures only.

8.3.3.3 Feature Matching For matching best feature vectors from the eigenmatrix, a similarity measure like Euclidean distance measure is used. When a new image from the test set is considered for recognition, the image is mapped to contourlet-PCA subspace and weights are calculated for the particular image.

Object identification module steps can be summarized as the following:

Let X_image and Y_image represent the training and testing data sets, respectively. For gaining the best feature vector from the training data set, at first, all the images are normalized

- Feature extraction and selection
  The following steps are performed for feature extraction:
  - The RGB image is converted into a grayscale image and resized to 64 × 64

- Filtering is applied to remove noise and to sharpen the image. Unsharp contrast enhancement filter is used for the preprocessing of face images. Thresholding is applied to retrieve the edge points
- Feature extraction is performed using a discrete contourlet transform and discrete curvelet transform
  - *Contourlet Transform*: Decompose each image into the contourlet transform. As a result of performing contourlet transform, coefficients of low frequency and high frequency in different scales and various directions will be obtained. Decomposed coefficients with the same size $k \times k$ as C_1, C_{2-1}, C_{2-2}... C_{n-1},... C_{n-u}, where u is the number of directions. These coefficients are used to reorder the column vector I_i of the images. All the coefficients are arranged to make a column vector.
  - *Curvelet Transform*: Decompose each image into the curvelet transform. As a result of performing curvelet transform, coefficients of low frequency and high frequency in different scales and angles are obtained. Decomposed coefficients of different sizes are obtained as C_1, C_{2-1}, C_{2-2}... C_{n-1}... C_{n-v} where v is the number of angles. These coefficients are used to reorder the column vector I_i of the images. All the coefficients are arranged to make a column vector.
- The feature image matrix $I = (I_1, I_2, I_3 \ldots I_P)$ is constructed from the coefficient column vector I_i, where i represents the number of images
- Feature matrix I is transformed to lower dimension subspace T^w using PCA
- T^w consists of the weight calculated for each image of the respective data set
- Euclidean classifiers are used to measure the distance between the images
- Feature matching and identification
  - *Euclidean Distance Classifier:* Feature matching is performed using Euclidean distance classifier and is used for object identification. In this classification method, each image is transformed to a lower-order subspace with

contourlet-PCA/curvelet-PCA using the above steps. Upon observing an unknown test image X, the weights are calculated for that particular image and stored in the vector w_x. Afterward, w_x is compared with the weights of training set T^w using the Euclidian distance with Equation 8.25.

$$D_e(p,q) = \sqrt[2]{[T^w - w_x]} \qquad (8.25)$$

If average distance does not exceed some threshold value, the weight vector of the unknown image w_x is matched with the training data set.

- *Neural Network Classifier:* Backpropagation Neural Network was created by generalizing the Widrow-Hoff learning rule to multiple-layer networks and nonlinear differentiable transfer functions. Input vectors and the corresponding target vectors are used to train a network until it can approximate a function, associate input vectors with specific output vectors, or classify input vectors in an appropriate way as defined by the Application. As shown in Figure 88.15. Networks with biases, a sigmoid level, and a linear output layer are capable of approximating any function with a finite number of discontinuities [5]. Neuron Model (tansig, logsig, purelin) is an elementary neuron applied to the inputs. Each input is weighted with an appropriate weight matrix. The sum of the weighted inputs and the bias, form the input to the transfer function f. Neurons use any differentiable transfer function f to generate the output. The feed forward neural network uses the initialization, activation, weight training, and iteration steps to perform the learning phase. For the training neural network, the weight matrix T^w of the training data set obtained from the contourlet-PCA/curvelet-PCA is used as the input node of the neural network as shown in Figure 8.16. Feature vectors from the query image are matched with the feature vectors of the training set. The images of the training data set whose distance measures are close to the query images and below the specified threshold value is displayed.

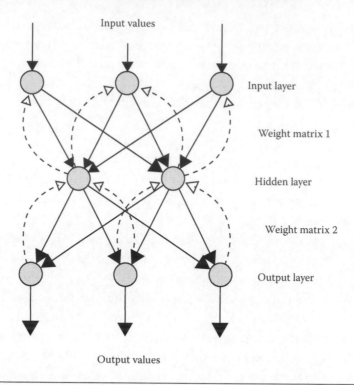

Figure 8.15   Feed forward neural network model.

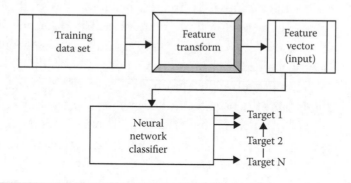

Figure 8.16   Learning phase of the neural network classifier.

For comparative analysis, two classifiers were used: Euclidean distance classifier and neural network classifier using a backpropagation method. For the training neural network classifier, weight matrix T^w of the training data set obtained from the contourlet-PCA is used as the input node of the neural network. Logarithmic sigmoid transfer function is used for the input layer and the hidden layer. Backpropagation training is implemented using gradient descent with momentum. For recognition of the query image, the weight vector of the query image is used to feed the respective neural network for obtaining the object recognition results. A threshold value near '1' represents the classification matching the target, and '0' represents the classification far away from the target.

Table 8.1a shows the comparative performance of the images using contourlet transform-PCA with a Euclidean distance classifier and a neural network classifier. Table 8.1b shows the comparative performance of the images using curvelet transform-PCA with a Euclidean distance classifier and a neural network classifier. Recognition rate with contourlet transform and curvelet transform with preprocessing and without preprocessing are compared according to Table 8.1a and 8.1b. Measurements with Euclidean distance and neural network with preprocessing are also compared for finding efficient distance measure. Table 8.2a and 8.2b report the time required to calculate the contourlet transform and curvelet transform using Euclidean distance and neural network with preprocessing and without preprocessing.

Table 8.1a Recognition Rate Using Discrete Contourlet Transform

DATA SET (JPEG IMAGE)	SIZE OF THE IMAGE (PIXEL)	CONTOURLET TRANSFORM WITHOUT PREPROCESSING EUCLIDEAN CLASSIFIER (%)	CONTOURLET TRANSFORM WITH PREPROCESSING EUCLIDEAN CLASSIFIER (%)	CONTOURLET TRANSFORM WITH PREPROCESSING NEURAL NETWORK CLASSIFIER (%)
Faces_94 female	180 × 200	92.57	97.27	90.90
Faces_94 Male	180 × 200	93.24	98.24	87.05
IIT_Kanpur Female	640 × 480	91.5	96	88
IIT_Kanpur Male	640 × 480	75.65	82	82

Table 8.1b Recognition Rate Using Discrete Curvelet Transform

DATA SET (JPEG IMAGE)	SIZE OF THE IMAGE (PIXEL)	CURVELET TRANSFORM WITHOUT PREPROCESSING EUCLIDEAN CLASSIFIER (%)	CURVELET TRANSFORM WITH PREPROCESSING EUCLIDEAN CLASSIFIER (%)	CURVELET TRANSFORM WITH PREPROCESSING NEURAL NETWORK CLASSIFIER (%)
Faces_94 Female	180 × 200	93.20	97.33	90.90
Faces_94 Male	180 × 200	94.6	91.76	79
IIT_Kanpur Female	640 × 480	90.55	90	80
IIT_Kanpur Male	640 × 480	74.8	78	61.6

TABLE 8.2a   Execution Time Required for Training and Testing Time of Face Images Using Discrete Contourlet Transform

| DATA SET (JPEG IMAGE) | PREPROCESSING TIME (S) | CONTOURLET TRANSFORM NEURAL NETWORK CLASSIFIER | | CONTOURLET TRANSFORM EUCLIDEAN DISTANCE CLASSIFIER | |
		TRAINING TIME FOR DATA SET (S)	TESTING TIME/FACE (S)	TRAINING TIME FOR DATA SET (S)	TESTING TIME/FACE (S)
Faces_94 Female	30.54	92.45	0.98	86.35	1.53
Faces_94 Male	37.10	93.06	1.11	88.23	1.54
IIT_Kanpur Female	15.98	52.37	1.52	46.35	2.18
IIT_Kanpur Male	16.30	56.02	1.54	50.05	2.32

Table 8.2b   Execution Time Required for Training and Testing Time of Face Images Using Discrete Curvelet Transform

| DATA SET (JPEG IMAGE) | PREPROCESSING TIME (S) | CURVELET TRANSFORM EUCLIDEAN DISTANCE CLASSIFIER | | CURVELET TRANSFORM NEURAL NETWORK CLASSIFIER | |
		TRAINING TIME FOR DATA SET (S)	TESTING TIME/FACE (S)	TRAINING TIME FOR DATA SET (S)	TESTING TIME/FACE (S)
Faces_94 Female	30.54	154.07	1.90	160.23	1.23
Faces_94 Male	37.10	184.63	2.13	190.05	1.56
IIT_Kanpur Female	15.98	61.10	2.35	65.89	1.67
IIT_Kanpur Male	16.30	63.61	2.65	69.60	1.89

Table 8.3   Recognition Rate Compared with Other Methods

METHOD	RECOGNITION RATE ON FACE94-DATA SET (%)	RECOGNITION RATE USING IIT KANPUR DATA SET (%)
Neural Network–PCA [39]	96	88
PCA [43]	89	—
ICA [43]	90	—
LDA [43]	93	—
Dual Wavelet Tree [44]	—	74.16 (Male)–86.66 (Female)
Discrete Wavelet Transform–Neural Network [40]	93.3	—
Discrete Contourlet Transform–PCA [42]	92.5 (Female)–93.2 (Male)	91.5 (Female)–75.6 (Male)
Discrete Curvelet Transform–PCA [41]	93.2 (Female)–94.6 (Male)	90.5 (Female)–74.8 (Male)
Discrete Contourlet Transform–Neural Network [41]	90.9 (Female)–87 (Male)	88 (Female)–82 (Male)
Discrete Curvelet Transform- Neural Network [41]	90.9 (Female)–79 (Male)	80 (Female)–61.6 (Male)

8.4 Comparisons with Other Methods

Comparative analysis of the recognition rate on the IIT_Kanpur data set and the Face94 data set using different approaches have been listed according to Table 8.3. PCA, LDA, and neural networks with wavelet transform and feature transforms are used. Different methods have used different numbers of images for training and testing data sets. Table 8.3 shows that the recognition rates of contourlet transform and curvelet transform outperformed the other methods used.

8.5 Conclusions

Recognition rates using the contourlet transform and curvelet transform with and without preprocessing are compared with different distance measures such as Euclidean distance classifier and neural networks. Recognition rates are compared finally as shown in the Tables 8.1 and 8.2. The recognition rate using contourlet transform with preprocessing and without preprocessing Euclidean distance classifier with preprocessing gives an improvement of almost 4% to 10% in the recognition rate compared with other methods. The neural network approach is faster, in terms of calculation, but provides a lower recognition rate compared to the Euclidean distance measure. The contourlet transform-PCA with preprocessing and Euclidean distance measure can be considered as the best classifier in terms of recognition rate as well as having a shorter execution time compared with curvelet transform-PCA with preprocessing.

References

1. R. Szeiliski, *Computer Vision: Algorithms and Applications*. New York: Springer, 2010.
2. M.T. Jones, *Artificial Intelligence: A Systems Approach*. Hingham: Infinity Science Press, 2008.
3. L. Wang, W.M. Hu, and T.N. Tan. Recent developments in human motion analysis. *Pattern Recognition* 36(3), 588–601, 2003.
4. R. Polikar. Pattern recognition in bioengineering. *Wiley Encyclopedia of Biomedical Engineering* 4, 2695–2716, New York: Wiley, 2006.
5. L.K. Jones. Constructive approximations for neural networks by sigmoid functions. In *Proceedings of IEEE* 78, 1586–1589, 1990.

6. S.M. Weiss, and C.A. Kulikowski, *Computer Systems that Learn: Classification and Prediction Methods from Statistics, Neural Nets, Machine Learning and Export Systems.* San Mateo, CA: Morgan Kaufmann, 1991.

7. S. Haykin, *Neural Networks: A Comprehensive Foundation.* Michigan University: Prentice Hall, 1999.

8. M.J. Swain and D.H. Ballard. Color indexing. *International Journal of Computer Vision* 7(1), 11–32, 1991.

9. S. Chand. Comprehensive survey on distance/similarity measures between probability density functions. *International Journal of Mathematical Models and Applied Sciences* 4(1), 300–307, 2007.

10. J. Mundy. *Object Recognition in the Geometric Era: A Retrospective,* In J. Ponce, M. Hebert, C. Schmid, and A. Zisserman, editors, Toward Category-level object recognition. Springer-Verlag, 3–29, 2006.

11. C. Harris, and M. Stephens. A combined corner and edge detector. In *Proceedings of the Fourth Alvey. Vision Conference,* Manchester, UK. 147–151, 1988.

12. D. Lowe. Distinctive image features from scale-invariant key points. *International Journal of Computer Vision* 60(2), 91–110, 2004.

13. H. Bay, A. Ess, T. Tuytelaars, and L. Van Gool. SURF: Speeded up robust features. *Computer Vision and Image Understanding* 110(3), 346–359, 2008.

14. M.A. Fischler, and R.C. Bolles. Random sample consensus: A paradigm for model fitting with application to image analysis and automated cartography. *Communications of the ACM* 24, 381–395, 1981.

15. K. Pearson. On lines and planes of closest fit to systems of points in space. *Philosophical Magazine* 2(6), 559–572, 1901.

16. M. Kirby, and L. Sirovich. Application of the Karhunen–Loeve procedure for the characterization of human faces. *IEEE Transactions on Pattern Analysis and Machine Intelligence* 12(1), 103–108, 1990.

17. M. Turk, and A. Pentland. Eigenfaces for recognition. *Journal of Cognitive Neuro Science* 3(1), 71–86, 1991.

18. T.H. Thi, K. Robert, S. Lu, and J. Zhang. Vehicle classification at night time using eigenspace and support vector machine. In *Congress on Image and Signal Processing,* Sanya, China, 424–426, 2008.

19. H.S. Sahambi, and K. Khorasani. A neural network appearance based 3D object recognition using independent component analysis. *IEEE Transactions on Neural Networks* 14(1), 138–149, 2003.

20. C. Zhang, X. Chen, and W.B. Chen. A PCA-based vehicle classification framework. In *Proceedings of IEEE International Conference on Data Engineering,* 17–27, 2006.

21. I. Daubechies. The wavelet transform, time-frequency localization and signal analysis. *IEEE Transactions on Information Theory* 36(5), 961–1005, 1990.

22. B.J. Woodford, and N.K. Kasabov. A wavelet based neural network classifier for temporal data. In *Proceedings of 5th Australia–Japan Joint Workshop on Intelligent and Evolutionary Systems,* Dunedin, New Zealand, 79–85, 2001.

23. M.N. Do, and M. Vetterli. The contourlet transform: An efficient directional multiresolution image representation. *IEEE Transactions on Image Processing* 14(12), 2091–2106, 2005.

24. J. Zhou, A.L. Cunha, and M.N. Do. Nonsubsampled Contourlet transform: Construction and application in enhancement. In *Proceedings of International Conference on Image Processing* 1, 469–472, 2005.

25. Y. Yan, R. Muraleedharan, X. Ye, and L. A. Osadciw. Contourlet based image compression for wireless communication in face recognition system. In *Proceedings of IEEE International Conference on Communications*, Beijing, China, 505–509, 2008.

26. B. Yang, S.T. Li, and F.M. Sun. Image fusion using nonsubsampled contourlet transform. In *Proceedings of 4th International Conference on Image and Graphics*, Chengdu, China, 719–724, 2007.

27. Ch. Srinivasan Rao, S. Srinivas Kumar, and B.N. Chatterji. Content based image retrieval using Contourlet transform. *International Journal on Graphics, Vision and Image Processing* 7(3), 9–15, 2007.

28. D.L. Donoho, and M.R. Duncan. Digital Curvelet Transform: Strategy, Implementation and Experiments. Stanford University, California, Technical Report 1999.

29. J.L. Starck, E.J. Candes, and D.L. Donoho. The curvelet transform for image denoising. *IEEE Transactions on Image Processing* 11(6), 670–684, 2002.

30. L. Dettori, and L. Semler. A comparison of wavelet, ridgelet and curvelet-based texture classification algorithms in computed tomography. *Computers in Biology and Medicine* 37(4), 486–493, 2007.

31. G. Hetzel, B. Leibe, P. Levi, and B. Schiele. 3D object recognition from range images using local feature histograms. In *Proceedings of IEEE International Conference on Computer Vision and Pattern Recognition* 2, Kauai, HI, 394–399, 2001.

32. H.F. Ng. Automatic thresholding for defect detection. *Pattern Recognition Letters* 27, 1644–1649, 2006.

33. R.C. Gonzalez, R.E. Woods, and S.L. Eddins. *Digital Image Processing Using MATLAB*, 2nd ed. Knoxville, TN: Gatesmark Publishing, 2009.

34. V. Jain, and A. Mukherjee. The Indian Face Database. http://vis-www.cs.umass.edu/~vidit/IndianFaceDatabase/, 2002.

35. Essex Face94 database. http://dces.essex.ac.uk/mv/allfaces/faces94.zip.

36. N.G. Chitaliya, and A.I. Trivedi. An efficient method for face feature extraction and recognition based on contourlet transform and principal component analysis using neural network. *International Journal of Computer Application* 6(4), 28–34, September 2010.

37. N.G. Chitaliya, and A.I. Trivedi. An efficient method for face feature point extraction & recognition based on contourlet transform and principal component analysis. In *International Conference and Exhibition on Biometric Technology (ICEBT)* 2, Coimbatoor, 52–61, September 2010.

38. E.J. Candes, L. Demanet, D.L. Donoho, and L. Ying. Fast discrete curvelet transforms. *Multiscale Modelling and Simulation* 5(3), 861–899, 2005.

39. N.G. Chitaliya, and A.I. Trivedi. Comparative analysis using fast discrete curvelet transform via wrapping and discrete contourlet transform for feature extraction and recognition. In *International Conference on Intelligent Systems and Signal Processing*, GCET, VV. Nagar, 2013.
40. N.G. Chitaliya, and A.I. Trivedi. Feature extraction using wavelet-PCA and neural network for application of object classification and face recognition. In *Proceedings of IEEE International Association of Computer Science & Technology (ICCEA)* 1, Bali, Indonesia, 510–514, 2010.
41. N.G. Chitaliya, and A.I. Trivedi. Automated vehicle identification system based on discrete curvelet transform for visual surveillance and traffic monitoring system. *International Journal of Computer Application* 57(1), 39–44, November 2012.
42. A.A. Bhurane, Face Recognition Using Dual-Tree Discrete Wavelet Transform. M.E. Thesis.
43. H.D. Vankayalapati, Evaluation of Wavelet Based Linear Subspace Techniques for Face Recognition.
44. M. Gupta, and G. Sharma. An efficient face recognition system based on sub-window extraction algorithm. *International Journal of Soft Computing and Engineering* 1(6): January 2012, ISSN: 2231–2307.

PART III
CASE STUDIES AND LARGE SCALE BIOMETRIC SYSTEMS

9

LEGAL ASPECTS AND ETHICAL ISSUES IN THE USE OF BIOMETRICS

A Study from Norway

ELHAM RAJABIAN NOGHONDAR

Contents

Abstract

The principles of purpose specification, confidentiality, proportionality, and subject consent are the main factors in the review of biometric technologies by the Data Protection Inspector in European Union member states. First, the purpose of data collection needs to be defined, transparent, and legitimate. Next, an evaluation of the proportionality for the collected data and the data processing should be made. The purpose principle specifies that proper protection is required against unauthorized use of biometric data for purposes except those the data was collected for. Confidentiality provides a minimum of protection by adequate tests that prove that the biometric data is accessible only by authorized individuals. Proportionality requires biometric data to be nonexcessive, relevant, and restricted to the requirements of the data collection's purposes. However, there is uncertainty about how the purpose and the proportionality principle should be applied to biometric data.

The main applications of biometrics are governmental, such as ID (identity) cards, e-passports, and boarding control. These biometric implementations are necessary to address identity theft, terrorism, illegal immigration, etc. There are also civil deployments of the biometric systems that raise ethical concerns relating to privacy, autonomy, and bodily integrity. Civil implementation of biometric systems should facilitate the utilization of social services for people. We provide an interpretation in the use of biometric systems in European countries with a special focus on ethical concerns and legislation in Norway.

This contribution will discuss the legal aspects and ethical issues in the use of biometrics. We review the regulations concerning the use of biometrics in European countries, and analyze the legislation based on the most recent biometric implementations in Norway. Privacy is the main concern but it is sometimes difficult to address all the privacy issues in a biometric system. Regulations are needed to prevent the misuse of biometric data. The ethical aspects cannot be underestimated because of the ethnic and cultural diversity in European countries. An extensive study is needed about information that might be revealed by biometric characteristics. It will provide a real understanding about how security and privacy concerns depend on each other. Some guidelines are also given to facilitate the use of biometrics, to increase user acceptance, and to consider privacy and ethical issues.

9.1 Introduction

Authentication technologies refer to some object you *have* (e.g., a key), information you *know* (e.g., a password), or something you *are* (that is a biometric feature). The most common and traditional authentication method is the use of a password [1]. Its main challenge, however, is that individuals may be required to memorize extreme passwords. Also, passwords can be simply hacked [14].

Biometric technology is an automatic pattern recognition mechanism that compares the measureable biological, physiological, and behavioral features of a person with a stored template to authenticate that person. Biometric systems are appropriate for applications that aim to identify individuals for a specific purpose [1]. They provide a link between a person and his or her identity based on the application context [3]. Biometrics have also been utilized to seek for patterns in normal people, for finding changes in bodily and psychological traits over time and in other health situations, and for providing a basis for ethnic classifications [6].

Physiological characteristics are normally more stable and consistent than behavioral characteristics. Therefore, physical characteristics can be suitable features primarily to identify individuals. Physical characteristics include fingerprint, palm print, hand geometry, finger vein, hand vessels, iris, retina, face, DNA, blood pattern, ear shape, body odor [12], and skin patterns [6]. Behavioral characteristics include voice, keystroke dynamics, signature and handwriting models, and mouse movements. Behavioral biometric characteristics are changeable according to psychological situations and environmental conditions. These human characteristics will improve through learning over time. They change as human ability improves. Hence, dynamic biometric systems are required to accept the human characteristics' changeability. Behavioral biometric characteristics introduce less invasive recognition methods that increase user acceptance.

Biometric systems can be utilized for various purposes such as military and civil applications, physical access control, e-commerce, e-health, automated teller machines, profiling groups of people, group screening, etc. [2]. Profiling people based on religion, sexual habits, political direction, and social activity is an explicit instance that works against anonymity. Currently, the recognition progress of biometrics is remarkable. In court, biometric technology has been utilized to detect or identify suspicious persons via fingerprints or DNA gathered at the crime scene [14]. Biometric systems are estimated based on two main characteristics: *distinctiveness* and *permanence*.

The authentication accuracy and applicability of a particular biometric feature depends on these two main characteristics for a specific population. As such, the nature and requirements of a biometric modality define whether it is appropriate for the target identification application. Face, fingerprint, iris, and hand geometry are the most common and unique features used in commercial biometric systems [15]. For instance, fingerprinting is a well-known biometric feature for access control to PCs, cellular phones, PDAs, and large-scale systems such as border control systems, voter registration, passport and visa documentation [15], elevator access control, identification of person in court, etc. [14]. Although hand geometry is an appropriate biometric for authentication and identification purposes because of the need for large sensors and increasing costs, a similar argument can be made for palm prints as well. It is a cost-effective authentication method and more features are required for extraction compared with fingerprints [15]. High-speed and accurate identification becomes essential for large-scale applications. The requirements of large-scale biometric identification systems differ from those of small-scale or medium-scale biometric identification systems [15]. Palm vein imaging is available for some commercial applications (for more information, see Jain and Kumar [15, p. 128]). However, there is no specific use for large-scale vascular biometric identification systems, which might be because of cost concerns and lack of sufficient research on vein specifications and stability [15]. Using biometric systems to identify people usually depends on the convenience of collecting the biometric features. The face, fingerprint, and iris are the most popular biometrics to employ at gate systems controls. The reason is that these three biometric features can be simply obtained at any time without assistance from any equipment. Currently, some countries use fingerprint recognition in border control systems, for example, the United States, Hong Kong/Shenzhen, Japan, Australia, Singapore, and some European countries [14].

Biometric commercial systems typically operate in two fundamental modes: authentication and identification [3]. The authentication or verification mode answers the question "am I who I claim to be?" The system may accept or deny our claim [4]. Shopping with a card, gaining access to resources, and boarding control are examples of authentication technology. Biometric authentication involves a "one to one" or (1:1) comparison of the sample actually presented by a user with the template already provided by the user. The identification mode includes a wider search in a large central database for a match through (1:n) or one-to-many searches [3]. The identification system answers the question "who am I?" without any primary claim for the identification [5]. Negative identification is another possible mode that cannot be found among the traditional authentication mechanisms. The system collects the biometric characteristics of individuals and defines whether the individuals have already enrolled within the biometric system. Negative identification prevents several enrollments of one individual. Thus, it should be considered as a permanent part of each biometric system particularly for large-scale biometric systems [1].

Biometrics technology is based on the following properties, which are either physiological or behavioral features:

- Universality: everyone should have the feature
- Uniqueness: two persons should not have the same biometric feature
- Permanence: the feature should be permanent over time
- Collectability: the feature must be measurable quantitatively and simple to achieve
- Performance: accuracy of the feature defines its performance
- Acceptability: the feature should be acceptable by people who use it
- Noncircumvention: the biometric characteristic should be difficult to fake

9.2 State of the Art

Biometric technologies introduce pros versus traditional authentication mechanisms. The important advantage is that biometric technologies discriminate between an imposter who has deceitfully achieved access to a biometric system and the legitimate user. In addition, traditional authentication mechanisms cannot support negative claims. For instance, a person who claims that he is not person X. Moreover, people do not have to carry a token or a key and passwords that could be lost and forgotten [16].

Biometrics deployment aims to authenticate and identify a vivid person. It is true that tracing people is possible by these means. This aspect needs to be argued, as people are concerned about their own privacy issues and related ethics. These two concerns should be discussed explicitly to reduce the fear of biometric technology. It is a fear of identity theft and misuse of personal information. Most recent efforts have contributed to the privacy rights and personal information concerns of people rather than their ethics concerns.

Another possible concern is being spoofed by biometric systems. For instance, the use of a fake fingerprint or facial picture to fool the capturing device. This kind of hacking scenario is feasible; although compromising biometric systems is rather difficult to practice.*

From the ethics aspect, people recognize biometrics as offensive and undermining their human dignity; therefore, this aspect of the use of biometric technologies needs to be addressed for all social groups. It works directly with the citizens' feelings about themselves. It can cause people to feel embarrassment and irritation, and might cause them difficulties in getting social services because not all members of society have biometrical technical knowledge.

There are some attempts to develop less privacy-invasive biometric systems. Even for highly secure government and business applications, there are still possibilities of misuse, for example, of private and health information. It is essential to wipe out obscurities related to the privacy aspects of biometric technologies. It will increase the citizens' trust in the undeniable benefits of biometrics. Considering the data-storing fashion, sharing and retention time of biometric information is critical to coping with the privacy problem. Ethical issues demand their own considerations, which will be discussed in Section 9.6 of this chapter.

In this chapter, we look at the expanding use of biometrics in e-commerce and online applications. Online biometric systems operate similar to offline biometric authentication systems. In the enrollment phase, a person offers his or her biometrics feature to an enrollment device. The biometric feature is typically a fingerprint. Next, a communication medium transfers the captured biometric information to the already existing database. An identification number is created for

---

* http://www.brighthub.com/computing/enterprise-security/articles/85687.aspx.

each user and stored in the database along with his or her biometric sample.

To begin an online connection, the user has to enter an identification number and living fingerprint sample. The middleware communication medium transfers the captured information to an authentication system. Then, the information can be verified with the stored information. The result of the verification will approve or reject the transferred information.

Five key components have been defined for online biometrics applications

- Enrollment device: a device that is connected to a PC, for example, via USB. The enrollment device includes a biometric finger scanner to capture the samples from a person
- Storage system: it is in charge of holding the biometric information obtained from the users
- Middleware: it handles the communication between enrollment device, storage system, and authentication system
- Authentication system: it compares the live sample provided by the user and the stored biometric information on the database. It is clearly responsible for performing the authentication operation
- Transaction processor: it monitors the whole online authentication

There is an opinion that the use of online biometric authentication can reduce the number of online transaction deceptions* through offering stronger access control than traditional authentication methods such as password and token.

9.3 Main Aspects of Biometrics Technology

First-generation biometrics concentrates on those features that directly distinguish the subject such as fingerprint, iris, palm print, face, hand geometry, DNA, foot dynamics, etc. These biometric systems have been improved to enhance precision, robustness, and security.

---

* http://techbiometric.com/articles/how-online-biometric-authentication-system-works/.

Second-generation biometrics or future biometrics generally focuses on multimodality, soft biometrics, behavioral biometrics, and electrophysiological biometrics. We review the second-generation of biometrics technology as the following:

- *Multimodal Biometrics Systems*: A multimodal biometrics system integrates multiple features to identify a person. It can be a useful alternative for people that typically have difficulties in enrolling in the biometric system. For instance, in case of a withered or injured fingerprint, face or signature recognition can be a substitution [6]. Multimodal biometric systems propose reliable performance and high-level security based on three contributions. First, reducing false acceptance rate and false rejection rate. Second, introducing other means of authentication if proper information cannot be extracted from a given biometric sample. Finally, challenging all attempts to spoof the system via fake data, for example, a forged fingerprint. However, biometric systems become more intrusive as they become more mature [8].

  Multimodal biometric systems may be organized into four main classifications based on attributes and sensors. The chosen features include "(1) single biometric feature and multiple sensors; (2) single biometric feature and single sensor, but multiple classification; (3) single biometric feature and multiple sensors and units; and (4) multiple biometric feature and multiple sensors" [17].

- *Soft Biometrics*: Soft biometrics comprises gender, age, height, weight, and ethnicity and can be deployed as secondary evidence besides a primary biometric feature for identification. Soft biometrics is not currently used during automatic authentication and identification. Soft biometric features do not provide the distinctiveness and permanence to identify a person uniquely and validly. It also can be simply spoofed; however, they introduce some information about individuals that can be useful (Figure 9.1). In other words, the information they give are helpful to distinguish individuals until identification aims [17].

- *Behavioral Biometrics*: Behavioral biometrics includes measurable behavioral features to identify an individual. For instance,

Gender, ethnicity, skin color, hair color
http://anthro.palomar.edu/adapt/adapt_4.htm
© Corel Corporation, Ottawa, Canada

Eye color
http://ology.amnh.org/genetics/longdefinition/index3.html
© American Museum of Natural History, 2001

Height
http://www.altonweb.com/history/wadlow/p2.html
© Alton Museum of History and Art

Weight
http://www.laurel-and-hardy.com/
goodies/home6.html © CCA

Figure 9.1 Soft biometrics.

vocal recognition, signature recognition, gait authentication, odor recognition, etc. Behavioral biometrics can also be divided into direct and indirect human–computer interaction (HCI). In direct HCI, a person directly interacts with input devices such as mouse dynamics, keystroke dynamics, e-mail activity, online gambling, and command line culture. Indirect HCI relies on analyzing evidences that are created by a person during work with different software, audit logs, network traffic, storage activity, and access to operating system applications like registry access.

Behavioral biometrics provides benefits particularly in combination with token-based authentication methods such as passwords and PIN codes. Behavioral biometrics is especially applicable for the authentication of a specific consent such as signature and voice recognition. However, they are weak because behaviors typically change over time and environmental conditions [6].

- *Electrophysiological Biometric Systems*: It records the electric signals of the human body's neural system to authenticate a person. They comprise recordings of heart electrical activity, brain electrical activity, eye movements signals, muscles activity signals, etc. These human biometric features are very unique and consistent and can be used to identify individuals. In addition, they are very accurate, universal, hard to spoof, small in size, and easy to implement in electronic devices such as laptops and cellular phones. The processing of the signal collection can be sophisticated because of the demand for wired sensors and environment noise. Wireless sensors, efficient filters to reduce noise, and signal amplification devices can empower the identification features of electrophysiological biometrics [6].

9.4 Analysis

A biometrics sample has proper quality if it is appropriate for personal discernment. Standard ISO/IEC 29794-1 has specified three components for biometrics sample quality:

- *Character*: it shows the intrinsic discriminative ability of the biometric source
- *Fidelity*: it is the level of resemblance between a biometric sample and its source based on each phase of the processing
- *Utility*: it discusses the effect of a biometric sample on the entire performance of a biometric system

The character of the biometric sample source and the fidelity of the processed sample affect the utility of the sample. In general, a quality metric should reflect the utility of the sample before other things. This means that quality should be perceived for recognition performance. However, the recognition algorithms' performance does not depend on similar features and factors. An appropriate quality measure is extremely related to the recognition algorithm type. Consider a face recognition algorithm that is not sensitive to environmental light changes, whereas another recognition algorithm can be seriously influenced by environmental light changes. A measure of illumination can be helpful to evaluate the performance of the latter recognition algorithm but not for the first one. Evaluation of quality typically depends on a specific recognition algorithm [18].

The use of standards comforts the interoperability and expansion of the biometric systems, although it threatens the biometric systems in some ways. The standards provide very sound and risky information about the biometric system functioning such as the format of templates that are stored. This exposes the system to indirect attack that is performed in the analog scope beyond the digital restrictions of the system. Thus, the typical digital protection routines cannot be utilized, for example, digital signature, digital watermarking, and semifragile watermarking [19]. Digital biometrics is different from traditional biometrics both quantitatively and qualitatively. The digital biometrics format enables us to collect, store, and proceed electronically a massive amount of data in a short time. It refers to quantitative traits of digital biometrics. Qualitative traits of digital biometrics give us numeric strings instead of icons. Digital formats show different qualities from analogical formats [6].

In the biometrics authentication procedure, indirect attack includes all attacks that can be done in all authentication levels except at the sensor level. Indirect attack can be transformed to direct attack through a high-quality iris print, and fake or gummy fingerprints extracted from reconstructed biometric images. A possible indirect attack is a Trojan horse, which passes the feature extraction and matcher modules. More information about possible attacks against a biometric system can be found in the study by Galbally et al. [19].

9.5 Legal Aspects in the Use of Biometrics in Norway

There are many discussions about the use of biometric technology and compliance with legal issues. The regulations must be considered before installation and during use of biometric systems to provide the necessary components, privacy and security, for the authentication and identification of people. The European data privacy principles are regulated with "Directive 95/46/EC of the European Parliament and of the Council of 24 October 1995 on the protection of individuals with regard to the processing of personal data and on the free movement of such data."

Some of the core principles of the law refer to data collection and some focus on data processing. The minimality or proportionality principle of data processing requires that the collected personal data be restricted to the needs of the data collection's aim(s). Proportionality emphasizes that personal data must be nonexcessive, relevant, and limited to the necessity of a certain purpose [9]. Proportionality also refers to the primary principle of the data protection law. Personal information should be processed fairly and lawfully. The fairness principle specifies that processing of private information should transparently address the individuals' privacy, autonomy, and integrity [9, p. 58].

There is an ambiguity about the definitions for the terms *excessiveness*, *relevant*, and *necessity*. The issue is not only in the use of biometrics in different contexts but also in the court system of European countries. For instance, the United Kingdom's data protection authority allows fingerprint recognition for students to get access to the schools' restaurant if such protections apply at that school. The law in France has denied the use of fingerprints for the same objective. In Germany, the data protection authority decided that the fingerprint image should be kept in a smartcard rather than in a database for similar purposes [3].

The major issues in the list of biometrics concerns include large-scale usage, biometric databases, medical usage, remote and covert biometrics (in relation to fairness information principles and, specifically, the proportionality principle), enrollment of vulnerable and disabled people, information sharing and system interoperability, technology conjunction, behavioral biometrics, and surveillance [6].

The European Data Protection Authority and the Data Protection Working Party, the consultative committee, have specified some criteria to implement the biometric systems based on the proportionality principle. The European Data Protection Authority clarifies that storing the biometric template involves less important information rather than the raw biometric image. It helps to mitigate privacy concerns, but avoiding any possible link between the template and sensitive information cannot be guaranteed because most of the biometric data potentially comprises sensitive data such as health information, origin, and physical situation [3].

Another concern is the reconstruction of the original image from the biometric template. More information about the reconstruction process can be found in the study by Galbally et al. [19]. The Data Protection Authority has also suggested preventing central storage or unnecessary storage for the authentication mode but not for the identification mode. Thus, the definition of authentication and identification is important for privacy protection [3]. Article 20 of the Data Protection Directive makes it clearer that, prior checking is needed for high-security applications. If the central storage regulation and prior checking are requirements for authentication installation, those should also be considered for identification installation because the identification mode involves the private data of many individuals. On the other hand, the Data Protection Working Party defines that prior checking is also needed for the identification installation. If the central storage is approved as being proportional, the implementation is accepted.

The Data Protection Directive discusses the retention times of biometric data as another important criterion. It clarifies that the storage length of the biometric data should not be more than required. The biometric data should be removed when the biometric system is no longer in operation. An appropriate selection of the biometric system can decrease security risks. For example, implementation of hand shape and hand vessels instead of fingerprints that remains on the surfaces.

Making a decision about the deployment of a biometric system based on the proportionality principle also refers to the consent principle: personal data ought to be processed only with agreement of the data's subject, unless there is a specific condition that is specified in the law. On the other hand, Article 7 of the Data Protection Directive restricts processing of personal data to the legal aims where it conflicts with the primary rights of the data subject, such as privacy and integrity. In addition, if the personal data consists of sensitive information, further agreement is necessary. European countries may comply with consent regulation based on discretion of their court system. For instance, Norwegian regulation about consent determines that a complete change of the collected biometric data is not allowed even with the data subject's consent [3].

9.5.1 Case Study

Decision makers allow or deny the use of biometric systems based on these main points: the necessity of the system, the legitimacy of the system, and the purpose of usage. The Data Protection Tribunal and the Data Protection Inspector make decisions to accept or reject the installation of biometric systems in Norway. Among magnitude utilization of the biometric technology, biometrics cases do not introduce a large percentage in Norwegian industry. Three biometrics cases are studied with respect to privacy concerns.

9.5.1.1 REMA 1000   REMA 1000, the famous chain store in Norway, needed a method to control working time registration for their employees. The personnel entered their personal ID number for authentication on the system. REMA 1000 decided to change the ID number authentication into fingerprint recognition to prevent the personnel from sharing their personal ID number and registering for each other.

Based on Article 12 of the Data Protection Directive, REMA 1000 had an actual objective required for identification. It needed to be clear whether that objective complied with the necessity principle or not. This means that the proportionality and purpose principles should also be fulfilled. The proportionality principle should take into account when the concern is about security levels, spoofing attack, effect of human factors, social, cultural and legal issues, or economic and technical issues. In other words, the consequence risks need to be checked versus the benefits. The Data Protection Tribunal explained that there are alternatives for REMA 1000 in this intrusive authentication method. Clearly, the legal need was not given. The Data Protection Tribunal believed that fingerprint recognition has a deeper meaning compared with simple registration. It proves that there is a suspicion of the employees. The Data Protection Inspector also mentioned that, although the biometric technology offers an accurate authentication, it distrusts and subverts the relationship between the employees and the employer.

In this case, risk and result derived from the use of biometrics were compared with the advantages and the security needed. The Data Protection Inspector also considered that REMA 1000 could deploy a less intrusive authentication method such as personnel number or a combination of ID number and password [3].

Each authentication technology has its own weaknesses and challenges, even though the authentication implementation should be based on several elements, for instance, security necessities, user acceptance, cost, environment, proportionality between incoming benefits and risks for all parties of a system, etc. Biometric systems should not be considered as the last and complete solution for every identification issue or as a replacement for traditional authentication methods. It is possible to spoof the fingerprint deployment for this case and the employees can still register for each other through a printed fingerprint, for instance. The use of an aliveness detection sensor could be a countermeasure; although it could reveal some sensitive information, such as an abnormal heartbeat [20]. This can be interpreted as a personal integrity violation.

9.5.1.2 Bunnpris   In March 2012, the Bunnpris retail chain aimed to use fingerprint identification for self-service shopping for beer and tobacco. The fingerprint template would be stored on a smartcard with only the individual's age. If individuals enrolling in the system are old enough, they will receive a token with their fingerprint. Next time, the individuals can buy beer and tobacco unsupervised because the token and their fingerprint match. It proves that the people are old enough to purchase age-limited products. There are four parties involved in this biometric case: the customer, the company using the biometric solution (Bunnpris), the vendor company of the solution (IT vendor Visma), and the government.

This use of biometrics is for access control; therefore, this is an authentication mechanism. The Data Protection Inspector rejected the scheme because the authorities believed that there is no strong necessity. Proportionality principle is the basis for this decision. The Norwegian Data Protection Inspectorate has a similar policy toward biometric technology with the Data Protection Working Party within the European Union's committee. It rejects the use of biometrics when other less intrusive alternatives exist.

Necessity can be discussed within two aspects. First, it is related to the availability of other less intrusive alternatives. Second, it is about the consequences, risks, and loss one may suffer from the deployment of biometrics versus the benefits it can bring such as preventing spoofing or applying a balance test.

Which of the parties benefit from this discussion is uncertain. From the customers' viewpoint, the benefits generally should be included at the individual's convenience—a user-friendly, reliable, and privacy-friendly system. Easy access or convenience is provided for a group of adults because there is no need for identity card checks to authorize the purchase of age-limited products. On the other hand, convenience might not be completely provided for older people because fingerprints are less readable with ageing. Furthermore, those customers who cannot provide a clear fingerprint sample also need to be considered because of their physical job, skin problems, or specific origin. Skin color and the structure of the papillae on the fingertips affect authentication. More information about skin diseases and their origins can be found in the study by Drahansky et al. [13]. Thus, this biometric case can refer to discrimination against aging and discrimination in society; unless an alternative is embedded into the system. From this standpoint, it can be inferred that the first aspect of the necessity element is not fulfilled for this biometrics implementation.

Article 12 of the Data Protection Act clarifies that biometrics may soon be utilized as an authentication method when necessary. In this case, the fingerprint template is stored in a smartcard and the data subject can control his or her biometric data. This refers to a privacy protective application. Hence, according to Article 12, it is not considered a privacy intrusive authentication method. Article 12 also clearly states that consent criteria should not be excluded as a legitimate part of processing. In addition, other alternative or voluntary options should be provided for individuals not willing to utilize the biometric application. It is of the opinion that consent addresses *human dignity*, an important ethical concept.

The Data Protection Inspector and the Privacy Advisory Board had different viewpoints in the Bunnpris biometrics case. As mentioned previously, the Data Protection Inspector could not find "strong necessity" of using biometric identifiers for the implementing company, Bunnpris. Therefore, the Data Protection Inspector believed that it would conflict with the Personal Data Act. The Privacy Advisory Board acknowledged that the fingerprint would not be used for identification; it only proves a person's age.

This disagreement shows the need for a clear definition for three dimensions of proportionality law and the exact meaning of nonexcessive, relevant, and necessity. In other words, based on what list of criteria is used, the *necessity* of a biometric implementation is defined and from the viewpoint of which parties is discussed. Bunnpris had explained that this authentication method reduced the chances of identity theft and that it would make life safer for these individuals.

If the system stored only the age of an enrolled person and no other personal information, identity theft would not be possible. In addition, the use of a smartcard to store individuals' fingerprints will provide some benefits including the avoidance of a massive attack on a common database and it will make a user responsible for protecting the stored fingerprint as that person should also protect the fingerprints that he or she leaves in everyday life.

There is an ambiguity about security for the fingerprint data on the smartcard, but the assumption is that the storage memory of the smartcard used is secure. Thus, the fingerprint information would not be easily available to a person holding the smartcard. It will be the individuals' responsibility if they lose their purse including other identifiers and Bunnpris' fingerprint token.

This situation can be threatening, in case other implementations of biometrics should be developed in the future in Norway. There would be threats against individuals' privacy and likely their identity if fingerprint recognition were implemented for other social services whereas a fingerprint, which is a strong identifier, can be utilized for high-security systems like e-banking and e-passports. This was also mentioned clearly in Article 12 of the Norwegian Personal Information, a fingerprint is a "unique identification measure"; therefore, it should not be used when no actual objective exists and the biometrics method is not *necessary* for such identification. The fingerprint authentication method was used from autumn 2012 in Bunnpris' chain stores.

9.5.1.3 Fitness24Seven   In May 2012, the Data Protection Inspector in Norway issued another rejection for the use of fingerprint recognition. Fitness24Seven demanded the use of smartcard fingerprints to control access to the center during evening and night shifts (the center is staffed during the day). The Data Protection Inspector denied the use of fingerprint recognition at the Fitness24Seven center. He believed that the use of fingerprint authentication violated the privacy of the individuals. According to Article 12, it has to comply with the objective and necessity regulations. There is an actual objective need for accurate authentication if there is no agreement that unauthorized access to the fitness center is less important than providing security for an organization's database. The use of a biometric smartcard minimizes the privacy and security risks if the data subject can decide to what extent or purpose the data can be used. This supports personal data, consent, and correction rights for individuals. However, if an individual decides not to utilize his or her biometric data or lacks consent, a question arises: Is there an alternative for biometric recognition to access the social service?

The necessity criterion is also fulfilled because some people might not be able to go to fitness centers during the daytime. These people will not be excluded from access because of their daytime occupation. It also brings financial benefit for the company using the biometric solution, Fitness24Seven, and the vendor company.

There is ambiguity about personal information that might be found on the smartcard. Hence, there is an uncertainty relevant to the loss and benefit a person can achieve that implies proportionality and weakens the *necessity* of the biometric implementation.

Legislation against misuse of biometrics data and standardization play a crucial role in the balance test. It can alter the benefits that are achieved by the parties. Both Bunnpris and Fitness24Seven are developing a privacy enhancing measure that is a match-on-card biometric system. Although the data does not leave the card, the reading device is an external element. It means that the individual still has to trust that the reading device has no storage of any template. Although there are many ways to misuse a system, regardless of whether the system is a biometrical system or not, the concerns about biometrical systems are linked to the nature of biometrics data systems, which can disclose private and valuable information.

There are possibilities to spoof the Bunnpris and Fitness24Seven systems. For instance, a person can present a gummy or silicone finger to the reader when there is nobody else around at the fitness center during the night shifts [10]. It is recognized as an attack at the sensor level or as a direct attack because the attacker needs no specific information about the internal function of the biometrics system such as the matching algorithm, feature extraction, feature vector format, storage mechanism, etc. [19]. Supervision and surveillance systems might be deployed to fight the spoofing attack. However, the supervision systems are privacy intrusive, as they can be run covertly and individuals have no control of their data during the data processing phase [10]. It would be a sensible strategy if negative identification were embedded into Fitness24Seven's biometrics system. This stops opportunity to enter the fitness center for another person in addition to an already enrolled customer.

The following guidelines contribute to addressing the privacy concerns:

- Define a sample quality that is not higher than needed. This minimizes the data collection that is suitable for function creep and people profiling [6]. Function creep is always a potential fear that could pull down public trust and ruin reliance on a given system. Although some instances of function creep are justly harmless, when it results from an intentional purpose, it refers to an important ethical breach. High sample quality creates extra data and introduces redundancy, not a better authentication mechanism. Biometrics redundancy refers to collecting additional information on people's age, gender, medical details, ethnicity, etc. High sample quality can be utilized to recreate artificial biometric features to spoof the system. More information can be found in the study by Mordini [6], which is about function creep incentives.

- Make the individuals aware of biometric method applications. This will create trust and increase user acceptance. Lack of knowledge about the benefits of biometrics technology should not result in the rejection of biometrics usage. Although awareness creates trust and increases user acceptance, it might also educate irresponsible persons to understand the technology of the biometric system and misuse it.

- Biometric data might be misused like nonbiometric data. This is no reason to not take the benefits of biometric authentication technologies. There is a need for legislation to support individuals' rights. Standards and certification procedures should be introduced to increase trust and protect privacy; otherwise, the benefits of biometric systems could become negligible. Fingerprint recognition has been well standardized, but facial and hand geometry recognition are two samples that lack standardization [10].

- Deploy biometric technologies that have been proposed in a privacy-enhancing way. This will increase the trust of individuals, the company using the biometric solution, and the government.
- The biometric systems, especially in case 2, should be implemented voluntarily or an alternative should be available for individuals who do not want to use the biometric application.
- Security needs, cost of spoofing risk or loss, and the consequences of human behavior must be considered with respect to biometric concepts.

9.6 Ethical Issues

Ethical issues are important when the purpose of using biometrics is in simplifying social services. The reason is that in most European countries, the legal regulations for biometric technology focus on human rights [7]. A serious discussion is appearing about whether biometric technology brings society any substantial benefits over other forms of identification methods and whether it forms a risk against privacy and becomes "a potential weapon in the hands of authoritarian governments" [6]. Some social groups may be offended by the use of biometric systems, including individuals with physical or learning disabilities, individuals with mental problems, disabled people, old people, specific ethnic groups, believers of particular religions, and homeless people. Homeless people might become victims of identity forgery [7].

The other concerns regarding the use of biometrics consists of large-scale applications, biometric databases, covert biometrics, health information, behavioral biometrics, fear of surveillance, and unauthorized purposes.

Some disabled people will have trouble enrolling because their biometric sample may not be sound enough. Furthermore, enrollment times and the authentication process are long, for instance, in fingerprint, face, and iris recognition. Also, some elderly people may not want to use biometric technology. The enrollment phase takes more time particularly for those 60 years of age and older. Some ethnic groups, such as people with colored-skin and dark irises, may experience difficulty during the enrollment phase for fingerprint recognition, face recognition, and iris recognition. Homeless people do not have a specific address to set up an enrollment time. Biometric data is not confidential for homeless people, even in case of getting a card because of their health situation, deficient weight, and untidy skin [7]. In large-scale systems, such as in border control, the ethical cost of an error rate can be higher than a simple rejection and delay. It might cause the subject to be identified as a criminal and cause travel restrictions [11].

Excluding these members of society from biometric authentication systems is unacceptable. Old people may need access to health and social services more than some others do. The exclusion can be discussed from an ethical aspect as some social groups might make sacrifices to benefit the others. There is a clear requirement for balance between public rights and the rights of minorities in society [7]. Human rights, in designing a new technology, can be defined to consider people's quality of life, which is chained to having autonomy and liberty [12].

Sensors that are used in the enrollment phase are a controversial part of biometric systems. They generate information about time and location; extra information such as age, gender, and ethnicity; emotional status in face recognition; or health-related information, among others.

Health information can be disclosed through some ways in this phase. For example, injuries or alterations in health situation can deter the enrollment of an individual into the biometric system. Although most biometric technologies have no ability to define the reasons of recognition failure, biometric systems might be able to determine these reasons in the future. In addition, comparing real-time samples and initial biometric feature samples can also provide medical information. Moreover, infrared cameras or sensors can define surgical amendments such as plastic surgery, scar removal, added internal materials, dental and body implants, etc.

Biometric data can also be used as a covert source, which is useful for researchers to determine individuals' susceptability to diseases or seeking linkage between a behavioral feature and a specific health status.

Although all the considered ethical concerns are results of the human body's nature, some actions can be adopted to address these ethical issues. First, any biometric system that will be implemented should always disclose its potential for gathering medical information. Doctors should have a proactive role in the sensor's designs to define medical elements that should not be embedded. Furthermore, individuals have to be notified about biometric devices capturing information at certain locations. This seems an impossible demand due to covert applications for screening and surveillance, and the use of biometric sensors in ambient intelligence perimeters.

European Data Protection Directive, Article 7, part 1 emphasizes that individuals need to be warned about the presence of biometric sensors, whereas Article 7, part 2 neutralizes this obligation. The regulation clarifies "Processing of data relating to offences, criminal conviction or security measure" needs no awareness by the people about the biometric sensors at a location. However, warning people about the existence of the sensors cannot necessarily refer to the data subject's consent.

The aliveness checking approach, which prevents the use of fake biometric features, can also reveal extra information. Aliveness can be checked by extracting physiological vital signs such as blood pressure, pulse, papillary reflex, etc. For aliveness checking, the use of biometrics such as iris recognition, which hardly reveals health and physiological status, can be recommended. However, function creep attacks remain an important risk in the aliveness checking process. The incidence of function creep can be decreased by not using biometric sample resolutions that are higher than needed. Biometric templates can be protected with effective encryption and storage of data.

Reconstructing original physiological and behavioral biometric features has raised lots of debate. *Template reverse engineering* is not possible, as the required data has been discarded in most biometric systems. However, the biometric template can be utilized to recreate a fake biometric characteristic to spoof the system. Spoofing attacks, identity theft, and people profiling risks should be avoided by appropriate encryption methods.

Electrophysiological biometrics is utilized in medicine to recognize abnormalities in physiological organs such as brain, heart, nerves, and muscles. Electrophysiological biometric technologies are novel authentication and identification methods that can be used in multimodal recognition systems. However, there are ethical, legal, privacy, and political issues to using these biometric characteristics. The ethical issues are due to the collection of medical and extra information by sensors being invasive psychologically [6].

Regardless of biometrics and application type, data collection should not consist of any form of individual humiliation. However, there is always the possibility that it can be deduced as such because of individuals' cultural diversity. For instance, a fingerprint is sort of degrading in some portions of Africa and Asia. In addition, facial recognition is distressing for Muslim women when they have to show their naked face to a male security officer. On the other hand, one might refuse data collection for a palm print recognition. It is clear that there is a need for clear definition for what is according to and what is against human dignity [2]. People's religious freedom should be protected. There should be a perception about inconvenience with biometric software that can be stepped up because of unfamiliarity with biometric technologies versus religious and ethical aspects.

The legitimate use of biometric technologies is more a topic of discussion in academia than a concrete political and ethical concern. Based on the European Charter, the dignity of the people is an implicit value and must dominate other values [20]. We think there is also a requirement for clear perception of what could be defined as an offense to human dignity. For example, there is random body checking in some airports. People who are chosen for the body checking probably have a different understanding and feeling about the action in front of others, particularly with insufficient awareness that the random selection is behind the system. This can also be discussed as degradation of humanity, if we accept that everyone deserves the same level of human rights, according to Chapter 1 of the Fundamental Rights in the European paramount framework.

It is not easy to create a balance between people's irritation and the needed security, specifically in large-scale systems. It seems that more security leads to more humiliation. According to the example above, we would think that persuading a person to display his or her naked face/body is an aspect of humiliation.

Biometric technologies are not deployed to undermine human dignity, but the technology can affect future expansion processes. Thus, it would be helpful to consider human dignity for future designs of biometric systems [20].

The European Union specifies the advantages of the use of biometrics as a technical tool to improve security and accuracy when authenticating people. Thus, biometrics is working against identity theft. Biometrics as a technical tool will improve and simplify citizens' lives, as well as those of other people in some applications such as border control and e-government. In addition, the European Union is aware of the special nature of biometrics. Therefore, it specifies that in processing biometrics identifiers, proper procedures must be accessible whenever either collecting people's biometrics is not possible or an inaccurate biometrics is offered because of a result of damaged capturing. The procedures should be performed and applied to respect the dignity of individuals who are not able to offer biometric data of the necessary quality. This will avoid individuals' suffering the consequences of defects of the system [17].

9.7   Conclusion

Proportionality is the core principle that needs to be considered in data collection and data processing. The proportionality components consist of nonexcessiveness, relevance, and necessity. Proportionality also refers to fairness and lawful data processing. In fact, it works for individuals' privacy, autonomy, integrity, and consent of the data subject. The use of biometric technology demands some caution with respect to security, privacy, and ethical issues. Although the token-based authentication methods may disclose the identity of the individuals, when losing, like biometric authentication methods, biometrics refers to sensitive information unlike traditional authentication methods. Thus, there is a requirement for legal support against the misuse of biometric and nonbiometric data. In addition, there should be established legislation, standards, testing procedures, and experts involved in the manufacturing process of sensors and biometric systems. This will propose a privacy-friendly technology, eliminate ethical concerns, and increase user acceptance. The role of awareness factor is crucial for both legal decision makers and users of the biometric systems.

User acceptance as an ethical aspect of biometric systems should be considered in the future design of biometric systems. Engineers and technical experts can play key roles in this respect. We think that privacy, user acceptance, and cost of implementation are the three main elements that hinder the deployment of biometric technology.

References

1. Matthew Lewis. 2007. *Biologger A Biometric Keylogger. An IBM Research white paper.*
2. Holly Ashton and Emilio Mordini. 2012. *Trusted Biometrics Under Spoofing Attacks.* TABULA RASA Euproject. 21–22.

3. Yue Liu. 2009. *The Principle of Proportionality in Biometrics*. University of Oslo, Norway. sciencedirect. 2–3.
4. Anil K. Jain, Arun Ross, and Salil Prabhakar. 2004. *An Introduction to Biometric Recognition*. IBM T. J. Watson Research Center, Digital Persona Inc. Siemens Corporate Research. 1–2.
5. Hugo Gamboa and Ana Fred. 2006. A Behavioral Biometric System Based on Human–Computer Interaction. *The International Society for Optical Engineering. Proc. SPIE 5404.*
6. Emilio Mordini. 2011. Seventh framework programme (Theme 3 Information and Communication Technologies). *The European Journal of Social Science Research*, 23:193–197.
7. Jeremy Wickins. 2007. *The Ethics of Biometrics: The Risk of Social Exclusion from the Widespread Use of Electronic Identification.* Springer Science. 6–7.
8. Shyam Sunder Yadav, Jitendra Kumar Gothwal, and Ram Singh. 2011. Multimodal biometric authentication system: Challenges and solutions. *Global Journal of Computer Science and Technology*, 11.
9. Jeremy Wickins. 2007. *The Ethics of Biometrics: The Risk of Social Exclusion from the Widespread Use of Electronic Identification.* Springer Science+Business Media B.V.
10. Mireille Hildebrandt and Eleni Kosta. 2009. *Biometrics: PET or PIT.* FIDIS Consortium. 8–12.
11. Anemarie Sprokkereef and Paul de Hert. 2007. Ethical practice in the use of biometric identifications within the EU. *Law, Science and Policy*, 3:4–6.
12. Jaana Leikas. 2009. *Life-Based Design: A Holistic Approach to Designing Human Technology Interaction.* VTT Technical Research Centre of Finland. 181–199.
13. Martin Drahansky, Eva Brezinova, Dana Hejtmankova, and Filip Orsag. 2010. Fingerprint recognition influenced by skin diseases. *International Journal of Bio-Science and Bio-Technology*, 2:5–8.
14. Patrick S.P. Wang. 2011. *Pattern Recognition, Machine Intelligence and Biometrics.* River Publishers Series in Information Science and Technology. 335–344.
15. Anil K. Jain and Ajay Kumar. 2010. *Biometrics of Next Generation.* Second Generation Biometric Springer. 2–6.
16. Peter Sloot, David Abramson, and Anne Trefethen. 2012. *Grid Computing and eScience.* Institute of Electrical and Electronics Engineers. 9.
17. Emilio Mordini. 2012. Global governance of privacy: The case of biometrics. *The European Journal of Social Science*, 23.
18. Fernando Alonso-Fernandez, Julian Fierrez, and Javier Ortega-Garcia. 2011. Quality measures in biometric systems. *IEEE Computer Society*, 10: 5–11.
19. Javier Galbally, Raffaele Cappelli, Alessandra Lumini, Guillermo Gonzalez-de-Rivera, Davide Maltoni, Julian Fierrez, Javier Ortega-Garcia, and Dario Maio. 2010. An evaluation of direct attacks using fake fingers generated from ISO templates. *Journal of Pattern Recognition*, 31:3–7.
20. Emilio Mordini and Sonia Massari. 2008. Body, biometrics and identity. *Bioethics* ISSN 22:2–5.

10

Biometric Identification

Device Specification and Actual Performance Considered for Operations of the Unique Identity Authority of India

HANS VARGHESE MATHEWS

Contents

Abstract

Mistaken identification is a particular problem in the biometric identification of a large population. The chance of mistaken identification, which is the conditional probability that individuals are different even though their biometrics match, will increase as more and more individuals are identified. The government of India is currently engaged in biometrically identifying its more than 1 billion citizens, and we find that the probability of mistaken matches will increase considerably between the initial and final stages of the exercise. Here are some indicative estimates: that probability is expected to increase from 0.006776 in the first 10 million identified to 0.618596 in the last 10 million, and from 0.064006 in the first 100 million identified to 0.609574382 in the last 100 million. The actual number of matches that will occur in the final stages is not negligible: 1,280,208 matches are expected for the last 100 million identified (out of which 780,382 will be mistaken). The work to be done in deciding when a match is mistaken will depend on how many previously identified persons a given individual is matched with. We are able to conclude, with the case at hand, that only rarely will there be more than one such matching person. Biometric devices may not perform as well in the field as they do in a laboratory when they are used for the rapid identification of a large population. The accuracy of a device is measured as the probability that a match will occur between two randomly chosen individuals. Manufacturers of devices specify accuracy through laboratory estimates and, for the devices being used by the government of India, we estimate that accuracy in the field is sixfold lower than the specified accuracy.

10.1 Introduction

The Unique Identity Authority of India, the UIDAI for short, is currently engaged in the biometric identification of the entire population of India. We shall be attempting an assessment of that ongoing exercise: and our primary concern is to appropriately assess the actual performance of the identification procedure, in the field, against such performance as might be expected from the technical specifications of the devices being used and the matching protocol that is being followed. In the next section, we shall more precisely define what a *biometric* is, identify the relevant technical specifications of the devices that produce them (i.e., exactly what matching amounts to), and then derive, from all this, the particular measures we shall need for our operational assessment. We begin with our findings.

10.1.1 Summary of Findings

A biometric device intended for the identification of individuals is supplied with a specified error rate: an experimental estimate of the probability that the biometrics of distinct individuals will match. When more than one device is used, and a suite of biometrics identifies an individual, the chance of such identification errors can be derived from the specified error rates of the individual devices. For the matching protocol that the UIDAI seems to follow, we compute $0.115512486 \times 10^{-11}$ as the specified identification error.* Manufacturers estimate error rates under laboratory conditions—when they are used for the rapid identification of a large population, as in our case, their performance in the field might fall short of what their specified errors promise, and we find that *identification error in the field exceeds by a factor of 6 (almost) the specified identification error for the UIDAI's matching protocol.*

We are able to draw our conclusions by examining the results of an experiment performed by the UIDAI when 84 million citizens were registered in their biometric database. The process of obtaining and storing biometrics is usually termed *enrollment*, and the stored suites of biometrics are called templates. The experiment estimated the chance of a false-positive match, which occurs when the suite of biometrics of a new individual, one who is not actually enrolled, happens to match some or other stored template. Therefore, the chance of a false-positive match is the conditional probability of a match occurring given that the individual is not enrolled, and it is usually called a "false reject rate." The rate depends on the number of individuals already enrolled. Write $\varphi(n)$ for what the false reject rate will be when n individuals have been enrolled: the identification error is the chance that the biometrics of a new individual will match any one given template; therefore, we have $\varphi(n) = 1 - (1 - \xi)^n$ when ξ is the identification error. Then, for a specified identification error of $0.1155001 \times 10^{-11}$ and an enrolled base of 84 million, the false reject rate should be $0.97020084 \times 10^{-4}$ at most; however,

---

* The UIDAI uses iris scanners and fingerprint scanners. It has made their specified error rates available to researchers at the Takshashila Institute, who have made them public. The specified error for their model of the iris scanner is reported as 1/13,100; the specified error for the fingerprint scanner is 1/500. The UIDAI has not published its matching protocol, but our investigations have led us to conclude the following: a match is taken to occur if both irises match and if any one digit also matches.

the UIDAI obtained an estimate of 0.57725×10^{-3} from its experiment. The bound on this rate comes from the relation $1 - (1 - \xi)^n \leq n\,\xi$, which holds for $0 < \xi < 1$ generally; from this, and from the relation of $\varphi(n)$ to ξ just given, one can obtain the bounds:

$$\varphi(n)/n \leq \xi \leq -\log[1 - \varphi(n)]/n \tag{1}$$

We have estimated the identification error in the field by using UIDAI's experimental value as a reliable operational estimate of $\varphi(n)$ for $n = 84$ million, and $0.687400801 \times 10^{-11}$ is our estimate of what ξ must be in the field.

The false reject rate is one measure of the operational accuracy, in the field, of a suite of biometric devices. An equally important measure is its converse: the conditional probability that an individual is not actually enrolled, given a match between his or her biometrics and some or other stored template. We shall term this *mistaken identification*. Our principal finding is that *the probability of mistaken identification increases considerably between the initial and final stages of enrollment by a factor of almost 10 between the first and last tenths of the population enrolled.*

We have proceeded by estimating the total number of matches expected, and the number of false matches among these, for the successive millions of individuals enrolled for whom we have used the lower of the bounds on $\varphi(n)$ given by

$$n\,\xi\,(1 - \xi)/(1 - \xi + n\,\xi) \leq 1 - (1 - \xi)^n \leq n\,\xi \tag{2}$$

The actual numbers are not negligible. For example, the UIDAI should expect 534,010 matches to occur for the first 100 million enrolled, out of which 34,180 will be false matches. However, a total of 1,280,208 matches are expected for the last 100 million enrolled and, of these, fully 780,382 would be false matches.*

---

* The discrepancy is more extreme for small initial and final subsets: we estimate 50,325 matches for the first 10 million, of which only 341 would be false matches; but 131,050 matches are expected for the last 10 million, out of which 81,607 would be false matches. The bounds on $\varphi(n)$ come from Professor Nico Temme of the CWI in The Netherlands, whose help we gratefully acknowledge. To count the number of matches and mistaken matches one needs, besides identification error, the chance that enrolled individuals will try to register again; and the chance of a match for an already enrolled person. The UIDAI has conducted an experiment that estimates the latter, and it has estimated to its satisfaction the former as well.

When a match occurs, the UIDAI must decide whether or not the individual is already enrolled, for which templates matching that person's suite of biometrics must be examined. The amount of work here depends on how many templates will match a given suite of biometrics, generally, when a match does occur. We get an upper bound of 10,922,437 on the total number of matches when the entire population of 1.2 billion has been enrolled: of which 4,924,539 would be false ones. However, we estimate that only 11,267,203 matching templates will have to be examined, at most, to decide which of these matches are false. Our last finding is that *only rarely will more than one matching template have to be examined, when a match occurs, to see if the match is a false one.*

Suppose n individuals are enrolled and ξ is the identification error: the computation requires an upper bound on the probability $\psi_q(n)$ of finding q or more matching templates, for any $q > 0$, should a false-positive match occur, and we use

$$\psi_q(n) = 1 - \sum_{0 \le r < q} C_{n,r} \xi^r (1 - \xi)^{n-r} \le [\xi^q/(q-1)!] \prod_{0 \le r < q} (n-r)$$

(3)

Here, $C_{n,r}$ counts the ways of choosing r distinct objects out of a collection of n distinct objects. We have $\psi_1(n) = \varphi(n)$ of course, and the standard identification of $\psi_q(n)$ with the value $I\xi\,(q, n - q + 1)$ of the incomplete beta function yields this bound.

10.1.2 A Further Consideration

The biometric identification of a large population is complicated by the following circumstance: enrollment will have to be conducted through several venues simultaneously. We must distinguish here between different instances of a given biometric device. Each venue will be served by one instance of each device being used. A biometric obtained from one venue, with one instance of a particular device of some make and specification, will have to be matched against the biometrics obtained from every other venue with other instances of the same device. The requirement now is that all instances of a device, of a given make and specification, be operational clones of each other. Section 10.4 specifies the conditions that operational clones must satisfy, and considers briefly how they might be practically met. However, for lack of data, we cannot gauge how well the UIDAI's operations might meet the requirement.

10.2 Quantitative Preliminaries

A biometric is a numerized representation of some generic physical or physiological feature of an organism: for precision and brevity, we shall call such a feature an organic object, using the word "object" in a less than daily way. The numerized representation is typically a real or binary vector, which must be of suitably large dimension if the biometric is to be used for the identification of organic individuals. We shall only be considering such identificatory biometrics. A device or arrangement for obtaining these numerized representations will first scan the organic object in some way. It is important to keep in mind that *a biometric is always the output that a particular device produces when it is given as input an organic object of the sort it was designed to scan.* The crucial circumstances now are

(a) the numerized representations obtained from any two scans of the same organic object are almost never *precisely* the same

(b) specifying *in advance* how numerized representations of different organic objects will themselves differ, with any exactitude, seems impossible

These inconvenient imprecisions arise in two ways: from unavoidable variations in the physical process of scanning, and from the peculiarities of whatever algorithm converts the signal or image produced by scanning into a numerized representation. Circumstance (a) allows the identification error already noted: because the numerized representations of two distinct organic objects may differ only as much as the representations produced by different scannings of one or another of those objects. The biometric produced from a particular scanning of an object may sometimes also appreciably differ from some identifying representation produced from a prior scanning of that object, which may occasion what one might call verification error, and we shall specify both identification and verification error more precisely in a moment. Therefore, circumstance (a) necessitates the measurement of similarity and difference: one has to decide how similar the two biometrics must be to be accounted numerized representations of the same organic object, and how different they must be, conversely, to be accounted representations of different organic objects. Circumstance (b) ensures that these difficulties may be met in an empirical way only: measures or means to decide similarities and differences for the biometrics produced by a particular device can be obtained only by sampling its output.

One usually proceeds here by deciding on some suitable distance between the numerized representations that a device produces, upon which certain distributions of these distances are experimentally estimated. Let X^δ denote the random variable whose values are distances between numerized representations of *distinct* organic objects, of which a random sample of $C_{n,2}$ values may be obtained from n objects after scanning each once. Let X^σ denote the variable whose values are distances between different numerized representations of the *same* organic object, of which n values may be obtained upon scanning each object twice; although special care may have to be taken to ensure that the sample is properly random. The primary requirement in the design of the device may now be stated thus: one must be able to find a number τ such that the probabilities $P(X^\delta < \tau)$ and $P(X^\sigma > \tau)$ are both miniscule. The chance that a value of X^δ lies below τ, on the one hand, and the chance that a value of X^σ lies above τ, on the other, must both be very small.

We emphasize that the variables X^δ and X^σ depend on the device that produces the biometrics. Let f^δ and f^σ denote their distribution functions. The decisive number τ above is called an *error threshold*, and experimental estimates of f^δ and f^σ must allow a ready choice of threshold. These estimates must allow the secure estimation of the probabilities $P(X^\delta < \tau)$ and $P(X^\sigma > \tau)$ as well. The first of these is what we called the *specified identification error* for the device, and *specified verification error* seems a good name for the second. Biometrics produced by a device are said to *match* if the distance between them falls below a chosen threshold, and to *falsely match* if they are numerized representations of distinct organic objects. We shall sometimes say that the objects themselves match or falsely match. We have said "identification error" for the chance of a false match: misusing words for the sake of brevity, and the specified identification error for a device, for a specified threshold, is its manufacturer's estimate of the probability of a false match. Verification error will not figure a very great deal, but we note that it is usually called the probability of a *false nonmatch*.

For numerized representations that are real vectors, the most common measure of difference would be Euclidean distance, or the Mahalanobis distance, if the vectors may be taken for values of a multivariate normal distribution whose covariance matrix can be reliably estimated. When the biometrics are binary vectors, a common measure would be the Hamming distance—provided the vectors are not sparse, which would most likely be the case. One might ask how realistic it is to treat such distances as values of a random variable, arising as they do from a particular device. However, the design of the device is presumably detailed enough to produce others which are operationally identical to it, and so the device may be regarded as one "black box" among many that each produce like outputs for like inputs. The matter is considered again in a different context in Section 4. Where f^δ and f^σ are integrable functions, $P(X^\delta < \tau)$ is the integral of f^δ over the interval $(-\infty, \tau]$ and $P(X^\sigma > \tau)$ is the integral of f^σ over $[\tau, \infty)$. We note that X^σ is like the genuine distribution used by Wayman [1], whereas X^δ is like the intertemplate distribution, but not quite the same (see Section 10.5). The graphs of f^δ and f^σ will peak, ideally, around means or primary modes that are widely separated, given their respective variances (see slide 49 in the study by Barrett [2]). One would like the mass of f^σ concentrated around a mode far to the left of where the mass of f^δ accumulates, and the threshold τ should lie many standard deviations to the left and to the right, at once, of the primary modes of f^δ and f^σ, respectively. The choice of a threshold τ, and determining the associated identification and verification errors, is a complicated affair in practice [1]. Moving τ to the left will decrease identification error and increase verification error, whereas moving it right will increase the first and decrease the second. Plotting estimates of the probability $P(X^\delta < \tau)$ against estimates of $P(X^\sigma > \tau)$, for varying values of the threshold τ, provide a curve called the *receiver operating characteristic* for the device which, under ideal circumstances, would display how changes in either identification error or verification error inversely affects the other.

We must note that "identification error" and "verification error" are not standard ways of referring to the probabilities they denote. They are often referred to as "error crossover rates," and the first, which we shall be most concerned with, is sometimes called the chance of a false-positive match for the device in question, or the false reject rate for the device. However, these latter terms find their proper use in the context of creating and maintaining biometric databases, as we shall shortly see.

We confine ourselves from herein to the biometric identification of human individuals. Suppose that more than one physical or physiological feature will be used to do so. Let $\{F_1, F_2, ..., F_K\}$ be the features whose numerized representations will provide a suite of identificatory biometrics for an individual, and suppose further that, for some considerable population of individuals, one such suite of identifying representations for each individual is to be stored in some biometric database. The process of gathering and storing identificatory biometrics is usually termed enrollment, and these stored representations are called templates. Therefore, in the situation we envisage, there are keepers of identity. Let us, melodramatically enough, style so the administrators of the biometric database are charged with obtaining and storing, for each individual in the population, a suite $\{b_1, b_2, ..., b_K\}$ of templates in which each b_k is a numerized representation of the feature F_k for each k in $\{1, 2, ..., K\}$. There will be a device M_k to scan F_k, whose manufacturer will have supplied the keepers of identity with a crossover threshold τ_k for the device, as well as the specified errors ρ_k and υ_k of identification and verification, respectively, which are associated with that threshold. The threshold and the associated errors will have been obtained by estimating the distributions of random variables X_k^δ and X_k^σ, which are the counterparts of X^δ and X^σ above, and ρ_k is the manufacturer's estimate of the probability $P\left(X_k^\delta < \tau_k\right)$, whereas υ_k is the like estimate of the probability $P\left(X_k^\sigma > \tau_k\right)$.

In the typical situation of enrollment, the keepers of identity are facing a putatively new enrollee: a person whose biometrics is not yet in their database. Let us call this individual S. Numerized representations $\{v_1, v_2, ..., v_K\}$ of the features $\{F_1, F_2, ..., F_K\}$ are obtained from S, and before they are entered into the database as his or her suite of biometric templates, they must be compared with every other suite of templates already in the database, of course, because each suite is meant to identify one and only one individual. Therefore, suppose that n persons have already been enrolled, and let $\{P_1, P_2, ..., P_N\}$ be a listing of these. For each index i in $\{1, 2, ..., n\}$ let $\{b_{1,i}, b_{2,i}, ..., b_{K,i}\}$ be the templates of the person P_i. We shall now suppose that each suite of biometrics in the database does correspond to a distinct individual: we suppose that there are no duplications, that is, in the database. For each k in $\{1, 2,..., K\}$ let $x_{k,i}$ be the distance between v_k and $b_{k,i}$: assuming that S is not already enrolled, the number $x_{k,i}$ can be taken for a value of the random variable X_k^δ, and it does seem realistic, assuming this, to regard the collection $\{x_{k,1}, x_{k,2},..., x_{k,i},..., x_{k,N}\}$ as a random sample of values drawn from X_k^δ.

As ρ_k estimates, the chance that any given value of X_k^δ will fall below τ_k, we may expect that ρ_k values from the sample will fall below this threshold; assuming, of course, that S is not actually enrolled. For each k in $\{1, 2,..., K\}$, let $\Gamma_k[S]$ denote the subset of those enrolled persons for whom such falling below the corresponding threshold happens, that is, P_i is in $\Gamma_k[S]$ when $x_{k,i} < \tau_k$. So the chance of finding any given enrolled person in $\Gamma_k[S]$ is ρ_k; and when the number n is suitably large—large enough for each quantity $\rho_k\, n$ to appreciably exceed 1, for instance—we must expect that none of the sets $\Gamma_k[S]$ will be empty. That is no reason to suppose, of course, that any one person will be found in each of these sets: it may be that the intersection $\Gamma[S]$ of all the $\Gamma_k[S]$ is actually empty. However, if we assume that each variable X_j^δ is now independent of every other X_k^δ, then for any enrolled person P_i, we can estimate the probability that he or she will be found in $\Gamma[S]$: that will happen only if $x_{k,i} < \tau_k$ for every index k in $\{1, 2,..., K\}$ of course, so the product $\rho_1, \rho_2... \rho_K$ estimates that probability now.

Suppose next that finding any P_i at all in $\Gamma[S]$ provides grounds enough for the keepers of identity to doubt that S is not already enrolled: the circumstance that $\Gamma[S]$ is not empty, then, when S is actually not enrolled, is usually termed a *false-positive match*. Let us say that S and an enrolled P_i are *matched at* the feature F_k if $x_{k,i} < \tau_k$: the condition of finding an enrolled P_i in $\Gamma[S]$ specifies a matching protocol followed by the keepers of identity, and here, a match occurs between an enrollee and any given enrolled person just in case they match at every numerized feature. Set $\xi = \rho_1, \rho_2... \rho_K$: we shall call this the *specified identification error for the matching protocol*, which, to make it entirely explicit, is the estimated probability that a match will occur between an unenrolled individual and any given enrolled person. The quantity ξ is a prior estimate of that probability, of course, obtained from the errors specified by their manufacturers for the devices being used and the conditions of their use in the process of enrollment that, in the field, may be expected to differ from the laboratory conditions of their testing. We shall focus on this question later.

In our terms here, the chance of a false-positive match is the probability that $\Gamma[S]$ does not turn out empty even though S is not enrolled, and we can make a prior estimate of this latter chance in terms of the identification error ξ for the matching protocol. Because ξ estimates the probability that any given enrolled person is found in the set $\Gamma[S]$, we may take $(1 - \xi)$ for the complementary probability that a given enrolled person *is not found* in $\Gamma[S]$. It seems licit to assume the following: whether or not any one enrolled person will be found in $\Gamma[S]$ is independent of whether or not any other enrolled person will be found there: thus, when n distinct persons have already been enrolled, we have $(1 - \xi)^n$ estimating the chance that $\Gamma[S]$ is empty. Therefore, the probability that $\Gamma[S]$ is not empty, which is the chance of a false-positive match here, is the quantity $1 - (1 - \xi)^n$.

Because $0 < \xi < 1$, we have $0 < (1 - \xi) < 1$ as well, so $(1 - \xi)^n$ decreases as the number n increases, and so the false reject rate will increase as enrollment proceeds. The increase in the false reject rate keeps pace with enrollment. We have

$$1 - (1 - \xi)^n = n \, \{\text{the integral of } (1 - t)^{n-1} \text{ over } [0, \xi]\} \leq n\,\xi \qquad \text{(i)}$$

as $0 \leq t \leq \xi < 1$ implies $0 < (1 - t) < 1$ and so $0 < (1 - t)^{n-1} < 1$ as well. Because it depends on the number of individuals enrolled, we shall write $\varphi(n) = 1 - (1 - \xi)^n$ for what the false reject rate comes to when n individuals have been enrolled. To summarize, we shall simply say *a match occurs* when the biometrics of an enrollee matches some stored template. Then, $\varphi(n)$ is the probability that a false-positive match will occur for the next *unenrolled* individual S who is to be enrolled: the chance that, even though he or she is not enrolled, the biometrics of S will match the templates of some or other enrolled person P.

That the chance of a false-positive match remains low is an evident desideratum. That enrolled persons trying to enroll again should be detected would be equally important. We must next consider the chance that an already enrolled individual will succeed in enrolling again. The probability of such an event is usually called the *false accept rate*. Let us write α simply for the false accept rate: the keepers of identity may expect this rate to depend on the specified verifications errors υ_k only or, more properly, on what the corresponding errors will be in the field. However, let us suppose for the moment that their devices perform as they are expected to.

Let D denote the biometric database, for brevity, and suppose next that S is an already enrolled person seeking to enroll again (using an alias, presumably). The templates taken at his or her prior enrollment will have created an avatar $P[S]$ for S in D, for example, a different virtual or spectral person from the perspective of the keepers of identity, and υ_k is their estimate, provided by the manufacturer of M_k, of the chance that S and this spectral $P[S]$ are not matched at the feature F_k. The probability that enrolled persons and their avatars do match at F_k should be estimated as $(1 - \upsilon_k)$ then. Write υ for the probability that *no match occurs* between an enrolled person P and his or her own avatar $P[S]$. Given the matching protocol they are following, and assuming again that matching at one feature is independent of matching at any other feature, the keepers of identity should estimate

$$1 - \upsilon = \prod_{1 \leq k \leq K} [1 - \upsilon_k] \tag{ii}$$

as the chance that a match will occur between an already enrolled person and his or her own avatar in D because a match is taken to occur only when matches occur at every feature. Note that whether or not matching at distinct features is independent, this complementary probability—which is the probability that an attempt to enroll again will be detected—actually decreases when more than one device is used. However, if K is a small count and if each υ_k is a miniscule quantity, the decrease should be negligible. In the mean, we have

$$\upsilon = 1 - \prod_{1 \leq k \leq K} [1 - \upsilon_k] \tag{iii}$$

$$1 - \alpha \geq 1 - \upsilon \tag{iv}$$

Inequality iii only restates Inequality ii of course. Inequality iv is obtained because the probability of a match occurring between an already enrolled applicant S and some or other enrolled P is at least as great as the chance of a match occurring between S and his or her own avatar $P[S]$; and from Inequalities iii and iv, we finally get the upper bound

$$\alpha \leq \upsilon = 1 - \prod_{1 \leq k \leq K} [1 - \upsilon_k] \tag{v}$$

We record once again that our bounds on the false reject rate and false accept rate derive from assuming that matching at any one feature F_k will be independent of matching at any other feature F_j: a circumstance we shall call the *independence of the metrized features*. Assuming that such independence obtained amounts to assuming that $\left\{ X_k^\delta \right\}_{1 \leq k \leq K}$ is a collection of independent random variables, and the collection $\left\{ X_k^\sigma \right\}_{1 \leq k \leq K}$ likewise; we note that these assumptions are generally made.

Consider next the converse of a false-positive match: the circumstance that an individual is not enrolled, in fact, even though a match does occur for him or her. We shall cast matters in the usual language of probability. Suppose that a number of persons have already been enrolled, and let S be the next individual presented to the keepers of identity. Let A now denote the circumstance that S is already enrolled, and A^c the complementary circumstance that he or she is not. Let B denote the circumstance that a match occurs for S, and B^c the complementary circumstance of no match occurring. The false reject rate is the conditional probability $P(B \mid A^c)$ then: the chance that a match occurs given that S is not actually enrolled. The false accept rate is the conditional probability $P(B^c \mid A)$: the probability that no match occurs given that S is already enrolled.

Now $P(A^c \mid B)$ is the probability that S is not actually enrolled, given that a match occurs: the chance of what was termed *mistaken identification* in the introductory summary of findings. Write $P(E)$ for the probability of any event or circumstance E; write $P(E \text{ and } F)$ for the probability of the conjunction of events or circumstances E and F; the formula

$$P(A^c \mid B)\, P(B) = P(A^c \text{ and } B) = P(B \mid A^c)\, P(A^c) \tag{vi}$$

relates the probability of mistaken identification to the false reject rate; therefore, we could estimate the former from the latter if we could estimate $P(A^c)$ and $P(B)$. Let us suppose that S is a randomly selected individual. The probabilities $P(A)$ and $P(A^c) = 1 - P(A)$ may now be taken generally to depend on the compulsions of individuals in the population that is being enrolled. Estimating them would, nonetheless, be very risky. But suppose the population is very large, as it is in our case, where UIDAI is engaged in biometrically identifying every resident of India. Suppose as well that, when a substantial number have been enrolled, the keepers of identity may reasonably take themselves to have sampled the population randomly. They may estimate $P(A)$ then, provided that they have been very successful in detecting attempts to enroll more than once. The personnel of the UIDAI have been bold enough to do so in fact, as we shall discuss next. Now $P(B)$ is the probability of a match occurring regardless of whether or not S is already enrolled, and the formula

$$P(B) = P(B \mid A^c)\, P(A^c) + P(B \mid A)\, P(A) \qquad\qquad \text{(vii)}$$
$$= P(B \mid A^c)\, P(A^c) + [1 - P(B^c \mid A)]\, P(A)$$

computes the chance of a match occurring for S, from the false reject rate and the false accept rate, and from the general probability that an enrolled individual will try to enroll again. The specified verification errors yield the upper bound on the false accept rate given in Inequality iv: from which the keepers of identity may expect that these probabilities will not change appreciably as enrollment proceeds. Therefore, when a substantial number have been enrolled, they could try to estimate (with a suitable experiment) what the false accept rate is for their matching protocol; and the personnel of the UIDAI have done so in fact.

In the following section, in which we consider the operations of the UIDAI in detail, we shall be using their experimentally obtained estimates of $P(A)$ and $P(B^c \mid A)$ to estimate the chance of mistaken identification. To do so accurately, we require an estimate of what the false reject rate will be in the field: which depends on the identification error (in the field) for the matching protocol they are following. As we mentioned in our introductory summary, after enrolling a substantial number, the UIDAI conducted an experiment to estimate the false reject rate. We use that to estimate identification error in the field. We end this preparatory section by directing the interested reader to the derivation of the bounds given by the Formulae 1, 2, and 3 in the summary of findings, which may be found in Section 10.1 of the technical supplement to this chapter, which is available online at (URL at PUBLISHER's WEB-ADDRESS) and may be freely downloaded from there. Some more of the detailed calculations needed are contained in the other sections of this supplement.

10.3 Calculations

In a note appearing in the online journal, *Pragati* [3], pertaining to the workings of the UIDAI and authored by a senior research associate at the Takshashila Institute, it was asserted that "the error crossover rate for fingerprinting and iris scans are 1 in 500 and 1 in 131,000, respectively." These are error rates supplied by their manufacturers, presumably, for the biometric devices used by the UIDAI. The author does not say if these rates are particularly for errors in identification or for errors in verification. But a standard way of proceeding is to choose the error threshold for a device in such a way that identification error and verification error are identical. Therefore, we shall suppose that the specified identification errors are such.

10.3.1 Step 1

The UIDAI itself has recently circulated an article titled *The Role of Biometric Technology in Aadhar Enrollment* [4], which reports an experimental estimate for the chance of a false-positive match. The estimate was made when 84 million individuals had been enrolled. The experiment consisted of 4 million trials with the following description: in each trial, a template is picked from the database and compared against the remainder to see if a match occurs (see Section 4.1 of the UIDAI report [4]). Assuming that the database contains no duplicates of the sampled templates, the number of times a match occurs should allow us to reliably estimate the chance of a false-positive match, which, remember, is the probability that a match occurs given that the person is not enrolled. The report stated that a match occurred 2309 times out of 4 million. There is no mention there of error crossover rates for the devices being used, and the UIDAI proceeds on the basis of its experiment to take $2309/4 \times 10^6$ for what the probability of a false-positive match was when 4 million had been enrolled. The matching protocol they are following is not specified either; therefore, one must look about a little to see if the experimental estimate accords with the specified identification errors for their devices. However, taking $r = 2309/4 \times 10^6$ (which comes to 0.00057725) as a reliable estimate of $\varphi(n)$ when $n = 84 \times 10^6$, we may estimate the identification error in the field: writing ξ for identification error in the field, and using Formula 1 from the summary of findings, we have

$$r/n \leq \xi \leq [-\log(1-r)]/n = \sum_{1 \leq k \leq \infty} r^k/(kn)$$

for bounds on ξ, and because $r^4/(4n) < 10^{-21}$ for the particular values of r and n that we have here, and as we have $(1.2) \times 10^9$ for an upper limit on the number to be enrolled, it should suffice to set

$$\xi = r/n + r^2/(2n) + r^3/(3n) = (0.687400801) \times 10^{-11} \qquad (\dagger)$$

with $r = 2309/4 \times 10^6$ and $n = 84 \times 10^6$. We must now contrive to discern the matching protocol: to do so, we must consider various possibilities and compute the specified identification errors for these matching schemes from the identification errors specified for the devices.

However, we need to consider a few variants only because one can make a good guess, from the report itself, at what the UIDAI's matching protocol must be. The physical features being metrized here are two irises and the insides of fingers and thumbs. The UIDAI's stated reason for using irises is that "people working in jobs that require repeated use of fingers—for example, in fireworks factories or in areca nut plantations—often find their fingerprints degraded, which makes iris useful in ensuring uniqueness," and further remarks made apropos of the need for using irises suggest how the decision might be made. The "proof of concept" exercise that the UIDAI had conducted before enrollment was begun *en masse* is said to have "clearly demonstrated that iris capture was indeed necessary, and along with fingerprint, it was sufficient to de-duplicate and uniquely identify the entire population" and "the accuracy of the combined system is an order of magnitude better" the report goes on to say "than fingerprints alone or iris alone." One "order of magnitude" is a factor of 10 here, and the second remark tempts one to guess that deciding on matches is done as follows: a match is taken to occur between an individual S presented for enrollment and an enrolled P if S and P are matched at both irises and at any one digit. The immediate motive for this guess is that the chance of a false match occurring at some or other digit, between an unenrolled S and an enrolled P, is now roughly 1/50, given a specified identification error of 1/500 for fingerprint scanners and again assuming the independence of the metrized features.

However, to make good on our guess, we should compute specified identification errors for close variants of this matching scheme. A few preliminaries are in order. Set

$\rho_\iota \equiv$ specified identification error for the iris device

$\rho_\delta \equiv$ specified identification error for the fingerprint device

$$\rho_{\delta,k} \equiv \sum_{k \leq s \leq 10} C_{10,s} (\rho_\delta)^s (1 - \rho_\delta)^{10-s}$$

For $1 \leq k \leq 10$, the quantity $\rho_{\delta,k}$ is the probability that, when S is not enrolled, comparing the numerized representations of his or her fingers to the representations of P's fingers, digit to corresponding digit, will result in at least k matches: $\rho_{\delta,k}$ is the probability, in short, that an unenrolled S and an enrolled P are matched at k digits at least.

Let ξ_0 denote the specified identification error generally for the matching protocols being considered, we have $\xi_0 = (\rho_\iota)^2 \rho_{\delta,1}$ now for the matching protocol that is our guess, assuming (to note it once more) the independence of the metrized features. Then we summarize that scheme and its closest variants, and their specified identification errors, with $\rho_\iota = 1/500$ and $\rho_\delta = 1/131{,}000$: the first two columns list required matches.

IRISES	DIGITS	ξ_0
2		$(\rho_\iota)^2 = 0.582779560 \times 10^{-10}$
2	≥ 1	$(\rho_\iota)^2 \rho_{\delta,1} = 0.115512486 \times 10^{-11}$
2	≥ 2	$(\rho_\iota)^2 \rho_{\delta,2} = 0.103776040 \times 10^{-13}$

Our conjectured matching protocol is the second one here, and given the estimate in Formula † for identification error in the field, the guess seems a good one because the difference between specified error and field error is the least for that choice. Note also that, in going from the first to the second of the variants listed above, the specified identification error does decrease by somewhat more than "one order of magnitude." We shall take our conjectured one to be the matching protocol followed by the UIDAI then, and for this scheme, the ratio of field error to specified error is 0.687400801/0.115512486 = 5.950878773 or approximately 6.

We are assuming here that, whatever the matching protocol of the UIDAI might be, both irises will be scanned. We also noted the "one order of magnitude" decrease in the specified identification error when going from using only irises to our conjectured matching protocol. To secure our guess, and for completeness, we shall summarize a few other possible matching schemes. Set $\rho_{1,1} \equiv 1 - (1 - \rho_1)^2$ as a preliminary: this is the probability that an unenrolled S and an enrolled P will match at *one or other* iris. With $\rho_{\delta,k}$ as it was defined above, and with the values of ρ_1 and ρ_δ just given, the following table lists possible matching schemes and specified identification errors. The first two columns list required matches, as before; for the first four of the listed schemes only one iris is scanned; for the last three both irises are scanned, but a match occurring at either will do.

IRISES	DIGITS	ξ_0
1	≥1	$\rho_1\,\rho_{\delta,1} = 0.151313186 \times 10^{-6}$
1	≥2	$\rho_1\,\rho_{\delta,2} = 0.135953906 \times 10^{-8}$
1	≥3	$\rho_1\,\rho_{\delta,3} = 0.725230000 \times 10^{-11}$
1	≥4	$\rho_1\,\rho_{\delta,4} = 0.256474002 \times 10^{-13}$
≥1	≥2	$\rho_{1,1}\,\rho_{\delta,2} = 0.271890000 \times 10^{-8}$
≥1	≥3	$\rho_{1,1}\,\rho_{\delta,3} = 0.145036500 \times 10^{-10}$
≥1	≥4	$\rho_{1,1}\,\rho_{\delta,4} = 0.512914410 \times 10^{-12}$

Consider the third matching scheme summarized here. Only one iris is scanned now, and all 10 digits. A match will be taken to occur if a match occurs at the iris and at *any three* corresponding digits. The specified identification error here is nearly an order of magnitude less than the scheme that uses only the two irises; therefore, this scheme is also a candidate for the matching protocol the UIDAI is actually using and, in that case, the specified identification error would be very close to the estimate in Formula † for identification error in the field. However, if the use of fingerprints is risky because "people working in jobs that require repeated use of fingers... often find their fingerprints degraded," then it would be prudent to use as few digits as possible for the matching protocol, and the specified identification error for our conjectured scheme is considerably less (by more than a factor of 6), than the error for candidate we have just looked at, and that should have decided UIDAI to choose the former scheme over the latter; surely, were both being considered. Moreover, if using three digits poses little risk, then using two digits poses even less and, in that case, the best strategy would have been to use the stricter variant of our conjectured scheme, which was summarized in the third line of the previous table, in which a match would be taken to occur if matches occurred at both irises and at *any two* digits. The specified identification error of $0.103776040 \times 10^{-13}$ would have been three orders of magnitude less than the error of $0.582779560 \times 10^{-10}$ for the scheme using matches only at both irises; therefore, the UIDAI should surely have gone with that if they were willing to go with the candidate we first looked at here. Therefore, we shall stay with our conjectured matching protocol.

10.3.2 Step 2

As we are now considering the operations of the UIDAI in particular, we shall refer to individuals presented for enrollment as applicants (for a UID or a "unique identity" precisely). Following the report of the experiment to estimate the false match rate $P(B \mid A^c)$ for the next unenrolled applicant after 84 million had been enrolled, the UIDAI report describes an experiment designed to estimate the false accept rate, which is the conditional probability $P(B^c \mid A)$ that a match will not occur given that, on the contrary, the applicant is already enrolled. We have already noted that the false accept rate does not depend on the number of individuals already enrolled. In Formula v of the previous section, we had derived an upper bound for this probability from the specified verification errors of the devices being used. The second experiment consisted of 31,399 trials of the following description: in each trial, an enrolled person is selected at random from the database and a fresh suite of biometrics is obtained from that person. That suite is then compared against each suite of templates in the database to see if a match occurs. One expects matches now, particularly because the fresh suite is being compared against the template of that enrolled individual, among others. In 31,388 of these trials, a match did indeed occur; therefore, 11/31,399 is the UIDAI's experimental estimate of the false accept rate $P(B^c \mid A)$. (The results of this experiment are reported in Item 3, Section 4.1 of the UIDAI report [4].) From the relation

$$P(B \mid A) + P(B^c \mid A) = [P(B \text{ and } A) + P(B^c \text{ and } A)]/p(A)$$

$$= p(A)/p(A) = 1 \qquad (10.1)$$

we get $P(B \mid A) = 1 - P(B^c \mid A)$, and 31,388/31,399 is the estimate we now have of this probability, which we shall regard as fixed because, as we have noted, the complementary false accept rate does not change as enrollment proceeds.

One might wonder if it is proper to estimate both $P(B \mid A^c)$ and $P(B^c \mid A)$ with just such experiments: by computing suites of distances $\{x_1, x_2,\ldots, x_K\}$ between the templates of enrolled persons or between the latter and freshly taken biometrics of such persons. However, complications would arise only if appeal were made to the distributional properties an x_k would have when it is regarded as a value of X_k^σ: and that cannot be done, obviously, when $P(B^c \mid A)$ is being estimated. No such appeal is being made, however, in the calculations. We have suites of distances obtained in two distinct ways: by template-to-template comparisons first, in which the elements of a compared pair are derived from distinct persons, and then by comparisons of fresh biometrics to templates. In the latter case, the elements of a compared pair will not always be derived from distinct persons. We may now identify the conditional circumstances $(B \mid A^c)$ and $(B^c \mid A)$ with concatenations of certain numerical events, which are determined by how each value x_k lies to the threshold τ_k only, without regarding the number as a value of either X_k^δ or of X_k^δ, or as a value of any distribution, for that matter, and our *interpretations* of these numerical circumstances as recognizable eventualities are secured by how these suites of distances have been obtained.

Our ultimate interest here is in the probability $P(A^c \mid B)$ of mistaken identification: the computing of which requires the converse $P(B \mid A^c)$ and the simple probabilities $P(B)$ and $P(A^c)$ as well, as we noted in Formula vi. From Formula vii, we see that an estimate of either $P(A^c)$ or its complement $P(A) = 1 - P(A^c)$, together with estimates of $P(B \mid A^c)$ and $P(B \mid A)$, will allow us to estimate $P(B)$. After the report of the second experiment, one finds that the UIDAI has determined to its satisfaction a "current 0.5% rate of duplicate submissions," which seems to say that 0.5% of the applicants turned out to have been enrolled already by the time 84 million had been enrolled. Assuming that the entire population to be enrolled had been randomly and sufficiently sampled by then, we may take $P(A) = 0.005$ and $P(A^c) = 0.995$ for stable estimates of these probabilities, and the UIDAI is prepared to assume, we note, that the "rate of duplicate submission" will neither decrease nor increase as enrollment proceeds (again, see Item 3 in Section 4.1 of the UIDAI report [4]).

10.3.3 Step 3

We can now proceed with the calculations for our other two findings. Our first object is to compute the probability of mistaken identification for various subsets of the population, which is estimated by the ratio of false matches to all matches. We shall begin by estimating the number of matches that will have occurred by the time enrollment is complete, and estimate the number of false matches among these. The population of India is said to be 1.2 billion; therefore, for each number n between 1 and $(1.2) \times 10^9$, we must consider what the false reject rate $\varphi(n)$ becomes by the time n individuals have been enrolled, and the lower bound from Formula 2 of the *Summary of Findings* gives the safe approximation

$$\varphi(n) \approx [n\xi\,(1 - \xi)]/[1 - \xi + n\xi] \qquad (10.2)$$

of $P(B|A^c)$ for the next individual to be enrolled. Using the value of ξ from Formula †, the easiest way to go would be to obtain a linear estimate for last term; otherwise, we shall have to make 1.2 billion estimates. We shall come back to the question.

Write $\beta(n)$ for the probability that a match will occur for the next individual to be enrolled: we get $\beta(n) = \varphi(n)P(A^c) + P(B \mid A)P(A)$ then from Formula vii, which we had for $P(B)$ above. The estimates of the UIDAI give us

$$P(B \mid A)\,p(A) \approx [31{,}388/31{,}399] \times (0.005) = 0.004998248$$

$$P(A^c) \approx 0.995$$

Set $\gamma = 0.004998248$ for convenience. Suppose a total of Q many individuals are to be enrolled; let $m(Q)$ denote the total number of matches we expect. Assuming that the occurrences of matches are independent of each other, as is usually done and as we well may, for the expected number of matches we now have the formula

$$m(Q) = \sum_{1 \leq n < Q} \beta(n) = \sum_{1 \leq n < Q} [\varphi(n)P(A^c) + P(B \mid A)P(A)] \quad (10.3)$$

$$\approx P(A^c)\left[\sum_{1 \leq n < Q} \varphi(n)\right] + \gamma(Q-1)$$

For a quick count of $m(Q)$, note first that $\varphi(n) \geq [n\xi(1 - \xi)]/[1 - \xi + Q\xi]$ always. Setting $\lambda = 0.687400801$ for convenience as well, we have $\xi = \lambda \times 10^{-11}$ from Formula †; and with and $Q = (1.2) \times 10^9$ we will, with a little calculation, obtain the approximations

$$[\xi(1 - \xi)]/[1 - \xi + Q\xi] \approx \lambda/[10^{-9}\,(10^{-2} + (1.2)\lambda)]$$

$$= (0.68177) \times 10^{-11} \quad (10.4)$$

$$P(A^c)\,[\xi(1 - \xi)]/[1 - \xi + Q\xi] \approx (0.678368115) \times 10^{-11} \quad (10.5)$$

Set $\eta = (0.678368115) \times 10^{-11}$: from Equations 10.2, 10.3, and 10.5, we have

$$m(Q) \geq \eta\left[\sum_{1 \leq n < Q} n\right] + \gamma(Q-1) = \eta Q(Q-1)/2 + \gamma(Q-1) \quad (10.6)$$

then. Next, note that we will have $(Q - 1) = (1.2) \times (10^9 - 1) + (0.2)$ when $Q = (1.2) \times 10^9$ because $(a10^q - 1) - a(10^q - 1) = a - 1$ generally; thus, the approximations

$$Q - 1 \approx (1.2) \times (10^9 - 1)$$

$$Q(Q - 1) \approx (1.2) \times 10^9(1.2)(10^9 - 1) = (1.44) \times 10^9\,(10^9 - 1)$$

may safely be used for estimation, given the values declared for η and γ here; and direct calculation shows that $m(Q)$ will now be approximately equal to 10,882,148. The estimate in Formula 10.4 above, which was used to obtain the factor η, may be found in Section 10.2 of the technical supplement to this chapter.

We underestimate $m(Q)$ here by using a uniform lower bound for $\varphi(n)$, and we shall provide a more accurate estimate later. However, one should expect more than 10.88 million matches to have occurred, at any rate, by the time enrollment is complete. Let us now count the false ones among all the matches. The probability $P(B \text{ and } A^c)$ is what we must attend to: so let $\varepsilon(n)$ denote the chance that, once n individuals have been enrolled, the next applicant is not enrolled but that, nonetheless, a match does occur. As $P(B \text{ and } A^c) = P(B \mid A^c) P(A^c)$ we get

$$\varepsilon(n) = \varphi(n)P(A^c) \approx \eta n = (0.678368115) \times 10^{-11}n$$

from Equations 10.2, 10.3, and 10.5 again. Let $d(Q)$ denote the total number of unenrolled applicants for whom a match will have occurred by the time enrollment is complete, that is, the total number of false matches. Assuming that such matches are independent of each other as well, we get $\sum_{1 \leq n < Q} \varepsilon(n)$ as our estimate of this number, whence

$$d(Q) = \sum_{1 \leq n < Q} \varepsilon(n) \approx \eta \sum_{1 \leq n < Q} n = \eta Q(Q-1)/2$$

The expression for $d(Q)$ is the first summand in the expression for $m(Q)$ above, and direct calculation shows that $\eta Q (Q - 1)/2$ is approximately 4,884,250. To summarize, by the time enrollment is complete, the UIDAI should expect to have adjudicated matches for more than 10.88 million applicants, and more than 4.88 million among these will have been false ones.

To be brief, let us call an applicant, whose suite of biometrics matches that of someone already enrolled, a matched applicant who will be falsely matched if he or she happens not to be enrolled. Now the numbers 10.88 million and 4.88 million may seem trifling when they are set beside 1.2 billion, and perhaps they are. However, there is an asymmetry here which one should note, as we shall discuss next: the number of matches, and the number of false matches among these, will vary considerably between the initial and final stages of enrollment.

To estimate the difference here, we need to refine our estimate of the factor η above by using small values of Q. Repeating the calculation that gives (10.4) with $\lambda = 0.687400801$ and $Q = 10^6$, we get

$$[\xi(1 - \xi)]/[1 - \xi + 10^6\xi] \approx [\lambda \, 10^5]/[10^{11} (10^5 + (1.2) \lambda)]$$

$$= 0.687395131 \times 10^{-11}$$

$$P(A^c) [\xi (1 - \xi)]/[1 - \xi + 10^6 \xi] \approx 0.683958155 \times 10^{-11}$$

Setting $\eta_1 = 0.683958155 \times 10^{-11}$ and with γ as above, and using η_1 just as we have used η, the matches expected for the first million enrolled are

$$\sum_{1 \le n < Q} \beta(n) \approx \eta_1 10^6(10^6 - 1)/2 + \gamma(10^6 - 1) \approx 3 + 4998 = 5001$$

approximately, and only three among these will be falsely matched applicants. However, the number of matches to be expected for the last million enrolled, and the falsely matched applicants among them, will be considerably larger. To estimate these numbers, set $Q = (1.2) \times 10^9$ once again and $M = (1.2) \times 10^9 - 10^6$; using Equations 10.2, 10.3, and 10.5 as before, the total number of matches expected in the last million is

$$\sum_{M \le n < Q} \beta(n) = \sum_{M \le n < Q} [P(A^c)\varphi(n) + P(B \mid A)P(A)]$$

$$\approx \left[\sum_{M \le n < Q} \varepsilon(n) \right] + \gamma \left[\sum_{M \le n < Q} n \right]$$

$$\approx \eta \left[\sum_{M \le n < Q} (n) \right] + \gamma(Q - M) \approx 8137 + 4998 = 13{,}135$$

of which 8137 are false matches. The total number of matches in the first and last millions enrolled is comparable, but we see that the number of false matches expected has increased disproportionately. To summarize, one expects approximately 5001 matches for the first one million enrolled, and three among the matched applicants should be falsely matched. In the last one million enrolled, one expects approximately 13,135 matches, and among these matched applicants, some 8137 should be falsely matched.

These exercises can be repeated for the sets or batches formed by successive millions of applicants. Let N_k denote the expected number of matches among the kth million applicants, and let F_k denote the expected number of falsely matched applicants among these; we must now estimate a factor like η for different values of the index k. Setting

$Q_k = k \times 10^6$ and repeating the calculations for Equation 10.4 with Q_k in place of Q, we get

$$[\xi(1 - \xi)]/[1 - \xi + Q_k \xi] \approx \lambda/[10^6 (10^5 + k \lambda)]$$

with λ as above; and for each index k and for values of n given by

$$[(k - 1) \times 10^6] = Q_{k-1} \leq n \leq [k \times 10^6 - 1] = Q_k - 1$$

we have $P(A^c)\varphi(n) \approx [P(A^c)\lambda]/[10^6(10^5 + k\lambda)]$ for the factor analogous to η here; which we shall denote by η_k. Therefore, with $\gamma = P(B \mid A)$ $P(A)$ as above and calculating as we did for Equation 10.3, we obtain the formulae

$$N_k = \sum_n \beta(n) = \sum_n [P(A^c)\varphi(n) + P(B \mid A)P(A)]$$

$$\approx P(A^c) \lambda [(2k - 1) 10^6 - 1]/2 (10^6 + k\lambda) + \gamma[(Q_k - 1) - Q_{k-1} + 1]$$

$$\approx \eta_k [10^6 [(2k - 1)10^6] - 1]/2 + \gamma 10^6$$

$$F_k = \sum_n \varepsilon(n) \approx N_k - \gamma 10^6$$

where $\sum_{r \leq j \leq s} j = (s - r + 1)(s + r)/2$ gives us, in the second line, the sum of the numbers lying between Q_{k-1} and $(Q_k - 1)$.

Using these formulae, we can estimate and compare matches and false matches for the first and last m million applicants, respectively, for varying values of m. Write $N_\alpha(m)$ for the matches among the first m million, and $F_\alpha(m)$ for the false matches among these; write $N_\omega(m)$ for the matches among the last m million and $F_\omega(m)$ for the false matches among those. Here are some estimates of these counts, for a few values of m, among the first and last aggregated millions.

m	$F_\alpha(m)$	$N_\alpha(m)$	$F_\omega(m)$	$N_\omega(m)$
1	5001	3	13,135	8137
2	10,011	13	26,264	16,267
5	25,077	85	65,609	40,168
10	50,325	341	131,050	81,067
100	534,010	34,180	1,280,208	780,382
200	1,136,318	136,665	2,493,042	1,493,392
250	1,463,057	213,490	3,074,167	1,824,605

In its report [4], the UIDAI asserts that "the system will be able to scale to handle the entire population without significant drop in accuracy." The ratio of false matches to total matches expected, for any substantial subset of the population, seems an appropriate measure of accuracy here: the lower the ratio—the lower the chance of mistaken identification, that is to say—the more accurate the system will be. So the ratios $F_\alpha(m)/N_\alpha(m)$ and $F_\omega(m)/N_\omega(m)$ are what we must attend to now: and here they are for the values of m for which we have previously computed the numbers:

m	$F_\alpha(m)/N_\alpha(m)$	$F_\omega(m)/N_\omega(m)$
1	0.00059988	0.619489912
2	0.012858556	0.61936491
5	0.00338956	0.619091893
10	0.006775956	0.618595956
100	0.064006292	0.609574382
200	0.12027003	0.599024004
250	0.145920494	0.593528263

The expected ratio of false matches to total matches increases considerably between the initial and final stages of enrollment. One or 10 million may not count as substantial subsets of a population, but a hundred million surely does in a population of 1.2 billion; and we see from the fifth line here that, as recorded in the summary of findings, the chance of mistaken identification will increase almost tenfold between the first and the last 100 millions enrolled. The probability of mistaken identification will only increase, of course, with any increase in the total population. Should the population of India reach 1.5 billion, for instance, we estimate that the false matches to total matches in the final 100 million will stand at 981,954 to 1,481,779, giving a ratio of almost 2:3 between them.

Keeping the population at 1.2 billion, however, we see that matters improve somewhat between the first 250 million enrolled and the last 250 million because the decrease in accuracy is now less than fivefold; but note how dramatically accuracy decreases as enrollment increases. The expected number of matches in the second 100 million is 1,136,318 − 534,010 = 602,308; the expected number of false matches among these is 136,665 - 34,180 = 102,485, and the ratio between these numbers becomes 0.170153808 for the second 100 million enrolled, whereas it was only 0.064006292 for the first 100 million. This last maneuver suggests the appropriate way to summarize the drop in accuracy: estimate and display the number of matches, and the false matches among these, for each successive million enrolled. Let us call these *false match ratios* for brevity. The graph in Figure 10.1 shows the results: it plots both the cumulative and successive false match ratios as enrollment proceeds. The lower curve charts the cumulative ratios, in which the ratio of false matches among all matches, of course, when a given number have been enrolled. The horizontal axis counts the population in millions, whereas the vertical axis records the respective ratios; the numerical labels display actual counts at each hundredth million.

Computing and summing with the formulae for N_k and F_k above gives us our revised estimate of 10,895,510 for the total count $m(Q)$ of matches expected: among which one may expect 4,897,609 to be false matches. These are lower bounds for these counts: we have underestimated them by using the lower bound in Equation 10.3 for the probabilities $\varphi(n)$. However, using the upper bound $n\xi$ will not change

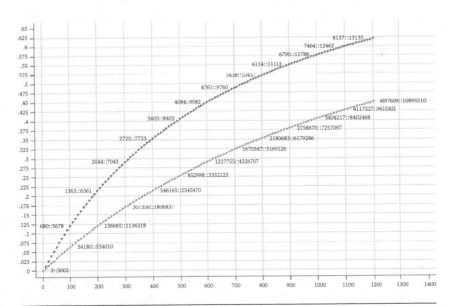

Figure 10.1 Successive and cumulative false match ratios, above and below, respectively, plotted for millions enrolled.

things too much. Writing $m^+(Q)$ for the upper bound on the total number matches, we have

$$m^+(Q) = \sum_{1 \le n < Q} [P(A^c)n\xi + \gamma] = P(A^c)\xi Q(Q-1)/2 + \gamma(Q-1)$$

then. Repeating the calculation for $m(Q)$ above, with $Q = 1.2$ billion again and with $P(A^c)\xi$ in place of η there, yields 10,922,437 as an upper bound on matches, and 4,924,539 as an upper bound on false matches. The differences between the upper and lower bounds here are 0.002471385 and 0.005498601 as fractions of the respective lower bounds, and as these are marginal for the largest of our counts, we may safely go with the numbers listed above. The graph in Figure 10.2 plots the differences, for successive millions, between false matches counted with the upper and lower bounds for $\varphi(n)$, respectively; and Figure 10.3 plots these differences for all matches. Notice that these differences grow in the same way as enrollment proceeds; therefore, using the upper bound for $\varphi(n)$ should make neither more pronounced nor less, the differences between initial false match ratios and final false match ratios.

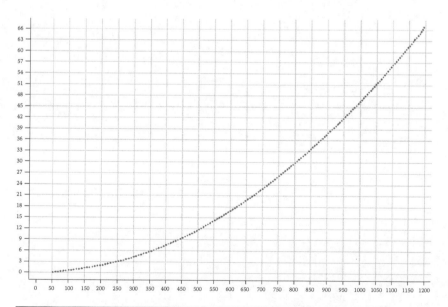

Figure 10.2   The difference between upper and lower bounds for all matches, plotted for successive millions enrolled.

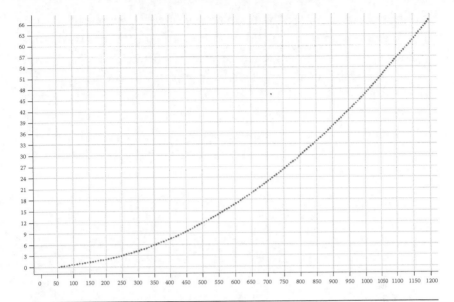

Figure 10.3 The difference between upper and lower bounds for false matches, plotted for successive millions enrolled.

10.3.4 Step 4

When a match occurs for a putatively new applicant, his or her suite of biometrics may match more than one suite of templates in the database. Let us call such a suite of matching templates a *matched record*, and each matched record will now have to be examined to determine whether or not the match is a false one. To measure how efficient the process of enrollment is, we shall have to estimate the total number of matched records that will have been found, by the time enrollment is complete, for all the matched applicants the UIDAI should expect. The process of estimation here is somewhat tortuous. Let $q < n$ and suppose n individuals have already been enrolled. Let $R_q(n)$ abbreviate the following circumstance, that at least q suites of templates in the database will match the biometrics of the next applicant. We must estimate its probability, and keeping with the notation we have been using, to do that we require the probability of the conditional circumstance $[R_q(n)|A^c]$: the circumstance that at least q suites of templates in database will match the biometrics of the next applicant S given that he or she is not in fact enrolled. The probability of a match occurring for S is $1 - (1 - \xi)^n$ recall, which is the chance that his or her suite of biometrics will match the templates of *some or other* enrolled individual, and that is the probability $P(R_1(n)|A^c)$ also; then, the chance of finding at least one matched record for an unenrolled applicant. The chance that exactly one suite of templates in the database will now match the biometrics of S is $n\xi(1 - \xi)^{n-1}$. Again, assuming that matching with any one suite is independent of matching with any other, and with this assumption of independence, the probability that exactly j suites of templates will thus match is $C_{n,j}\xi^j(1 - \xi)^{n-j}$; therefore, we have

$$P(R_q(n)\,|\,A^c = \sum_{q \leq r \leq n} C_{n,r}\xi^r(1-\xi)^{n-r} = 1 - \sum_{1 \leq j < q} C_{n,j}\xi^j(1-\xi)^{n-j}$$

The quantity on the right is the term $\psi_q(n)$ of Equation 10.4 in the summary of findings: which gives us the upper bound on $P(R_q(n)|A^c)$ that we shall be using. It seems reasonable here to set $P(R_{m+1}(n) \,|\, A)$ equal to $P(R_m(n) \,|\, A^c)$: the chance of finding at least $(m + 1)$ matched records when the $(n + 1)$st applicant *is* already enrolled should approximate, surely, the chance of finding at least m matched records were he or she *not* enrolled. Therefore, we have

$$P(R_q(n)) = P(R_q(n) \,|\, A)\, P(A) + P(R_q(n) \,|\, A^c)\, P(A^c)$$

$$= \psi_{q-1}(n)P(A) + \psi_q(n)\, P(A^c)$$

for $q > 1$. We may assume the independence of matches for different applicants: the chance that at least q matched records will be found for one applicant is not affected by whether or not that happens for any other. Write N for the total number of individuals who are to be enrolled, and for $q > 1$ set

$$T_q = \sum_{1 \leq n < N} P(R_q(n)) = P(A) \sum_{1 \leq n < N} \psi_{q-1}(n) + P(A^c) \sum_{1 \leq n < N} \psi_q(n)$$

T_q will equal or exceed the total number of matched records found for those matched applicants whose suite of biometrics matches q suites of templates, *at least*, in the database. Write S_q for this latter set of matched applicants: the set S_q will contain the set S_{q+1} of course, and for the total count T of matched records we shall then have

$$T = (T_1 - T_2) + 2(T_2 - T_3) + 3(T_3 - T_4) + \ldots + r(T_r - T_{r-1}) + \ldots$$

which comes to $T_1 + T_2 + \ldots + T_{N-1}$, where N is the total population because $T_r = 0$; of course, when r equals or exceeds that total. However, we may very reasonably expect to have $T_r \approx 0$ before r gets at all large, and we shall now approximate the few terms that we need to safely count T. We use the upper bound in Formula 3 in the *Summary of Findings* as our approximation for $\psi_q(n)$ here. We have T_1 already, which will equal the total number of matched applicants, of course, and at the end of the last section, we had computed that number as 10,922,437 using $\psi_1(n) = 1 - (1 - \xi)^n \approx n\xi$ as our approximation. Now for $N = (1.2) \times 10^9$, we obtain the approximations

$$T_2 = P(A) \sum_{1 \le n < N} \psi_1(n) + P(A^c) \sum_{1 \le n < N} \psi_2(n) \approx 274{,}545.4$$

$$T_3 = P(A) \sum_{1 \le n < N} \psi_2(n) + P(A^c) \sum_{1 \le n < N} \psi_3(n) \approx 219.9$$

$$T_4 = P(A) \sum_{1 \le n < N} \psi_3(n) + P(A^c) \sum_{1 \le n < N} \psi_4(n) \approx 0.6$$

$$T_5 = P(A) \sum_{1 \le n < N} \psi_4(n) + P(A^c) \sum_{1 \le n < N} \psi_5(n) \approx 0$$

The calculations are in Section 3 of the technical supplement. Because T_r only decreases as r increases, we shall need only these approximations to estimate T.

We may take $T \approx T_1 + T_2 + T_3 + T_4$ then, and because we have computed with upper bounds for our probabilities $\psi_q(n)$, we may safely suppose that

$$T \approx 10{,}922{,}437 + 274{,}545 + 220 + 1 = 11{,}267{,}203$$

is what the count of matched records will come to, *at most*, by the time the entire population of 1.2 billion has been enrolled. At the end of Section 3.3, we had computed an upper limit of 10,922,437 on total matches, and an upper limit of 4,924,539 on false matches among these: and with 11,267,203 for an upper limit on matched records, we see that, as asserted in the summary of findings, to determine which matches are false, only rarely will more than one matched record have to be examined, and things should be so through the entire course of enrollment, even though the number of matched records examined for each match will increase somewhat in the final stages.

10.3.5 Step 5

We now close the main part of our essay by registering a very minor complication. We have taken a biometric for a real or binary vector, which it usually is. The "numerized representations" of fingerprints may sometimes be two-dimensional patterns, although of certain "minutiae" that are characteristic of them: see [6] for a discussion. However, no grave consequences follow for the calculations done here: the specified probabilities of distances falling below or above a threshold will only have to be replaced with the chances of spatial patterns matching either too closely, on the one hand, or not matching closely enough, on the other.

10.4 Operational Clones

At the end of the introductory section, we touched on a particular complication that will attend the biometric identification of a large population, which is that enrollment must be conducted simultaneously through several venues. The UIDAI would have to enroll applicants for a UID through hundreds of venues, surely, if the biometric identification of 1.2 billion people is to be completed in good time. Then the suite of identifying biometrics obtained from an applicant at any one venue will have to be compared against those obtained from applicants at every other venue, and one must ensure that matching will be uniformly done regardless.

The question had been broached, in passing, in Section 10.2—we consider it here in a somewhat different light. Let F be some particular identificatory feature. We must distinguish once more the scanning of F—which produces the *image* we mentioned in Section 10.2—from the *processing* of that image into a numerized representation of the feature, and the combined process of scanning and processing may be termed the *metrizing* of F. We must now regard a biometric device as a scanner paired to an image processor, and where many scanners are paired to one processor, we shall take each such pairing for a different *instance* of the same biometric device. Let M be some make of a device to metrize the feature F: there will now be one instance of M for each venue. Let u denote, generically, the numerized representation of F produced by any instance of M. For any such representation u, let $O(u)$ denote the *particular instance* of F which was scanned, by *some or other* instance of M, in producing it. For any two such representations u_1 and u_2, let $S(u_1, u_2)$ denote the circumstance that they were both produced by the same instance of M; and let $\neg\, S(u_1, u_2)$ denote the circumstance that they were produced by different instances of M. Let $d(u_1, u_2) = x$ denote the distance between u_1 and u_2 under whatever metric has been chosen to measure their difference. In the notation of Section 10.2, the distance x may be taken for a value of the random variable X^δ if $S(u_1, u_2)$ is obtained but $O(u_1)$ *is not* the same as $O(u_2)$; and for a value of the variable X^σ if, on the other hand, $S(u_1, u_2)$ is obtained and $O(u_1)$ *is* the same as $O(u_2)$. Now the following seems a reasonable condition to impose if many instances of M are all to be regarded as operational clones of each other:

C^1 $P(x < \tau \mid \neg\, S(u_1, u_2)) = P(x < \tau \mid S(u_1, u_2))$ if $\neg\, [O(u_1) = O(u_2)]$ for any choice of threshold τ

The condition asks that, given different instances of the feature F, the chance of a match being the same whether or not their numerized representations are produced by the same instance of the device M. This will ensure that identification error does not vary between venues. For verification, we need to ensure as well that given any one instance of F, the chance of no match occurring between different representations will be the same whether or not these are produced by the same instance of M: and the analogous condition would be

C^2 $P(x > \tau \mid \neg\, S(u_1, u_2)) = P(x > \tau \mid S(u_1, u_2))$ if $[O(u_1) = O(u_2)]$ for any choice of threshold τ

There would be other ways, surely, in which operational clones could be specified. However, the literature does not seem to address the problem, most likely because, for most uses of biometric identification, templates will be formed with a single instance of a device. A manufacturer may undertake to guarantee that each instance of a biometric device it makes is an operational clone of every other: but they do not seem to do as a matter of course. Therefore, when many venues are used for enrollment, the keepers of identity will very likely have to confirm for themselves that all their instances of a single device are indeed operational clones of each other. There would be many ways, again, to test whether or not many instances of a device are such, but some standard way of testing for the equality of distributions should serve for a rough and ready check here.

The classic Kolmogorov–Smirnov method, for instance, could provide a simple check: here is one way in which that might be used. Comparisons will most often be made between numerized representations produced by different instances of the device. For (u_1, u_2) where $\neg [O(u_1) = O(u_2)]$ and $\neg S(u_1, u_2)$, we might now regard the distances $x = d(u_1, u_2)$ as the values of a random variable X_0^δ, which is analogous to the distribution X^δ we have for the device M of course. Let G_0 be the cumulative distribution function of $X_0^\delta : G_0(x) = P\left(X_0^\delta \leq x \right)$ for any real number x. With any good-sized random sample from X_0^δ, and for any suitably small number $\varepsilon > 0$, one can construct bounding curves $G_{0,\varepsilon}^+$ and $G_{0,\varepsilon}^-$ such that

$$P\left[G_{0,\varepsilon}^-(x) \leq G_0(x) \leq G_{0,\varepsilon}^+(x) \right] = 1 - \varepsilon$$

for each real number x: so for any value x of X_0^δ, the probability is ε, only, that $G_0(x)$ does not lie in the interval $\left[G_{0,\varepsilon}^-(x), G_{0,\varepsilon}^+(x) \right]$. The keepers of identity should be able to construct such bounding curves quite soon after enrollment has begun. For any instance of M they should then be able to obtain a random sample of pairs (u_1, u_2) with $\neg[O(u_1) = O(u_2)]$, which have been produced by that instance itself, and the distances between the elements of each pair here may now be taken for a random sample of values drawn from X^δ. These values can be used to construct an estimate G of the cumulative distribution function of X^δ: whose construction should be such as to allow one to readily check whether or not, for each x, the value $G(x)$ lies in $\left[G_{0,\varepsilon}^-(x), G_{0,\varepsilon}^+(x) \right]$. With any luck, that will be the case, and should each instance of M pass this test, we may suppose that condition C^1 has been met. How such a procedure might be repeated for C^2 should be evident: provided only that a random sample can be drawn from the analogous distribution X^σ. For that, the keepers of identity will have to obtain, from each of a suitably large random collection of applicants, pairs (u_1, u_2) of numerized representations whose elements are produced by different instances of M, which requires that each of these applicants have the feature F scanned at two distinct venues, as well as twice at one other venue, obviously, to get sampled values of X^{σ}.

Our treatment might seem overly elaborate. Practically considered the constraint is that, for a biometric device or arrangement of a given make, the images produced by different instances of the scanner should be indistinguishable to the processor that converts these images into numerized representations. This condition might be routinely satisfied by certain sorts of devices. For a given make of a fingerprint scanner, for instance, the usual protocols of "quality control" might ensure that the scans output by different machines would even be indistinguishable to any available method of processing them into numerized representations, and such would very likely be the case whenever the image produced by a scanner is simple enough to be humanly scrutable. However, matters would be otherwise when the output of the scanner is informationally dense, as the image produced by scanning an iris would surely be, and only empirical testing could then ensure that the images produced by different instances of the scanner are indeed indistinguishable to the processor.

There is no indication, in their publications, that the UIDAI has sought to ensure that different instances of their devices will be operational clones of each other. Discovering that they are not, once enrollment has proceeded far, will be inconvenient. But we note again that the literature not seem to consider the matter. The biometric identification of the Philippine population was undertaken a few years ago, and the process seems to have been well assessed. Curious readers may look at the relevant articles in the studies collected by Wayman [5]. None of these take up our question, but we note that only fingerprints were used there.

10.5 Two Caveats

It seems prudent to record a caveat regarding the templates that are stored in biometric databases. Where time and resources permit, a template is constructed by summarizing more than one numerized representation of an organic object, which object would be, of course, an instance of some identificatory feature F here. The word "sample" is now used for the primary numerized representation. If each representing sample is a real vector, the template is often just the mean of the samples, such as in the book by Wayman [1]. When these samples are binary vectors, there would be ways, presumably, of extracting some binary summary as a template; however, we have not encountered any discussions under this heading. Where templates are summaries representing samples, the random variable X^σ in Section 10.2 records the distribution of distances between samples and templates representing identical organic objects, whereas the random variable X^δ records the distribution of distances between samples and templates representing distinct objects, and these are the genuine and intertemplate distributions, respectively, used by Wayman [1]. (One could also compare a sample representing one object to a template representing another organic object, and these distances could be taken as the values of a third random variable, which Wayman [1] calls *the impostor distribution*. But the utility of the latter seems to lie in comparing biometric devices of different makes, so we have not considered it.) The UIDAI is very likely using representing samples themselves as templates. We do not know how the manufacturers of their devices have tested them, but if the specified errors were estimated using summarized templates, then some difference between specification and actual performance should have been expected, and perhaps the observed scale of the difference was to be expected as well. Another reason for the considerable difference between specification and performance might lie in our assuming, mistakenly perhaps, the independence of the metrized features. There is reason to suspect that such independence cannot actually be obtained for fingerprints, and that is the other caveat we must register.

References

We have referred more than once to the article by Wayman [1], and Section 10.2 mentions Barrett's [2] in work the course of discussing specified errors. The collection of studies edited by Wayman [5] expands on the complexities of biometric identification, and all three documents are freely available online on the World Wide Web. We also considered the UIDAI [4] article in some detail (available on their web site at http://uidai.gov.in/). Our source for the specified errors of their devices was the article by Srikanth [3], which appeared online in the journal *Pragati* early in 2012, and presumably remains available.

1. J.L. Wayman. Technical testing and evaluation of biometric identification devices. *Biometrics: Personal Identification in a Networked Society*, edited by A.K. Jain, R. Bolle, and S. Pankranti. Kluwer Academic Press, Norwell, M.A., U.S.A. 1999.
2. W. Barrett. Evaluation of Biometric Identification Systems. Summary. U.S. National Biometric Test Centre, San Jose State University, San Jose, CA, 1997.
3. R. Srikanth. Securing the identity. Pragati, Roundup Section, January 6, 2010.
4. Unique Identity Authority of India (UIDAI). The Role of Biometric Technology in Aadhar Enrollment, pp. 17–19. http://uidai.gov.in/.
5. J.L. Wayman (ed.). *National Biometric Test Center Collected Works*. U.S. National Biometric Test Center, San Jose State University, San Jose, CA, 1997–2000.
6. A.K. Jain, A. Ross, and S. Pankanti. Biometrics: a tool for information security. *IEEE Transactions on Information Forensics and Security* 1(2): 125–145, 2006.

Index

Page numbers followed by *f* indicate figure and those followed by *t* indicate table.